THE COMPLETE FILMS OF
EDWARD G. ROBINSON

THE COMPLETE FILMS OF
Edward G. Robinson

BY ALVIN H. MARILL

A Citadel Press Book

PUBLISHED BY CAROL PUBLISHING GROUP

First Carol Publishing Group Edition 1990

Copyright © 1990 by Alvin H. Marill

A Citadel Press Book
Published by Carol Publishing Group

Editorial Offices
600 Madison Avenue
New York, NY 10022

Sales & Distribution Offices
120 Enterprise Avenue
Secaucus, NJ 07094

In Canada: Musson Book Company
A division of General Publishing Co. Limited
Don Mills, Ontario

Designed by A. Christopher Simon

Carol Publishing Group books are available at special discounts
for bulk purchases, for sales promotions, fund raising, or
educational purposes. Special editions can also be created to
specifications. For details contact: Special Sales Department,
Carol Publishing Group, 120 Enterprise Ave., Secaucus, NJ 07094

Library of Congress Cataloging-in-Publication Data

Marill, Alvin H.
        The complete films of Edward G. Robinson / by Alvin H. Marill.
            p.   cm.
        "A Citadel Press book."
        ISBN 0-8065-1181-8 : $15.95
            1. Robinson, Edward G., 1893-1973--Criticism and interpretation.
        I. Title.
        PN2287.R67M37   1990
        791.43'02'092--dc20   90-48017
                                                                        CIP

Manufactured in the United States of America
10 9 8 7 6 5 4 3 2 1

ACKNOWLEDGMENTS

I am indebted to John Cocchi, whose celebrated, hawk-eyed attention to film credits and the names of screen players is second to none.

To Jerry Vermilye, whose incomparable photo collection was vital to the fruition of this book.

To James Robert Parish, whose admiration of Robinson's work brought both of us together in a book venture the first time around.

To John Behrens (of CBS), Jack Dukesbery, Guy Giampapa, Pierre Guinle, Norman Miller, Lyle W. Nash, the late Dr. Marvin Robinson, Lou Valentino and David Williams.

And thanks to the various film studios which gave us The Complete Films of Edward G. Robinson: Warner Bros., Columbia Pictures, Metro-Goldwyn-Mayer, RKO Pictures, United Artists, Paramount Pictures, 20th Century-Fox, Walt Disney Productions, American-International and Cinerama.

CONTENTS

FOREWORD

I have been asked to write the introduction to this wonderful book about one of the dearest men I know, Edward G. Robinson. To write an introduction about him is very simple, as he is a very simple man and a very great man. He is a great humanitarian and a great actor, having made *Little Caesar* as well as *Five Star Final* with me . There is nothing that I could say about this great artist that would really praise him enough. I wish there were more actors in the world like him and more who had his heart.

— Mervyn LeRoy

EDWARD G. ROBINSON
—"*A Man of Great Kindness*"
(THE NEW YORK TIMES obituary)

THE COMPLETE FILMS
OF EDWARD G. ROBINSON

16

INTRODUCTION

"If I were just a bit taller and I was a little more hand-some or something like that," Edward G. Robinson once admitted, "I could have played all the roles that I have played, and played many more. There *is* such a thing as a handicap, but you've got to be that much bet-ter as an actor. It kept me from certain roles that I might have had, but then, it kept others from playing *my* roles, so I don't know that it's not altogether balanced."

Edward G. Robinson was probably the foremost example of an actor making the most of his disadvan-tages. Lacking both looks and height, and working against type by making the "little man" the dominating character, he managed to carve out a career which made him the most successful leading man in films (as opposed to the starring "love interest") during the 1930s and early 1940s. "I remember just before going onto the soundstage," he said, "I'd look in my dressing-room mirror and I'd stretch myself to my full 5′5″ or 5′6″—whatever it was—to make me appear taller and to make me able to dominate all the others and to mow them down to my size."

Robinson's versatility was indeed far greater than the type-casting as the arch-gangster character with which most always identified him. True, his Rico Bandello in *Little Caesar* created a sensation—a landmark on which he built an illustrious screen career, as well as the defini-tive style that became the model on which virtually all other actors would pattern their own gangster charac-terizations. The Robinson "gangster" imitation for dec-ades was standard repertoire for nearly every impressionist in show business, although Robinson maintained that it was they who have created this leg-end and the image of this gangster.

Nevertheless, *Little Caesar* was the prototype. There was never a picture like it before and there was never an Edward G. Robinson before. And the Brothers Warner were quick to realize this and turned a tidy profit by almost completely cornering the market on this fast moving, genuinely exciting, totally unsubtle genre of social film.

As a motion picture, *Little Caesar* was far from the best of its type; in fact, it has always been considered only slightly better than average, and is viewed today primarily as a curio. However, Robinson's portrayal of the title character as an analytical study of a merciless killer still holds up (taken in the proper context) as a superb conception by exactly the right performer whose acting abilities and physical traits melded perfectly to the universal—or, if you please, Warner—image of such a character. And when Robinson goes down under a fusillade of police bullets in the final scene, gasping "Mother of Mercy! Is this the end of Rico?", one knows for certain that he will be back and back and back—as Joe Krozac, as Remy Marco, as Little John Sarto, as Johnny Rocco, as Vincent Canelli as Leo Smooth. . . .

But Robinson's film career neither began nor ended with *Little Caesar*. Of the more than eighty films he made subsequently, only a quarter of his roles called for gangster portrayals. In about an equal number, he was the unswerving, if occasionally unappreciated, upholder of law and order. He also limned five "real" people, appearing in two of the finest biographical films ever made; he won and lost the girl an equal number of times (nine); and he confronted Humphrey Bogart five times (usually preceding a shootout), four as the good guy.

And before *Little Caesar*, Robinson spent sixteen years on the New York stage, perfecting his craft in more than thirty plays, eleven with the Theatre Guild and "about ten with Arthur Hopkins, who was perhaps the most literate producer we had on Broadway."

He was born Emanuel Goldenberg in Bucharest, Rumania, on December 12, 1893, the fifth of six sons of Morris and Sarah (Guttman) Goldenberg. His father, a builder by trade, decided—partly because of religious persecution—to take the family to America. He took his three older sons with him, and young Manny followed shortly thereafter with his two other brothers, their mother and her mother. He was nine when he arrived in Manhattan, but he later said, "I was born when I came to America." As a minor, he automatically acquired United States citizenship when his father obtained final papers.

The family lived in an East Side tenement before moving uptown to the Bronx, where Morris Goldenberg ran a candy store, and later became an antiques dealer. One of young Manny's brothers, who had been seriously injured in a street fight back in Bucharest, died not long after the family moved to America, and the other three older ones eventually drifted into the jewelry business. The youngest was to become a dentist. Said Robinson: "I was number five. I became the black sheep of the family, since nobody in it had ever had anything to do with the theater."

Young Manny reportedly gave the longest Bar Mitzvah speech in the history of the Rumanian Synagogue on Rivington Street; it was such a success that he gave more than a passing thought to becoming a rabbi. "For about six weeks, I became a fanatic, and I drove momma and poppa crazy, and I wanted them to take me down to the seminary and enroll me there. But then I realized that I would probably have to be a moron or a charlatan to pose as a sancrosanct gent, you know, twenty-four hours a day—and I gave up that idea. The reason I wanted to be a rabbi, though, is the same that motivated me to want to be a lawyer after that—a defense lawyer, but never a prosecutor. I wanted to instill the right sort of ideas into children."

He attended Public School 20 (whose alumni ranged from George Gershwin to Paul Muni to Senator Jacob Javits) and he was editor of the school paper. An exceptional student record provided him with the opportunity to enroll in Townsend Harris Hall, a preparatory school, where he became interested in acting. "I was trying to find my way," he told an interviewer. "I read Shaw's dramatic criticisms and I saw that acting was not all strutting and fretting. The thing got hold of me in my junior year at high school. Now, everyone has dramatic instincts, but I began to realize the scope of it. To be entrusted with a character was always a big responsibility to me."

In 1910, he entered City College of New York, and after reading Antony's soliloquy in *Julius Caesar* he was elected to the Elizabethan Society. Oddly, he was never to play Shakespeare professionally. On scholarship, he joined the American Academy of Dramatic Arts (AADA) in October 1911, where his closest friend was Joseph Schildkraut. The late actor once noted: "Manny stuck to his work, and I looked at the girls."

It was while with AADA that Emanuel Goldenberg became Edward G. Robinson. "Franklin Sargent told me that I had to get an Anglo-Saxon name, whatever that is," Robinson told UPI in 1963. "I kept the initials E.G. but I don't know to this day why I chose Robinson as a last name. If I had to do it again, I'd take a shorter name. You have no idea how long it takes to write Edward G. Robinson for a flock of autograph hunters."

Robinson's first exposure before a non-classroom audience was in 1913 when at Loew's Plaza's amateur night he tried out a monologue he had written. Calling his reading "The Bells of Conscience," he had put it together from generous portions of Henry James's **The Bells**—a murderer's confession under hypnosis. It helped him get his first professional job with The Stainach Stock Company in Binghamton, New York, and he made his stage debut as Sato in Eugene Walter's *Paid in Full* in April 1913. He then moved onto a repertory group out of Cincinnati, The Orpheum Players, and did twenty-two weeks with them.

Noted Robinson: "I was aware early in my career that the acting profession had to be created and carved out by oneself, so that I decided that I wanted to do a certain amount of stock to develop myself in a variety of roles and build my sense of projection bit by bit to be solidly founded. I wanted to start at the very beginning to ring the curtain up and down, and I played little bits in stock after I got out of the Academy. I wanted to spend a year with Shakespeare, but I revised those ideas when I found out that no individuality was permitted as far as interpretation was concerned —you had to read it a certain way, stand in a certain spot—and I realized that there was little chance for development. I also wanted to be with a circus, with a burlesque company, in vaudeville, to touch every branch of the entertainment world."

In 1914 he landed a role in Edward Knoblock's *Kismet* in a company touring Canada. "We were booked in the provinces," he recalled, "when the war came on and that absolutely killed the theater, and we had to shut down prematurely after about five or six weeks. I went to New York and started making the rounds looking for a job, and I found that nobody knew me and I thought, at the time, it was a very undignified business to be in. In those days, I would go for an interview and find myself competing with this other chap who would always be younger and taller and much handsomer than I. I would recognize immediately that the producer wasn't particularly sympathetic and I learned to say, out of intuition, 'I know I'm not much on face value, but when it comes to stage value, I'll deliver for you.'"

Robinson continued: "I was about to give up acting for teaching—again, to mold kids—but I was saved because I happened to know something about languages." He found that a play, *Under Fire*, by Roi Cooper Megrue, was being cast with German- and French-speaking parts needed to be filled. "Because I doubt whether my looks could have gotten me by, the sheer fact that languages had always been a hobby of mine and that I could play various ethnic types, gave me my first chance on Broadway. I was a French soldier, a Belgian patriot, a German. In the last act, I came in as an Englishman, a Cockney. They used to call me the League of Nations. After that I never left Broadway." The play opened on August 12, 1915, and he was billed as E. G. Robinson. He was not overlooked by the critic for *The New York Times*, who wrote: "In minor roles, exceedingly good work is done by Robert Fischer, Norman Thorp, E. G. Robinson and Henry Stephenson."

In October 1916, he was cast as Fagan in *Under Sentence*, a play Roi Megrue co-authored with Irvin S. Cobb, and he was again billed simply as E. G. Robinson.

Later in the season he turned up as a Japanese named Hushmaru in *The Pawn*, and used his full name for the first time. On February 4, 1918, Robinson opened in a rural comedy called *The Little Teacher*, and got himself a pair of good notices. Said *The New York Times* critic: "As the Canuck friend of the hero, Edward G. Robinson had the best opportunity and made the most of it." Alex Pierce wrote in the *Tribune*: "Edward G. Robinson created an amusing role as Batiste."

While in New York, Robinson made his first movie—a minor role in *Arms and the Woman*, being directed by George Fitzmaurice at the Astoria Studios in Queens. This credit never has been included in his filmography or even was mentioned in his autobiography, *All My Yesterdays* (Hawthorn Books, 1973). He wasn't to make another screen appearance for seven years.

A brief tour of duty with the U.S. Navy followed, but Robinson never left New York harbor and was only a subway ride from Broadway. "We were all secluded up there because of the flu epidemic," he recalled, "but the farthest I ever got as a sailor was in a rowboat in Pelham Bay. And when the Armistice was signed, I broke down and cried by myself in a YMCA hut, and I figured, 'Now what have I done to save the world for democracy?'"

Back on Broadway, Robinson was in the comedy *First Is Last*, which had a brief run at the start of the 1919-20 theater season, and of the young actor's performance Alexander Woollcott commented in *The New York Times*: "The present company, assembled by William Harris, Jr., is quite hopelessly handicapped, so that only Edward G. Robinson flares up in one scene of drink-befuddled oratory." In December of that season, Robinson was Satan in *Night Lodging*, a translation of Gorky's "The Lower Depths." Found the *Tribune*: "Edward G. Robinson carried off a scene in the last act with a true spirit of fire."

Looking back on those early days in the theater, Robinson reminisced: "On the stage, I never had to starve. Occasionally, my brothers would come to my aid. I never indulged myself in luxuries, although my tastes ran in that direction, and I had to be a success to satisfy my appetites. When I started out in a road show, people—actors—of my category would stop at a boarding house, and I would go along, but after a night or two, I didn't like it—the bed I had to sleep in, the kind of food. I wanted a good cigar, so I lived beyond my means. I'd change and go to a hotel and try to get a good dinner. I guess I just couldn't afford to be a failure."

In September 1920, he was Pinsky in Booth Tarkington's *Poldekin*, which starred George Arliss. The play was one of the very earliest to deal with anti-Communism. He followed this with the role of The Director in Sven Lange's *Samson and Delilah*, which brought the great Yiddish Art Theatre actor, Jacob Ben-Ami, to Broadway for the first time. The *Times's* Alexander Woollcott singled out Robinson for "a fine performance."

With Ben-Ami, Sam Jaffe and Louis Wolheim, among others, Robinson appeared, in December 1921, in the premiere English-language staging of the Peretz Hirshbeim play, *The Idle Inn* (which Wolheim adapted with Isaac Goldberg). "This was the most heterogeneous conglomerate company one could imagine," Robinson said. "There were Scotsmen, Irishmen, Cockneys and Americans all trying to play Jews. It was a folk story, produced by Arthur Hopkins, but in the translation from the Yiddish, the last act was left out."

The following month, Robinson was seen as Nordling in a revival of *The Deluge*, and then he joined The Theatre Guild and found himself cast as Louis in the French farce, *Banco*, a vehicle for Alfred Lunt. The Woollcott review was a negative finding, though: "The piece is delightfully acted with only Edward G. Robinson rather at a loss."

In early 1923, Robinson made what he always maintained to be his first motion picture (and his only silent film), playing a Spanish aristocrat in *The Bright Shawl*. Richard Barthelmess, Dorothy Gish and Jetta Goudal had the leads, Mary Astor was his daughter(!), and his AADA classmate, William Powell, also had a part. Said Robinson: "I did *The Bright Shawl* during an interval between plays. I had very few intervals. In order to do a lot of theater in a short time, you had to be in a few failures. Mine I considered distinguished failures. No sooner would one play finish, though, than I was rehearsing another one. But there was a rather long interval, and I had never been to Cuba, and it was right after Christmas time. John Robertson, a distinguished director in silent films, had seen me and thought that I would be great for this vehicle, to play this Spanish Don, an old man—and it was a trip to Havana, where those great cigars were made. That was the only silent part I ever played. I swore off after that because I didn't particularly like it, and I felt that the stage held more of a future for me."

The actor's notices were substantially better, for his next outing on Broadway, Ibsen's *Peer Gynt*, with his friend Joseph Schildkraut in the lead. Robinson played two parts, and Woollcott noted: "There must be a word

for the telling performance of Edward G. Robinson as the Button Moulder in the superb last act." Inexplicably (and possibly through a printing error), the actor was billed as *Edgar* G. Robinson when he played Shrdlu in Elmer Rice's *The Adding Machine* in March 1923. The first name notwithstanding, Woollcott singled him out for comment: "Excellent, too, it need hardly be said, is Robinson."

After Rice's avant-garde play, Robinson starred with William Courtenay in *The Voice* in Chicago ("The critics murdered us . . . the play was terrible"), and he returned to Broadway the following October, as Louis in Edna St. Vincent Millay's adaptation of Molnar's *Launzi*—and the *Edward* was back on the playbill but the *G.* was missing! One month later, he turned up in the Zoe Akins comedy, *A Royal Fandango*, starring Ethel Barrymore. Included among the supporting players was a young actor named Spencer Tracy. Ironically, Robinson and Tracy were never again to work together, although a number of Tracy roles four decades later were assumed by Robinson when his long-time friend was indisposed by a series of illnesses. He had less kind things to say about Ethel Barrymore and always referred to the play as *The Royal Fiasco*.

In 1924, Robinson played Octaviano in *The Firebrand*, in which Joseph Schildkraut starred as Benvenuto Cellini and Frank Morgan as The Duke of Florence, but it was in a pair of G. B. Shaw works in November 1925 that Robinson got his first "money" reviews. He played Caesar in *Androcles and the Lion* and Giuseppe in *The Man of Destiny* on one double bill. Writing in *The New York World*, Alexander Woollcott raved: "The role that suddenly, surprisingly, magnificently comes to life for the first time is that of Caesar, played with great gusto by that capital actor, Edward G. Robinson." The critic for *The New York Times* said: "As the Emperor Caesar, the mighty and omnipotent, Mr. Robinson also gave an enjoyable performance running to low comedy." And the *Tribune*, commenting on the second play, found: "It was easily Edward G. Robinson as Giuseppe who carried off histrionic honors."

With The Theatre Guild company (Alfred Lunt, Lynn Fontanne, Dudley Digges, et al), Robinson was next on view in Franz Werfel's *The Goat Song*, in January, 1926, and J. Brooks Atkinson wrote in *The New York Times*: "Mr. Robinson is refreshingly amusing as the peddler Jew." And two months later, he played the Stage Director in the Guild's production of Evreinov's *The Chief Thing*.

Then in August, he appeared in the Lawrence Langner farce, *Henry Behave*, and garnered this review from *The New York Times*: "The honors of the play go to Edward G. Robinson who has strayed from The Theatre Guild to donate a flawless portrayal of the smug oleageous VP of the realty company." Included among the supporting players were Pat O'Brien, Elisha Cook Jr., and an actress named Gladys Lloyd, who, on January 21, 1927, would become Mrs. Edward G. Robinson. (They had been seeing one another for several years.)

Miss Lloyd, née Gladys Cassell, was the daughter of the famed artist-sculptor C. C. Cassell, and had had a number of stage roles previously, including a part with the Astaires in *Lady Be Good*. She was in Robinson's words, "The quiet essential American Protestant" and had been married previously and had a daughter. It was some time before he could bring himself to introduce his wife to his parents who were devout Jews.

Back with the Guild, Robinson next appeared in three consecutive plays in four months. In October 1926, he was Porfirio Diaz in Werfel's *Juarez and Maximilian*; the following month he played a small role as a New England lawyer in Sidney Howard's *Ned McCobb's Daughter*; and at the start of the new year, he received some nice notices as Smerdiakov, the epileptic in *The Brothers Karamazov*.

And in March, performing in repertory with the Guild, he was Ponza in Pirandello's *Right You Are If You Think You Are*. Talking about the great turnover of roles in this particular period, Robinson recalled: "The runs were fairly short, since The Theatre Guild worked on a subscription audience that guaranteed you six weeks before you went into another play. That was attractive to me, because they [the Guild] were going to establish a repertory company, but they never did. You have a repertory company until you have a hit. Then you just keep running with it. The Guild didn't live up to its obligations in my mind."

Stardom followed with Robinson's next Broadway role.

Establishing him among the great young actors of the stage—and giving him his first starring role—was Bartlett Cormack's sensational play, *The Racket*, which opened on Broadway in November 1927. Robinson played the only gangster part he ever did on the stage—that of Nick Scarsi—in an interpretation which was chillingly close to the public's conception of Al Capone.

Wrote Arthur Ruhl in the *Herald-Tribune*: "Mr. Edward G. Robinson as the villainous boss was the only one whose make-up and manner clicked with pungent 'Theater' the instant he stepped on the scene. He was quite wicked enough to satisfy the hungriest melodrama fan, and it is reassuring to be able to report that he got 'his' in the end."

And this from the *New York World*: "Edward G. Robinson as the crook, stopping at nothing, was great, especially at the last when driven into a corner, threatening, desperate, but cold and calculating." *Theatre Magazine* called his performance "a masterly creation of character."

Robinson's sinister Italian gangster in the Chicago underworld was the forerunner of the Capone-like character he was later to develop on the screen and with which he would virtually single-handedly create a cinematic style to fit the national mood.

"We had a fair run in New York," Robinson recalled, "and we were booked into Chicago about the end of April, but Chicago wouldn't let us in because *The Racket* was much too true." He told an interviewer, "It was documentary, you see. As a result the season was aborted and disorganized, and some of us were offered a chance to come out for ten weeks to play it in Los Angeles and San Francisco. It was my practice not to leave New York. When a play went on the road, I went into another one, you see, but it was already what you would call *morte saison*—dead season for the actor. What could you do in April, May and June, and all that, except perhaps try out a play for the following season. So I came out [to Los Angeles] and these motion picture tycoons happened to see me in this particular role. That was my introduction to them. They wanted me to stay and do some pictures then—the pictures had just begun to talk—but I could not divorce myself from the theater and I went back."

Returning to Broadway where he at last had realized stardom, Robinson opened in November 1928 in what could be termed a three-act grand guignol—as Mr. Crispin in *A Man With Red Hair*, based on the Hugh Walpole novel. Here, in part, is the appraisal of his performance by the critic of *The New York Times*:

"Its titular character—a terrible monstrosity in the book—who is made almost as alarming on stage by Edward G. Robinson—believes in the religion of pain; that by undergoing it one acquires power and learns the innermost meaning of life . . . Mr. Robinson is, of course, an actor who has given some extremely good performances in this metropolis. His characterization of Crispin is not the high spot of his acting career, but it ranks well at the top. He brings out all the insane, demoniacal qualities in this cruelest of his stage portraits, depicting the sadist as among the maddest and most horrific of men."

Writing in *The New York Sun*, Stephen Rathburn said: "Seen last season as the super gangster in *The Racket*, Mr. Robinson proves in his present characterization of a sadistic lunatic that he is without a peer in this particular field on the legitimate stage. His only rival is Lon Chaney! The highest praise I can give Mr. Robinson is to say that if his acting career were not so well known and anybody had said that he was formerly a prominent member of the Moscow Art Theater, nobody in last night's audience would have doubted the statement."

It was during an engagement of *The Racket* in San Francisco and Los Angeles in 1928 when the film people came knocking at Robinson's door again, this time with an offer to appear in a movie to be shot in New York, and so in 1929 (while still on Broadway in *A Man With Red Hair*) Edward G. Robinson began what would be truly an illustrious cinema career. The vehicle that began it all, *The Hole in the Wall*, was not, however, the skyrocket to make his name a marquee draw. It did mark a number of "firsts" though. It was Claudette Colbert's first sound picture (like Robinson, she had previously made one silent film); it was the first feature-length talking motion picture to be shot at Paramount's Astoria Studio on Long Island; it was the first "talkie" to be directed by Robert Florey. In it, Robinson played a crook named The Fox whose love for Miss Colbert gets absolutely no response, primarily because she is too busy seeking retribution from a woman whose lies had sent her (Colbert) to prison for five years. (Although *The Hole in the Wall* was definitely Claudette Colbert's film, Robinson's name appeared first—and quite prominently—when Paramount decided to cash in on the actor's new popularity a few years later and reissue the film.)

Back on Broadway in February 1929, the playwright, presented himself, leaving his work in the trusted hands of Edward G. Robinson, the actor. In a three-act comedy, *Kibitzer*, which he wrote with Jo Swerling (they had tried it out in Atlantic City in the summer of 1927), Robinson starred as Lazarus, an Amsterdam Avenue cigar dealer. Of his role, *The New York Times* found: "The play is almost entirely Mr. Robinson and his performance. The portrayal of The Kibitzer by this actor of finish and variety is full-length, revealing him in nearly all his moods and aspects. . . . For Mr. Robinson, it constitutes a minor triumph; another scalp added to his list of histrionic achievements."

And this from *Theatre Arts Monthly*: "Hardly a season fails to demonstrate Edward G. Robinson's astonishing talent as a character actor."

Robinson's second talkie, *Night Ride*, starring his friend Joseph Schildkraut, gave him another role as a hood. Schildkraut later wrote in his book, *My Father and I*: "There was the part of a Capone-like gangster in the picture and I suggested my good friend and former classmate at the American Academy of Dramatic Arts, Edward G. Robinson, for the role. Carl Laemmle Jr. had never heard of him, and it took all of my persuasion to make Universal engage him. Robinson was magnificent, perfectly cast, and he 'played me right off the screen,' as the saying goes."

Irving Thalberg then engaged him to play Tony, the crippled grape-grower, in a new film production of *A Lady to Love*, MGM's sound version of Sidney Howard's *They Knew What They Wanted*. Filmed previously by Paramount as *The Secret Hour* with Pola Negri and Jean Hersholt (and in 1940 by RKO under the original Howard title featuring Carole Lombard and Charles Laughton in the leads), this talkie version was Thalberg's hope for easing Vilma Banky's transition to sound. The plan was a failure in that respect, but the picture did reveal Robinson to be a powerful screen performer in the role of a love-sick old man who wins over a mail-order bride by enclosing the picture of a younger man so she won't be disappointed. Noted *The New York Times*: "As Tony, Mr. Robinson is capital. . . . The range of acting as offered by [him] is most gratifying." *Cinema* (May 1930) commented: "Mr. Robinson is the life of the picture. . . . It is hard to imagine [the role] better acted."

Robinson also starred in the German-language version of the production which was filmed simultaneously with virtually the same cast (except for Joseph Schildkraut who replaced Robert Ames as the romantic lead).

The story goes that Irving Thalberg, realizing Robinson's screen potential, called the actor to his office and offered him a generous five-year million-dollar contract. Robinson, who still considered his loyalties to the stage, held out for a six-month pact to allow him time for some Broadway acting, and his agent was called in as intermediary in the negotiations which ended in a standoff. Robinson never again worked in a Thalberg film. (It would be interesting to ponder the direction of Robinson's career had he signed with MGM rather than with Warner Bros.)

Instead, he returned briefly to Universal, where *Night Ride* had been made; he took on another gangster role in Tod Browning's sound remake of his own 1921 film, *Outside the Law*, and then he played an Oriental half-caste—the chop suey king of San Francisco—in *East Is West*. That, too, was a remake—of a 1923 silent.

He followed that picture with the first of many he would do for Warners, *The Widow From Chicago*. He again played a gangster, but by now he had gained enough of a reputation so that *The New York Times* headed its review: "Edward G. Robinson In New Film."

The role of Caesar Enrico Bandello, "Little Caesar," came next.

Recalled Robinson: "I had the advantage of reading the book by Burnett, and when the script was first submitted to me, it was just another gangster story—the east side taking over the west side, and all that. Finally I was given a version that made some difference, reading more or less like a Greek tragedy. It's a man with a perverted mind, ambitions of a kind, who sets a goal more important than himself—that's what makes him a highly moral character in his perverted way. He is a man who defies society, and in the end is mowed down by the gods and society, and doesn't even know what happened. If Rico had expended his energies in another way, he would have been a great, great fellow. In his own mind, he thought he was doing the right thing, and that's the way you color him. You, as an actor, comment on him—subjectively and objectively. Rico in his way was like Macbeth and Othello and Richard—all of those great characters—and it was like a Greek tragedy or one by Shakespeare. Rico Bandello was not at all like Nick Scarsi [in *The Racket*]. Bandello was very naïve, while Scarsi was an extremely sophisticated character. But I think that the picture has sustained itself throughout these years because it was constructed as a Greek tragedy."

Within weeks of the film's release, the legend of the underworld character Robinson had created was already beginning to haunt him. Wherever he went, he was recognized not as Edward G. Robinson the actor, but as "Little Caesar." And for more than twenty years afterwards, critics, in reviewing his performances in any films, would judge his work against his portrayal of Rico Bandello—whether he was playing a gangster, a cop or a doctor, or doing broad comedy or stark drama. Somehow, a reference to "Little Caesar" would find its way into the critique.

(And it is not over yet. *Little Caesar* went into theatrical reissue again in the fall of 1970, receiving another Broadway run nearly forty years after its premiere there. Now, of course, there's the video market.)

Before *Little Caesar* was released in January 1931, Robinson returned to the theater for what turned out to be less than a success and his last legitimate stage appearance for more than two decades. He played the title role in *Mr. Samuel* by E. Fleg and Winthrop Ames, adapted from the Comedie-Française's *The Merchant of Paris*. "Since Edward G. Robinson plays the title part with colorful impetuosity," commented J. Brooks Atkinson in *The New York Times*, "the long stretches in which Mr. Samuel reduces conversation to soliloquy are completely engrossing. For Mr. Robinson is a versatile actor who can make a bootlegger in *The Racket* or a psychopathic busybody in *Kibitzer* or a rough-hewn grandee of business in the current play immediate and vivid figures."

The play ran a brief two weeks on Broadway, and Robinson later said in a *New York Post* article (1940): "That disaster decided me. I thought, What's the good of being true to the theater when in eighteen years, one hasn't built up a following big enough to support one in even his lesser efforts?" Robinson wasn't to act on the stage again for nearly twenty-one years.

Buoyed by the phenomenal success of *Little Caesar*, Warners teamed Robinson with James Cagney, fresh

Publicity shot for SMART MONEY (1931)

from *his* recent triumph in *Public Enemy*, in the only Robinson-Cagney combination ever put together—*Smart Money*. The film had Robinson playing a small-town barber who becomes a big-time gambler, with Cagney as the good friend he accidentally kills over the affections of costar Evalyn Knapp.

"When I did *Little Caesar*," said Robinson, "they wanted to star me, put me above the title, but I said to the Warners that despite the fact that I had been starred in many plays on Broadway, this is another field. I suggested that they try another picture, and if the public really accepts me as such, then they could put my name above the title. But once you do, I told them, since I am signing a long-term contract with you, you will continue to do it so long as I am working for you."

Following *Smart Money* came *Five Star Final*, with Robinson cast in a non-gangster part for a change. In this well-remembered attack on Yellow Journalism, he was the managing editor whose get-the-story-at-any-cost policy ruins a number of lives and causes a couple of suicides. The same story turned up five years later as *Two Against the World*, with Humphrey Bogart handling the Robinson role. As *Five Star Final* was playing at the Warner Theatre on Broadway, Edward G. Robinson opened a block and a half away on Seventh Avenue at the Palace (September 18, 1931) on a bill headlined by Kate Smith. Robinson was tagged in the ads and on the marquee as "'Little Caesar' himself," and got this notice

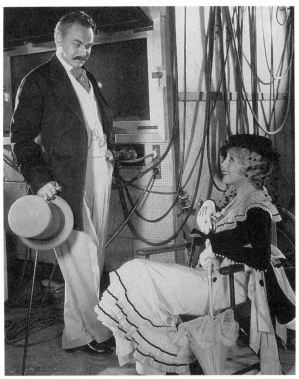

On the set of SILVER DOLLAR (1932) with Bebe Daniels

Silver Dollar gave to Robinson, however, a full-blown role worthy of his talents. Playing the legendary silver-mining senator from Colorado, H. A. W. Tabor, but called Yates Martin in the script, the actor was able to turn in a bravura performance of *Little Caesar* caliber. *The New York Times* headed its review: "Edward G. Robinson In Film Version of David Karsner's Biography of Haw Tabor." And the *Sunday Times* found that "Whatever Mr. Robinson did in *Little Caesar* is even more convincing here, notwithstanding that Yates Martin is a character from the past." Following the film's premier three days before Christmas, 1932, the Warners received this congratulatory wire from ex-Governor Al Smith: "Robinson is more Haw Tabor than Tabor himself could have been."

Edward G. Robinson's only son, Emanuel Robinson Jr., known nearly always as Manny (as his father always had been to his friends), was born on March 19, 1933, in Doctor's Hospital in New York. Harry Warner was his godfather.

Robinson's first screen comedy was *Little Giant*, released in May 1933. It was a bit of fluff about a former beer baron who decides to get some culture. In another departure for Robinson, this time he got the girl—Mary Astor.

In *I Loved a Woman*, from another novel by David

from *Variety*: "Two distinguishing points in the show are the new style MC-ing of Rick Craig and the astonishing adaptability to the two-a-day technique of Robinson. Of the two, the Robinson angle is probably more striking. The tough guy from Hollywood, it is to be remembered, comes to vaudeville on the crest of a wave of fan popularity. His background, except for a short time in pictures, is strictly legit. . . . [In] the Robinson number, which doesn't bear too much repetition, he gives little speeches between screen showing of scenes from *Little Caesar* and *Smart Money*."

Most of Robinson's 1932 film work, while quite profitable for the Brothers Warner, provided the actor with rather routine screen assignments. Robinson was a tong executioner in San Francisco's Chinatown in *The Hatchet Man*—a type of character he does not best essay. *Two Seconds*, in which he is a murderer who recalls his entire life in the seconds preceding his execution, gave him less than he returned to it. (This was his third picture with Mervyn LeRoy, who had also directed him in *Little Caesar* and *Five Star Final*.) In *Tiger Shark*, decked out in a spiffy, well-groomed mustache and a hook where his left hand should be, he played Mike Mascarena, the best tuna fisherman on the west coast ("portrayed splendidly by Edward G. Robinson," reported *The New York Times*), who loses his girl, Zita Johann (then Mrs. John Houseman), to his buddy, Richard Arlen, and his life to a shark.

Instructing Mary Astor on the fine art of gangsterdom between takes of THE LITTLE GIANT (1933)

Karsner, the author of *Silver Dollar*, Robinson played a beef baron who made a fortune selling tainted meat, lost his home when he began playing around with a money-grubbing opera singer (Kay Francis) whom he had promoted to stardom, and had a run-in with Teddy Roosevelt. Then he was a gambler who bets on and goes to the dogs in *Dark Hazard*. It came from a novel by W. R. Burnett, who had also written *Little Caesar* earlier and whose later claim to fame would be *The Asphalt Jungle*. *Dark Hazard*, incidentally, turned up just three years later remade as *Wine, Women and Horses*.

The Man With Two Faces, a film version of the George S. Kaufman and Alexander Woollcott play, *The Dark Tower*, gave Robinson the opportunity to don some bizarre makeup and attempt a French accent, and to play an egotistical actor who murders his brother-in-law to save the sanity of his sister. Louis Calhern was in the former role, Mary Astor in the latter. It was all done more meaningfully and suspensefully on the stage in the hands of Basil Sydney.

On loan-out to Columbia for John Ford's hilarious comedy, *The Whole Town's Talking* (from another W. R. Burnett novel), Edward G. Robinson hit another peak in his career and accepted rave reviews for his adeptness as a comedian. He played a dual role—as a timid clerk and a look-alike gangster. Curiously, it was the first of only five pictures in which he starred that ever played Radio City Music Hall, and his photo was used for the first time along side *The New York Times* review. It

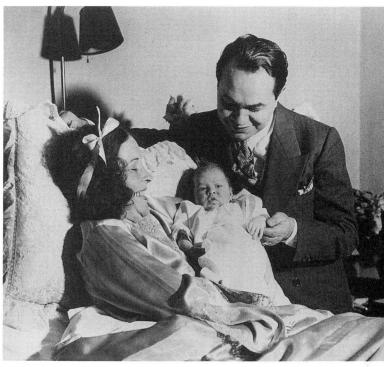

With wife Gladys and newborn son Edward G. Robinson, Jr. (1933)

would be nearly thirty years before Robinson would again work with John Ford.

In 1935, he also did another picture on loan-out—this one for Samuel Goldwyn, and the only time since

On the town with wife Gladys in 1934

Mr. and Mrs. Edward G. Robinson at home in Beverly Hills in 1934

With his trademark cigar, c. 1934

he became a star that he got less than top billing (in deference to Goldwyn regular Miriam Hopkins). The film was called *Barbary Coast*, directed by Howard Hawks from an original screenplay by Charles MacArthur and Ben Hecht. Robinson had the flashy role of Louis Chamalis, the owner of a crooked gambling house in the San Francisco of Gold Rush days, who transforms a naïve young lady into the Belle of Frisco and then watches her fall for a handsome, hard-luck Forty-Niner (played by Joel McCrea). Most of the critical attention, though, was focused on a young Walter Brennan, who virtually stole the picture as Old Atrocity—and probably would have won a supporting Oscar had they been awarded in those days. (The Supporting Actor/Actress awards began in 1936, when Brennan *did* win, repeating the feat in 1938 and in 1940.)

Robinson's next screen portrayal was to have been Duke Mantee in *The Petrified Forest*, and there are two stories of why it was not. This is the more well-known: Leslie Howard, who had starred opposite Humphrey Bogart in the Robert E. Sherwood play on Broadway, had agreed to do the film version on condition that Bogart also re-create his role. Warners, meanwhile, had already settled on Edward G. Robinson as Mantee. When Howard learned of this, he threatened to withdraw unless Bogart played the gangster.

However Robinson told an interviewer that he had himself turned down the role. "I didn't want to go along and keep doing gangster parts. I was then contracted to Warner Brothers and I kept insisting that I wanted to get away from the gangster category. And it was nice because it brought Humphrey Bogart back into pictures and then eventually he became a very important star."

He and Bogart made the first of their five films together in *Bullets or Ballots*. Said Robinson in retrospect: "In those days, I would play the leading role, and he [Bogart] would be opposite me, and we would shoot at each other perhaps a reel before the picture finished. Since I happened to be the so-called 'star,' he would die a reel ahead of me, and I would go on with a bullet in me right up to the last scene. In *Key Largo*, the last time we did a picture together, the situation was reversed. He was then their star and I was just a visitor, and we had our shoot-out as usual, but I died first and he went on for another reel."

Bullets or Ballots was the first picture in which Robinson moved over to the right side of the law. The film was based on the life of Johnny Broderick, one of New York's most famous detectives, and Robinson played the detective who pretended to be kicked off the force to get a line on and infiltrate the rackets. "It's no secret," reported *World-Telegram* film critic Douglas Gilbert in May 1936, "that Mr. Robinson, a sterling stage player,

At a gala with Ginger Rogers in 1936

has long tired of his bloody roles and is increasingly apprehensive lest he go down in film history as a type. It is said that he consented to make this film on condition that he be given the role of Beethoven in a contemplated picture of the great composer's life."

What Robinson was given, however, was a chance (by Columbia Pictures) to see London and to again show his comic flair. The project was *Thunder in the City*, an effortless little affair made in England, which did not materially help nor hinder his career.

On his return to Warner Bros., he starred in what would rank as another screen classic—*Kid Galahad* (ridiculously retitled *Battling Bellhop* for television), in which he and Humphrey Bogart again faced each other as rival fight managers who kill each other off at the fadeout. It was Robinson's only film with the queen of the Warner lot, Bette Davis (who played his girl friend), and it made a star out of young Wayne Morris in the sensational title role.

(Worthy of note as a sidebar is the infrequency of times Edward G. Robinson was teamed with the other Warner stars or with members of the lot's "stock company," considering the studio's penchant for working out various boxoffice combinations. Robinson, for instance, worked only once with Cagney, Garfield, Raft [while he and Robinson were both at Warners], Bette Davis, Kay Francis and Ida Lupino. He was never teamed with Errol Flynn, Ann Sheridan, Paul Muni or Olivia de Havilland.)

On the set of BULLETS OR BALLOTS with Humphrey Bogart, young Manny and George E. Stone in 1936

27

Wayne Morris spars with Edward G. Robinson, Jr., as dad watches between breaks in the filming of KID GALAHAD (1937)

Publicity pose c. 1937

Kid Galahad was reworked in 1941 as *Wagons Roll at Night*, with a carnival background substituted for the fight ring, and with Bogart in the Robinson role. And in 1962 it was resurrected as a vehicle for Elvis Presley, with Gig Young in Robinson's part as the trainer-manager.

MGM then borrowed the actor in 1937 for *The Last Gangster*, but that studio lacked the pizzazz for creating pictures of the social genre Warners had perfected in the thirties. Ironically, though, Robinson's role of Joe Krozac in *The Last Gangster* was the last "serious" gangster part he would do for eleven years.

On October 19, 1937, Robinson began a long run on the weekly CBS radio series, *Big Town*, starring as Steve Wilson, crusading editor of *The Illustrated Press*. Claire Trevor was the original Lorelei Kilbourne, and was succeeded by Ona Munson. "It was a very popular program," Robinson told an interviewer. "Jack Benny was number one and we were number two for many years. I played an editor of a newspaper and it dealt with the problems of the day. Then the war came on, and they still confined me to cleaning up the rackets, and I said 'Now this is an enterprising and alive editor. There's a war going on and I'd like to concern myself with some of the day's big questions.' And they said: 'Well, no, we can't do that. We can't have anything either factual or fictional about the war because it becomes controversial and they won't buy our soap' and that kind of thing. And so I got off—dropped it after five years."

On the screen, Robinson was induced by Warners to enter the world of Damon Runyon. He played Remy Marco in the screen version of *A Slight Case of Murder*, which Runyon and Howard Lindsay had written for Broadway a few years before. While the play could not be considered one of the great stage triumphs, the film enjoyed a huge success, and Robinson appeared to be thoroughly enraptured with the role of a gangster who made a Prohibition Era fortune with his needled beer, but forgot to stop needling it after he went straight. Warners remade it in 1952 as a semi-musical (!) entitled *Stop! You're Killing Me* with Broderick Crawford and Claire Trevor. Of *A Slight Case of Murder*, Howard Barnes commented in the *Herald-Tribune*: "'Little Caesar' died hard but his passing shouldn't grieve Mr. Robinson unduly if he can get more scripts like this one."

The Amazing Dr. Clitterhouse followed, and Humphrey Bogart was again the nemesis. Robinson had the title role, which Sir Cedric Hardwicke had done on the stage. John Huston and John Wexley wrote the screen adaptation of the Barre Lyndon play, and the star took the part of a psychiatrist who experiments with criminals to study their mentality—and then decides to become one himself "in the interest of medicine." Claire Trevor had the female lead as a lady fence.

Behind the CBS microphone in 1938

Then Robinson was loaned once again to Columbia for *I Am the Law*, playing a law professor-turned-racketbuster (named John Lindsay!) who, at the climax, herds the city's entire criminal population into a circus tent and attempts to reform it through a lecture and visual aids—visual aids that contain films of an actual electrocution.

On the home lot, Warner Bros. cast him as an FBI agent in *Confessions of a Nazi Spy*, a semi-documentary which was a daring film, at the time, having been based on a just-completed exposé and court case. Attempts were made to suppress the film, and its screenings for the press were held behind locked doors in various locations around the country.

Viewed more fifty years later, Anatole Litvak's then-controversial *Confessions of a Nazi Spy* is nothing more than an ordinary espionage melodrama in which Robinson's role is no more dominant than any of the others. But the time was 1939, and the picture was selected by the National Board of Motion Picture Review as Best American Film of the Year.

For MGM, Robinson was a fugitive from a chain gang (wrongly convicted, of course, since he was now playing sympathetic roles if not necessarily stalwart heroes) in *Blackmail*. The man who sent him to prison on a frameup (twice, yet!) was Gene Lockhart, in one of his dastardly villain characterizations.

Then Robinson got four exceptionally strong roles at Warners. The first, *Dr. Ehrlich's Magic Bullet*, considered by the critics one of the truly memorable biographical screen studies, is still thought by many fans as the best thing the actor has ever done on film, and, after *Little Caesar*, it is the one most closely associated with Robinson. As Paul Ehrlich, the bewhiskered, bespectacled Edward G. Robinson was the scientist who discovered 606, the specific against syphilis. "The most dramatic and moving medical film I have ever seen," Howard Barnes wrote in his critique in the *Herald-Tribune*, "due in no small part to the brilliant portrayal of Dr. Ehrlich by Mr. Robinson . . . an understanding performance which is in the first rank of biographical portraits."

Critical acclaim notwithstanding, Robinson was overlooked by the Academy of Motion Picture Arts and Sciences in its Oscar nominations. (Ironically, Edward G. Robinson, regardless of his stature as a finished actor, had never been nominated for an Academy Award nor a Tony for his stage work nor an Emmy for a television performance.)

"You can't imagine the pleasure I got out of playing Dr. Ehrlich," Robinson later remarked. "So far, most of the rats, detectives, prosecutors and editors I've played were two-dimensional characters, and it was up to me to round them out, to give them flesh and blood and qualities of human beings. But Ehrlich is a different matter altogether. The character is there —and a great character it is—and all an actor has to do is play it honestly and simply."

Jack Warner then handed Robinson the role of Little John Sarto in *Brother Orchid*, one of the truly funny gangster spoofs on film. As Sarto, Robinson progressed from erstwhile hard-boiled crook to lovable, orchid-growing monk. He was surrounded by a superb cast including Ann Sothern, Donald Crisp, Ralph Bellamy, Cecil Kellaway, Charles D. Brown, Morgan Conway (later, the screen's Dick Tracy), and, in another of their meetings, Humphrey Bogart playing Jack Buck, whose "protection racket" ensures the sale of the monastery's flowers.

Bosley Crowther noted in his review in *The New York Times* that Robinson had agreed to make this one last gangster film for Warners for the privilege of playing Dr. Paul Ehrlich. The critic went on to comment: "A funnier piece of hardboiled impudence hasn't been enjoyed hereabouts since Mr. Robinson's Remy Marco found his house cluttered up with certain parties, not so tastefully composed, in *A Slight Case of Murder*."

Another serious biographical study followed, with Robinson portraying Paul Julius Baron Reuter, the founder (in 1858) of the great English newsgathering

Lobby card for Robinson's 1938 comedy at the height of his Warner Bros. stardom

service which bears his name. *A Dispatch From Reuters* found the actor again heading a top drawer cast: Edna Best as his wife; Otto Kruger, Albert Basserman and Montagu Love, all of whom were with him in the Ehrlich film; Eddie Albert, Gene Lockhart, Nigel Bruce and Walter Kingsford.

Robinson's first film in 1941 was *The Sea Wolf*, and he offered a strange interpretation of Jack London's famed sea captain, Wolf Larsen. (This was the fifth of seven cinemizations of *The Sea Wolf*, although the story was also used by Warners in 1950 as the basis of *Barricade*, transplanted from the high seas to the High Sierras.) Through Robert Rossen's screenplay, the Robinson conception of Larsen was more psychological than that of his predecessors, and he made the captain of *The Ghost* a true sadist. This was the second of the actor's two pictures directed by Michael Curtiz (*Kid Galahad* was the other), and it was the only time he worked with either Ida Lupino (as the shady lady passenger) or John Garfield (as George Leach, the cabin boy), from the Warner contract player roster. The press preview for *The Sea Wolf* was held on the high seas—on a liner

between Los Angeles and San Francisco—and was attended by Robinson, Garfield, Miss Lupino, and Hobart Bosworth, who was the screen's first Wolf Larsen in 1913. (The others: Noah Beery Sr. in 1920; Ralph Ince in 1925; Milton Sills in 1930; Barry Sullivan in 1958; and Chuck Connors in 1975.)

Besides the interesting teaming of Robinson with both George Raft and Marlene Dietrich, *Manpower* offered nothing but a story which was more than slightly similar in plot to Warners' earlier *Slim* (1937). As is often the case, it was just three great talents getting all they could—and a bit more—out of a banal script. It was the first time Robinson and Raft worked together "live," although both had appeared as animated characters in a 1936 Merrie Melodies cartoon called *The Coocoonut Grove*. The next professional meeting between the two would be in 1955, and again they appeared as adversaries.

The fourth and final time Edward G. Robinson and Mervyn LeRoy were on the same picture was in the actor's next film, *Unholy Partners*, at MGM. Three screenwriters toiled on this one, among them Bartlett

30

Playing the Palace on Broadway with Kate Smith in the late 1930s

Cormack, the author of *The Racket*. Like *Manpower*, *Unholy Partners* was not really worthy of Robinson's talents, to say nothing of the others in the cast: Edward Arnold, Laraine Day, Marsha Hunt, et al. In it, Robinson was an erstwhile reporter who decided to publish his own tabloid, but lack of funds forced him to go into partnership with gangster Edward Arnold. Much of the footage was given over to confrontations between the two.

With *Larceny, Inc.*, Robinson wound up his long association with Warner Bros. An adaptation of the Laura and S. J. Perelman play, *The Night Before Christmas*, the film comedy had Robinson back in harness—as a gangster named Pressure Maxwell (who ends up as a pillar of society). Among the members of Warners' stock company in support were Jane Wyman, Jack Carson, Broderick Crawford, Anthony Quinn, Edward Brophy, Harry Davenport and Jackie Gleason. Of his three gangster spoofs for Warners, this would be the least successful. A brief announcement accompanying *The New York Times* review of the film noted that Warners had recently purchased an unpublished story by Guy Kilpatric saluting the Merchant Marines. It was to be the basis of a film called *Heroes Without Uniforms* and a vehicle for Robinson, Bogart, Raft and Sydney Greenstreet. When it finally reached the screen as *Action in the North Atlantic*, only Bogart remained from the original proposed lineup.

Free now from his long-term contract and from his weekly radio series, *Big Town* (which he left on July 2, 1942), Robinson spent some time in Europe on tours of various military installations, and then returned to make appearances in two omnibus films by French director Julien Duvivier, who produced them with Charles Boyer (who also acted in both). In each, Robinson had the opportunity to demonstrate his acting abilities in small parts, developing and socking over three-dimensional characterizations in his briefly allotted screen time.

In *Tales of Manhattan*, a compilation of stories revolving around a man's dress coat and the effect it has on the lives of those who come in contact with it, Robinson, in his portion, was a successful lawyer-turned-Bowery-alcoholic who wears the coat to his graduation class reunion at the Waldorf-Astoria—and is given a second chance at life. (An episode starring W. C. Fields, running approximately twenty minutes, was deleted from the final print because the film was too long and the sequence was the easiest to remove. It now remains a curiosity among Fields fans and cinema buffs.)

With Hope Hampton and Herbert Marshall in 1939

In *Flesh and Fantasy*, which has been likened to a cinema program of three one-act plays, Robinson appeared in the second episode, an adaptation of Oscar Wilde's *The Crime of Doctor Saville*. The actor was seen as an American attorney in London who is convinced by palmist Thomas Mitchell that he will commit murder. And he does—he murders the palmist.

The three Robinson cinematic contributions to the war effort were rather weak affairs. *Destroyer*, which Columbia Pictures ill-advisedly attempted to liken to the classic *In Which We Serve*, found Robinson in uniform as a real old salt who has his moment in battle and then relinquishes his job as Chief Boatswain's Mate and

Leading a Hollywood contingent to the White House: (l-r) Mrs. Pat O'Brien, Gloria Jean, Brenda Joyce, EGR, Dorothy Lamour, William Boyd, Eleanor Roosevelt, Grace Bradley (Mrs. William Boyd), Gladys Lloyd Robinson, Olivia de Havilland, Ona Munson and James Cagney

Publicity shot with Edward Arnold and Laraine Day for UNHOLY PARTNERS (1941)

the hand in marriage of daughter Marguerite Chapman to costar Glenn Ford. In *Tampico*, again playing an old sea dog, Robinson battled a Nazi spy ring, tangled with a young lady (Lynn Bari) who might or might not have been an enemy collaborator, and sparred with First Mate Victor McLaglen.

And as Wilbert Winkle, a tinkerer wed to a shrew, Robinson was an overage draftee who distinguishes himself as a war hero, in a film version of Theodore Pratt's novel, *Mr. Winkle Goes to War* (promoted by Columbia Pictures as "In the Great 'Mr. Deeds' Tradition"). It was an unsuccessful melding of comedy and drama, and even Robinson seemed to agree, through his performance, that he was uncomfortable in the role.

If the preceding three roles can be considered lesser Robinson, the three which followed more than compensated for the unpardonable waste of his talent. Billy Wilder's taut classic, *Double Indemnity*, a harsh examination of an almost perfect crime, came first. Wilder and Raymond Chandler fashioned a superb screenplay from a series of stories by James M. Cain, written for *Liberty Magazine* and allegedly based on a murder case of the 1920s. Wilder then convinced Paramount to let him cast their star light comedian, Fred MacMurray, as a villain (which they did since MacMurray was in the process of wrapping up his contract with the studio). Next the writer-director argued a good case with Barbara Stanwyck, who apparently did not relish the idea of playing a murderess—even in a blonde wig. To Edward G. Robinson, Wilder entrusted the role of the insurance investigator who is bothered by a suspicious claim and learns that this colleague is a murderer.

Although the entire film was done in flashback, with MacMurray tipping the plot with his opening line, "I've killed a man," Wilder delicately maintained the suspense to the last frame—and presumably beyond, since a long trial and execution sequence running about

Robinson in 1941

Publicity shot with Fred MacMurray and Barbara Stanwyck
for DOUBLE INDEMNITY (1944)

With Gladys and Manny on
the set of SCARLET STREET
(1946)

Robinson in the early 1950s

twenty minutes was deleted from the final print, which now ends with Robinson calling for a police ambulance to take the wounded MacMurray to the hospital. Much later Robinson said: "That scene that we did shoot but was never seen was good for the character I played in that he witnessed the execution of his only friend (MacMurray), and he feels that he is the one who has killed MacMurray because the gnawing of an inner person forced him (my character) to suspect that the original death was not suicide. And it was the reaction of that character witnessing the execution that was very, very dramatic." Robinson, it is universally agreed, came off best in this film, doing full justice to the role as written by Wilder and Chandler in this intriguing adult drama. (Robinson might have been given third billing, but his on-screen credit had his name much larger than that of his illustrious co-stars.)

An even greater part came to Edward G. Robinson in his next film, *The Woman in the Window*, the first of two he did under the direction of Fritz Lang. Again blessed with a literate script—this one by Nunnally Johnson from J. H. Wallis's novel, *Once Off Guard*—Robinson was cast as a psychology professor whose drab life is changed when he meets the model whose portrait in the window of a gallery near his club he has admired for some time. With her, he gives in to one moment of emotional weakness (hence the title of the original novel) and becomes involved in murder. Merle Oberon was originally signed to star opposite Robinson, but the role subsequently was taken by Joan Bennett. Most knowledgeable critics agree that the superior melodrama was compromised when director Lang "copped-out" with a trick ending—having Robinson awaken from a dream of all that had gone on before. Lang, however, defended it in an article, "Happily Ever After," he had written in 1948 for *Penguin Film Review* No. 5. He claimed it was necessary, since "if I had continued the story to its logical conclusion, a man would have been caught and executed for committing a murder because he was one moment off guard." Thought Robinson, in retrospect: "They were thinking, I suppose, of box-office. Why kill him since he was a sympathetic character. Perhaps they thought that would be too morbid—like *Double Indemnity*."

In his third successive Grade-A role, Robinson was Martinius Jacobson, a Norwegian-American farmer in Wisconsin, who helps awaken in his young daughter, played by Margaret O'Brien, the realities of life. The film was *Our Vines Have Tender Grapes*, and the Dalton Trumbo screenplay from George Victor Martin's novel allowed Robinson to create another of his memorable characterizations, and Thomas M. Pryor wrote of it in his review in *The New York Times*: "One of the finest performances of his long and varied career."

During the war years, after leaving "Big Town," Robinson did a variety of dramatic appearances on radio and was selected by *Motion Picture Herald* as "The most effective film personality on radio." In addition, he devoted a great deal of energy to various patriotic and religious causes. On screen, he spoke the English commentary for the feature-length Russian documentary, *Moscow Strikes Back*, in 1942, and the following year he was narrator for a short called *The Red Cross At War*. He, Paul Muni and Jacob Ben-Ami, along with a group of other actors, participated on March 9, 1943, at New York's Madison Square Garden, in a mass memorial to the Jews who had lost their lives during the Nazi regime. Entitled *We Will Never Die* and written by Ben Hecht, it was seen by 40,000 people during two performances. Ben-Ami narrated and as described by *The New York Times*: "Paul Muni and Edward G. Robinson, dwarfed by the great stone tablets [in a massive set erected in the Garden], came through the space between the Ten Commandments . . . [and] alternately they recited the record that Jews have written into world history, from Abraham and Moses down to our time."

During 1944, Robinson was heard as narrator on *Too Long, America*, a radio documentary about racial intolerance; toured France with a U.S.O. troupe; made propaganda broadcasts in various languages for the Voice of America; and, at the invitation of the British Ministry of Information, acted in a feature-length semi-documentary (for which he took no salary), *Journey Together*, as an American flight instructor involved in the training of R.A.F. pilots. (It was released in the U.S. in 1946.)

Following the war, Robinson was scheduled to star for Paramount in a motion picture called *Bright Journey*, from an original screenplay by Arnold Manoff to be directed by actor Paul Stewart. The project, in which Robinson was to portray a venal fight promoter, never got off the ground. The later *Body and Soul* was remarkably similar in story-line. John Garfield assumed the lead and Lloyd Gough took the role Robinson was to have played.

Edward G. Robinson's first postwar picture, thus became his second for Fritz Lang: *Scarlet Street*. It was produced independently (since no studio would touch the story because of its "adult" theme) by a company known as Diana Productions, headed by Fritz Lang, Walter Wanger, and his wife, Joan Bennett, and it reunited Robinson, Miss Bennett and Dan Duryea in an attempt to again spark the kind of electricity they had produced in *The Woman in the Window*. The new project had been adapted by Dudley Nichols from Georges de la Fouchardière's play, *La Chienne*, and had been previously filmed (in 1931) by Jean Renoir under that title.

Among the problems confronting *Scarlet Street* were the many similarities (probably too many) between it and *The Woman in the Window*. As in the picture it followed, *Scarlet Street* dealt with a middle-aged philanderer with a weakness that involved him with a shady young woman and, later, a murder for which another man is accused. While *Scarlet Street* played more with irony at its climax than with a trick ending, *The Woman in the Window* still towers above it as a tauter, more perfectly rounded melodrama (the fadeout notwithstanding).

In a lengthy Sunday piece about the film, Bosley Crowther wrote of *Scarlet Street*: "In picturing this slightly noxious story, Walter Wanger and Fritz Lang have combined some rather vivid movie-making with some pretty weak fictitious stuff, so that the whole thing comes out a variably absorbing and irritating show. Edward G. Robinson is mousy—perhaps a little too earnestly so—as the cashier, Dan Duryea is salty as the boy friend, and Joan Bennett makes a rather spiritless cat."

If *Scarlet Street* was not the success all involved had hoped, it was not for lack of publicity. Six weeks before its scheduled New York opening (January 1946), it was slapped with a ban by the Motion Picture Division of the New York State Department of Education. Rather than requesting certain deletions in this "adult drama," the Board of Review banned the entire film, an action taken only rarely against a major Hollywood production (like *The Outlaw*). On appeal, the Board announced that, in consideration of public opinion and the seriousness of the film's intentions (!), the motion picture would be licensed for exhibition if certain unspecified cuts were made—like, allegedly, elimination of six of the seven stabs which Christopher Cross (Robinson) inflicts on Kitty March (Bennett) with an ice pick, as well as certain isolated lines of dialogue. The cuts were made.

Next, Robinson worked for and with Orson Welles in *The Stranger*, from a screenplay by Anthony Veiller and John Huston. Taking the part originally intended for Agnes Moorehead, long a member of Welles' Mercury Players (but presumably without strong enough name value for marquee bait), Robinson was a war crimes commissioner posing as an art collector (type casting?) who tracks down the former commandant of a Nazi prison camp now posing as a school teacher in a Connecticut town. He got the majority of the critical notices on this film, which turned out to be an arch Wellesian exercise, both in cinematic techniques and in acting excesses (with the exception, of course, of Robinson).

Then, with producer Sol Lesser, Robinson formed a new production company called Film Guild Corporation, which turned out only one film—*The Red House*, a memorable chiller paced by the performances of Robinson and Judith Anderson and of four young players: Lon McCallister, Allene Roberts, Julie London and Rory Calhoun. With a screenplay by Delmer Daves (who also directed) from the novel by George Agnew Chamberlain, *The Red House* was embraced by the critics as a true adult hair-raiser.

Shortly after that film's release, some rather adverse publicity that would seriously affect Robinson's future movie career began appearing in print. Column and magazine items had begun to imply that the actor was a Communist, or at least a Communist sympathizer—or perhaps something less than 100 percent American.

During the Thirties, Robinson had become well-known to all kinds of fund-raisers in Hollywood as the softest touch in town. He had told an interviewer back in 1938, "Everybody on the Coast keeps hollering at me to do something about improving the world either in the movies or out. They want me to stump for this ism or that ism. I would but I don't know anything about isms. I'd rather listen to the worst violinist in the world than be the best politician." Instead, he apparently had lent his name and given his money to a whole spectrum of causes—and this generosity (or naïveté) came back to haunt him a decade later. *Newsweek*, for one, bluntly stated: "Edward G. Robinson is persistently found in Communist fronts." And in a news story headed "Civil Rights Group Called Red Front" (August 31, 1947), *The New York Times* said that Edward G. Robinson's name was included on the "initiating committee." The story went on to detail that, when contacted, Robinson did not recall whether he had agreed to be one of the committee, but "if I lent my name, I am sure it was in behalf of the best American ideals. I don't believe in Communism and I never lend my name to any organization that smacks of Communism."

In 1950, *Red Channels* listed Robinson as having been connected with eleven alleged Communist fronts. The publication made no mention of the more than 300 other groups he had patronized in one way or another.

Robinson insisted upon appearing before the House Un-American Activities Committee to clear his name ("I couldn't let anyone call me a Communist," he explained), and subsequently testified three times. On October 27, 1950, he submitted a twelve-page list of contributions over a ten-year period and detailed a full record of his war activities. Two months later, he again appeared, answering questions fully, repeating his war record, and telling members of the committee that he had sent a transcript of his earlier testimony to J. Edgar Hoover.

He also told the hearing: "You are the only tribunal we have in the United States where an American citizen can come and ask for this kind of relief. . . . I am sorry if I have become a little bit emotional . . . because I

think I have not only been a good citizen, I think I have been an extraordinarily good citizen and I value this above everything else."

Robinson made a final committee appearance on April 30, 1952, reading again into the record his war activities and his list of contributions. He was finally cleared with this finding from HUAC: "According to the evidence to this committee, you are a good, loyal and intensely patriotic American citizen."

The actor's friend, writer Jo Swerling, later said: "Eddie was terribly hurt by the Congressional hearings professionally. This is a very cool industry, unfriendly to anybody in trouble. He was broken up by it. It almost ruined his life. It cost him a fortune. Eddie spent, I'd say $100,000 in legal fees and for trips to Washington." Swerling also recalled that after the hearings had begun, producers stopped offering Robinson "the type of parts he was accustomed to getting."

The effect of all of Robinson's well-documented problems did not immediately reflect on the actor's career. Following *The Red House*, there had been four other films in the works before the HUAC investigation of Hollywood got under way.

First, there was the Chester Erskine screen adaptation of Arthur Miller's powerful play, *All My Sons*, with Robinson portraying the corrupt airplane-parts manufacturer who had caused the death of twenty-one flyers including his own son. The critical notices were mixed on the film version, but most agreed that Robinson came off well in his interpretation of Joe Keller, the part that Ed Begley had originated on Broadway.

Key Largo reunited him with Bogart back at the old lot (where Bogart was now the company's ace attraction just as Robinson had been a decade earlier), and Robinson gave another memorable performance as the ruthless Johnny Rocco. As Bosley Crowther put it in his review, "an expertly timed and timbered scan of the vulgarity, corruption and egoism of a criminal mind." In his book, *Agee on Film*, critic James Agee made this observation: "The first shot of Edward G. Robinson in *Key Largo*, mouthing a cigar and sweltering naked in a tub of cold water ('I wanted to get a look at the animal with its shell off') is one of the most powerful and efficient 'first entrances' of a character on record." And Robinson's scene forcing his alcoholic mistress, Gaye Dawn (Claire Trevor), to sing "Moanin' Low" before giving her the drink for which she had been begging, and then refusing to give it to her, further demonstrated that he had not lost his sadistic touch in the years since he played Rico Bandello. This was John Huston's follow-up to his superb *The Treasure of the Sierra Madre*, and he and Richard Brooks had virtually rewritten Maxwell Anderson's free-verse play. For her performance in the film, Claire Trevor won an Oscar.

Night Has a Thousand Eyes, with Robinson an ex-vaudevillian who finds himself endowed with clairvoyant powers and attempts to prevent a murder he has foreseen, turned out a rather tepid, unsuccessful cinemization of Cornell Woolrich's interesting novel.

The final film in this phase of Robinson's career, however, gave him wide latitude for another carefully etched and memorable characterization—as Gino Monetti, the barber from New York's Little Italy who had become a successful banker, and whose three sons fight to take over the empire he had created while the fourth, who had gone to prison for him, returns to avenge his father. The picture, *House of Strangers*, was shown at the 1949 Cannes Film Festival, and for his performance in it Robinson was chosen Best Actor of the Year.

Robinson also made a brief appearance spoofing his familiar gangster interpretation in Warners' Doris Day musical, *It's a Great Feeling*. Then he found his services were no longer in demand, and he went to Europe to seek roles.

He found only one, in the English film, *My Daughter Joy* (shown in the United States as *Operation X*). It was an adaptation of Irene Nemirowsky's novel, *David Golder*, and had been filmed under that title by Julien Duvivier in France in 1931 with Harry Baur in the leading role. In the new version, directed by Gregory Ratoff and minus its political and racial inferences (about a Jewish conspiracy to rule the world), Robinson was cast as a power-hungry millionaire who rose from bootblack in this study of megalomania.

Then he returned to the United States and asked HUAC to hear his testimony. Between his second and third appearances before the committee, Robinson returned to the stage for the first time in more than two decades, as Rubashov, the disenchanted Communist, in *Darkness at Noon*. While Claude Rains was playing the role on Broadway, Robinson headed the national company for a 26-week tour (September 28, 1951–April 26, 1952). Supposedly, Sidney Kingsley, the play's producer and co-author (with Arthur Koestler), had originally offered the role of Rubashov to Robinson, but the actor turned it down because it was too exhausting a part, requiring him to be on stage through every single minute of the action.

Until he was finally cleared by HUAC, the only motion picture work Robinson could obtain was in *Actors and Sin*, an independent two-part film written, produced and directed by his friend, Ben Hecht. Robinson appeared in the first story, "Actor's Blood," playing a fading star who attempts an odd revenge upon the boy friends of his actress daughter (Marsha Hunt) by making her suicide appear to be murder so that each will be a suspect.

The Hollywood work he at last *was* able to locate provided him with a series of rather undistinguished roles in some dreary B films. *Vice Squad* revolved around a routine day in the life of a big city police official and was told in semi-documentary style; *The Big Leaguer* had Robinson in a baseball uniform, playing the part of Hans Lobert, a real-life scout for the New York Giants who was put in charge of the organization's training camp in Florida, and was the first picture in his screen career which did not have a regular play-date in Manhattan (and odd, since it was produced by MGM—certainly a major studio—and since it dealt with baseball as played by a New York team); *The Glass Web* found him as a television researcher who is played off against TV writer John Forsythe by their mutual girlfriend, Kathleen Hughes, an enterprising young would-be actress. *The Glass Web* was, incidentally, Robinson's sole 3-D movie—and hardly worth the effort.

In *Black Tuesday*, he was once again a vicious snarling killer (to the joy both of critics and fans), and in *The Violent Men*, playing Barbara Stanwyck's crippled husband who finds himself cuckolded by his younger brother (Brian Keith), Robinson appeared in the first western of his career. The only apparent reason for *A Bullet for Joey* was the teaming again of Robinson and George Raft.

Tight Spot, a rather stagey film version of Lenard Kantor's play *Dead Pigeon*, had Robinson star as a U.S. attorney trying to keep material witness (Ginger Rogers) alive to testify against a gangster (Lorne Greene), with most of what action there was confined to a hotel room. And in *Illegal*, Robinson was a former District Attorney who makes a comeback as a defense lawyer for a crime syndicate. The film was Warners' remake of its *Mouthpiece* (1932) and its *The Man Who Talked Too Much* (1940); it was thought to be vaguely similar in structure to *The Asphalt Jungle* of W. R. Burnett (who, by coincidence, co-authored the screenplay of *Illegal*).

The vintage Robinson surfaced, though, in Warners' *Hell on Frisco Bay*. He was cast as Victor Amato, the vicious waterfront boss whose nemesis is an ex-cop he had framed (Alan Ladd). This was the Robinson of *Little Caesar*, older by twenty-five years, but excitingly alive in a meaty, incisive role, spiced with sharp dialogue (by Martin Rackin and Sydney Boehm), sardonic wit, and the perfect opportunity—with one snarl wrapped behind him—to act rings around the entire cast. And Edward G. Robinson was never one to let a good role slip by unmolded.

Nightmare, alas, was something else again—a weak programmer from another story by Cornell Woolrich (who wrote it under his pen name, William Irish), and previously filmed by Paramount in 1947 as *Fear in the Night* by the same director, Maxwell Shane. Again Robinson was a detective.

And, in a brief but telling role as a cruel Hebrew overseer who uses every opportunity to make points

With son Manny in 1952 at the HUAC hearings in Washington

with the Egyptians by betraying Moses, Robinson closed out another phase of his film career in DeMille's massive new version of *The Ten Commandments*. Replying to a comment about how, as the Hebrew leader Dathan, he looked as though he had just stepped from the pages of the Bible, Robinson said: "You sort of have to get into a role—to feel it and sense it and dwell on it and get inside it. Something I've always believed in: you may *look* the part but that doesn't mean you're going to play it. But if you *feel* the part, you'll look it. Sensing that role made me take on the look."

Also disappearing at this stage of Robinson's career was the Hollywood in which he ranked as the least star-like (in appearance) of all the major stars. He was asked to comment on the changing system, with businessmen replacing the moguls who had been absolute czars. "In retrospect," he felt, "seeing these college-bred men now, functioning on their own, I think the Mayers and the Goldwyns and the Warners served a great purpose. You can get any number of college men, but they don't often become very good picture-makers who are great gamblers and who have an intuitive feeling for what should be done on the screen. A great many of those older producers were very illiterate—I'm not going to mention names—but somehow they had that special something to produce pictures and to assemble the many, many talents that go into a production."

During this period, Robinson also began dabbling in television. He made his network debut (as did Bing Crosby) in a guest appearance on an NBC telethon for the U.S. Olympic Committee which was hosted by Bob Hope (June 21, 1952). His first dramatic work on the medium was on the *Lux Video Theater* (September 17,1953) in "Witness for the Prosecution"—it had nothing to do with the Agatha Cristie mystery that was to become a stage hit around that time. Then he did a pilot film for a proposed weekly series, *For the Defense* (1954), in which he had planned to star as a former

police captain turned criminal defense attorney. The series never materialized and whether this single half-hour episode was ever shown is undetermined.

He *was* seen, though, late in 1954 in a TV adaptation of Eric Ambler's *Epitaph for a Spy* for the CBS *Climax!* series. Robinson played an unsuspecting Iron Curtain refugee who is used as a pawn by a pair of French traitors while vacationing in Southern France. In January 1955, and again the following December, he appeared in teleplays on NBC's *Ford Theater*, and in late 1956, Robinson and Vincent Price, both acknowledged art authorities, put their expertise on the line over a four-week period on the popular, pre-scandal-plagued *The $64,000 Challenge*.

On February 25, 1956, Robinson's wife of twenty-nine years sued for divorce. According to Robinson's autobiography, she had become a manic-depressive many years earlier, had been in and out of sanitoriums since the early 1940s and had frequently started divorce proceedings and then withdrawn them. Gladys Lloyd Robinson died June 6, 1971 while attending the graduation of her granddaughter from Marymount, along with Robinson and his second wife, Jane. In August 1956, they arranged a settlement of $3.5 million in community property, plus 25 percent of all of the actor's future earnings. To meet these terms, Robinson was forced to sell what has been considered one of America's finest privately owned art collections, which he had begun when he purchased his first painting for two dol-

Publicity pose for BLACK TUESDAY (1954)

lars at a 1913 auction. (He had rebuilt much of his art treasury in the ensuing years since the divorce.) A page-one story in *The New York Times* (February 26, 1957) was headlined: "Edward G. Robinson Art Brings $3,000,000." Its purchaser was later identified as Greek shipping magnate Stavros Niarchos, who bought fifty-eight paintings and a Degas bronze. "I had put everything into pictures," Robinson explained, "and couldn't afford to buy my wife's share of their value."

Less than three weeks before the divorce announcement, Edward G. Robinson had returned to Broadway in Paddy Chayefsky's first stage play, *Middle of the Night*, and, as The Manufacturer, a middle-aged widower in love with a younger woman (Gena Rowlands), the star was in top form and scored a personal artistic triumph. Wrote *The New York Times'* Brooks Atkinson: "It seems like old times to have Edward G. Robinson back. . . . [He] gives a winning and skillful performance, and no one could be more relaxed about a part. But no one could give the character more warmth or kindness, or make an undistinguished man so notable. If the years have done nothing else to him, they have supplied him with a quarter century of living, which leaves its mark on the soul of everyone who is perceptive.

As Dathan in THE TEN COMMANDMENTS (1956) as makeup artist Paul Malcolm (right) applies the finishing touches to EGR's beard, while his boss, Frank Westmore, supervises

"If there is any technical difference that can be noted by a theatergoer with a short memory," Atkinson continued, "it is a deepening of authority. His acting is effortless. . . . It is good to be reminded of his easy skill and to have him back with us again."

And Richard Watts, commenting in the *New York Post*, said: "Thanks in great part to the superb acting and moving performance of Edward G. Robinson in the leading role, the result is a touching and interesting drama that combines realism with sentiment in expertly showmanlike proportions."

The show ran for 479 performances on Broadway, and then Robinson took it on tour during the 1957-58 season. Ironically, as happened with the film version of *Death of a Salesman*, which he very much had wanted to do, Robinson lost the role of The Manufacturer to Fredric March when *Middle of the Night* reached the screen in 1959.

Edward G. Robinson married again on January 16, 1958, while *Middle of the Night* was being performed in Washington, D.C. His new wife, Jane Adler (née Jane Bodenheimer), twenty-six years his junior, was with the production end of the show in which Robinson was starring.*

The following October, he made his only appearance on the prestigious CBS-TV series, *Playhouse 90*, in

With fellow art collector Vincent Price at a Los Angeles gallery in 1957

*She, too, shared her husband's love of art, and in 1971, she authored with Leonard Spigelgass a chatty book about his collection, *Edward G. Robinson's World of Art*.

Following wedding to Jane Adler, January 16, 1958

characters were changed from Jews to Italians with the leading role refashioned to fit the personality of Sinatra (who co-produced with director Frank Capra), but the best lines went to Edward G. Robinson and to Thelma Ritter who played the latter's wife. Bosley Crowther, writing in *The New York Times*, felt that "As the brother, a narrow-minded dullard, Edward G. Robinson is superb; funny while being most officious and withering while saying the drollest things." The role proved a good beginning to the latest part of Robinson's film career—as a superlative character actor. Together with *Hell on Frisco Bay*, it provided him with the best screen part he had during the 1950s.

He began the next decade by playing Daniel Webster in an hour-long television adaptation (by Phil Reisman Jr.) of Stephen Vincent Benet's *The Devil and Daniel Webster* (David Wayne was The Devil) on NBC—and rerun, curiously, on CBS two years later.

Robinson was seen on the wide screen in 1960 twice. In *Seven Thieves*, he took the part of an old-time crook who masterminds a $4 million robbery of the Casino at Monte Carlo and dies of a heart attack from the excitement of the caper. The film was a screen version of Max Catto's novel, *Lions at the Kill*, and was the first of many

Ernest Kinoy's "Shadows Tremble." Robinson was a retired toy manufacturer who decided to buy the historic Vermont home in which he had regularly summered, but the tradition-bound villagers did not take kindly to "immigrants" and he found himself virtually ignored by them. Early the next year, he made a pair of dramatic television appearances in fairly rapid succession. He starred on the *Goodyear Theater* in "A Good Name" (as a clothing manufacturer) in March, and four weeks later, he was seen on an episode of the *Zane Grey Theater*, acting opposite his son in a Civil War story called "Loyalty." This was the first time the two Robinsons had worked together professionally and followed a long, well-documented estrangement between the two which first became public in 1952. The younger Robinson talked freely of it in his autobiography, *My Father, My Son*, published in 1957.

Robinson's return to the screen was as Frank Sinatra's older brother in the film version of Arnold Shulman's play, *A Hole in the Head*. It was originally written for television and aired in 1955 under the title, *The Heart Is a Forgotten Hotel*. It was expanded for the Broadway stage where it opened in February 1957 as *A Hole in the Head*, and was turned into the musical *Golden Rainbow* eleven years later. For the film, the

With Manny on the set of TV's *Zane Grey Theatre* in 1959

in which Robinson would blueprint a complicated crime for others to execute—like *The Biggest Bundle of Them All*, *Grand Slam*, *Never a Dull Moment* and *Mad Checkmate*.

Next he turned up as a "guest star" in *Pepe*, which was an overblown, overlong movie written to exploit the talents of the Mexican star Cantinflas, but which virtually destroyed that brilliant clown's career in this country. Robinson was seen as a film producer (named Edward G. Robinson) who gives a down-and-out director (Dan Dailey) his comeback chance and who returns to Cantinflas a horse the diminutive Mexican had doggedly followed for 195 screen minutes (plus intermission).

Robinson was off the screen until mid-1962 (part of the time filming in Japan and in Italy), but he was seen on television in 1961 first on the *General Electric Theater* in a story called "The Drop-Out" and then in an episode of Robert Taylor's series, *The Detectives*, entitled "The Legend of Jim Riva." In "The Drop-Out," Robinson was a salesman who welcomes his high school drop-out son (played by Billy Gray) into the business and is satisfied to learn at the fadeout that the boy has doubts about leaving school after making the rounds

A film-wrap toast to A HOLE IN THE HEAD (1959) with Frank Sinatra and Frank Capra

Arriving in Israel for the filming of ISRAEL (1959)

In Manhattan with wife Jane in 1960

with his father. And as "Big Jim Riva," the last of the big-time gangsters, Robinson was a man who is released from prison and who plans a quiet retirement. At his homecoming party, though, he and his wife are wounded by a young hood and he decides to round up his old mob to avenge his shooting.

The following March, he narrated "Cops and Robbers," a documentary in NBC-TV's *Project 20* series, which combined old still photos and rare film footage to trace the growth of American law-breaking from the days of Colonial piracy through the workings of contemporary syndicate operations.

In 1962, again playing a movie producer, Robinson appeared in a visually beautiful but rather lightweight comedy-drama called *My Geisha*, with Shirley MacLaine and Yves Montand (whom producers were still intent on making an American "star"). In *Two Weeks in Another Town*, he was cast not as a movie producer but, for a change of pace, as a movie director. The best thing about the film—in which almost none of the characters are either likeable or believable—is that he was reteamed with Claire Trevor (as his wife) for the first time since *Key Largo*, and they played, as *Variety* concluded, "the only lifelike people in the story."

While on location in Nairobi, Kenya, in June 1962, filming *Sammy Going South* (shown in the United States in mid-1965 under the title *A Boy Ten Feet Tall*), Robinson suffered a heart attack, but returned to complete his role in that motion picture. Back in the United States, he narrated, with Betty Hutton, Cornel Wilde and Barbara Stanwyck, *The World's Greatest Showman*, a ninety-minute television tribute to Cecil B. DeMille in December 1963. Interestingly, the show was produced not by Paramount, where DeMille created his most memorable spectaculars, but by MGM; it has the unique distinction of being introduced by the familiar logos of both companies—the MGM lion and the Paramount mountain.

His next motion picture role, in 1963, was in MGM's *The Prize*, which Mark Robson directed from Ernest Lehman's screenplay of the Irving Wallace novel. Robinson played a dual role—a Nobel Prize-winning German physicist who is kidnapped on the eve of the awards ceremonies and the twin brother who, years before, had defected to the East, and who is substituted for the good doctor. As inane as *The Prize* was on the screen, it proved to be a fun movie and Paul Newman's presence in practically every scene helped insure it huge boxoffice success.

Good Neighbor Sam the same year was a 1960s attempt at screwball comedy with Jack Lemmon as an advertising account-executive whose coup was obtaining the business of a straight-laced, middle-American, Bible-spouting dairy magnate, played with good humor

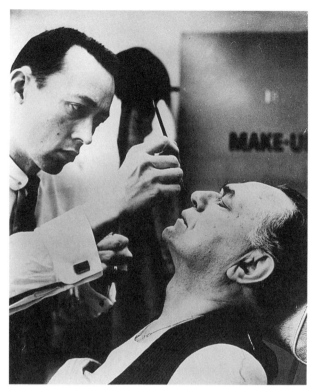

Being made up by Dick Smith for a TV production of THE DEVIL AND DANIEL WEBSTER in 1960

by Edward G. Robinson. And in *Robin and the Seven Hoods*, Robinson, in a gag appearance sans screen credit, played his briefest role in films, reprising his by-now personal gangster characterization and being killed off two minutes and twenty seconds into the story. A life-sized painting of him hung prominently, though, through much of the film as a reminder of who the boss was. And for Warner Bros., yet!

Billed simply as Con Man, Robinson was then in *The Outrage*, Martin Ritt's westernized version of Akira Kurosawa's *Rashomon*, perhaps the most famous of all Japanese films (at least in the Western world). Said A. H. Weiler in *The New York Times*: "Edward G. Robinson's portrayal of the bearded, seedy, cocky con artist is earthy and direct." And Wanda Hale wrote in the *Daily News*: "(He) is delightful as the cruddy old man, a cynic who hears the various versions of the crimes and believes none." He was next reunited with John Ford after three decades, turning up briefly in *Cheyenne Autumn* as Secretary of the Interior Carl Shurz, a role Spencer Tracy was originally to have played. As with his previous two or three screen appearances, this role could be considered not much more than a cameo.

Early in 1965, Robinson did more television, beginning with a dramatic reading on *Hollywood Palace*. Then he was seen in the TV drama *Who Has Seen the*

Wind? as the captain of a tramp steamer whose passengers include a family of stateless wanderers in the backlash of World War II, forced to spend their lives on shipboard because their country no longer exists. The program was the second in a series of ninety-minute dramas produced for the United Nations by Telsun Productions and underwritten by the Xerox Corporation. An international cast was featured (among the players: Stanley Baker, Maria Schell, Theodore Bikel, Gypsy Rose Lee, Victor Jory, Lilia Skala, Simon Oakland) and it marked the debut television assignment of director George Sidney.

And, at the end of 1965, he made an appearance on the popular TV game show, *What's My Line?*

A Boy Ten Feet Tall, which he had made in 1962 and in which he was the sole American, finally received an American release in May, 1965. In it, Robinson looked, as *Variety* noted: "like a slightly junior Ernest Hemingway," playing a grizzled diamond smuggler who helps a ten-year-old war orphan on his 2,000-mile trek from Port Said to Durban in search of relatives. In New York to promote the film, Robinson was interviewed by Howard Thompson of *The New York Times*, and the actor made these observations about his profession and about film-making in general:

There are certainly more jobs [for actors], but more problems from the standpoint of rounding one's talent. And acting is such a chaotic, haphazard profession, anyway, requiring so

With Kirk Douglas and Dahlia Lavi as Vincente Minnelli discusses an upcoming scene in TWO WEEKS IN ANOTHER TOWN

much careful handling and management. I searched deeply inside myself before I decided on it. When I was a kid of twelve, I first thought about the pulpit, then got over it. Then I thought about law. Then I did some amateur theatricals and finally made up my mind.

The danger today is being catapulted into an important decision too quickly. These people fall harder and more rapidly. I fought against the idea of being billed as a star here on Broadway before I went to Hollywood, and I fought again when *Little Caesar* came up. I told them to wait. The picture was a big hit. Still, I said to wait for a couple of more. I told them to go ahead, finally, on *Five-Star Final*. And I was a star.

As for film technique—well, I try to soak myself in the character. Sometimes it's strange and hard. You go over your lines, look for the key. Maybe it's in some little inflection. And it's not easy if you're handed a script on Friday and told to come in ready on Monday. I wanted to be loaded with my people. They talk about actors filling the screen. I think what they really mean is that loaded *character* filling it.

The director? That depends entirely upon him. But not many are helpful to we poor actors, I don't mind saying. You do maybe one or two takes, then they move the camera for new angles and you're frightened to death left all alone out there, knowing your sins are about to be recorded from generation to generation—and for television. Now, when I see some of my old pictures, I say to myself that I could have done this or that. I want to say, "Let's do that one again."

Although Robinson had gotten sole above-the-title billing in *A Boy Ten Feet Tall*, the starring role actually went to young Fergus McClelland, an unknown. Robinson had his best role in years, though, in his next

In Rome with Kirk Douglas in 1961 for TWO WEEKS IN ANOTHER TOWN

43

With Princess Margaret and Lord Snowden in 1963

role as an American CIA agent in a French film called *La Blonde de Pekin*, shot in late 1966 and first released in Europe in 1968. (It has never been shown theatrically in the United States.)

During the time he was away from American screens, Robinson's total professional exposure in the United States was a twenty-second walk-on (or head-out-the-window gag bit) on the *Batman* TV series in 1966. Late in 1967, after *Bonnie and Clyde* had gone into release and had begun to create the lingering controversy over violence in films and the current resurgence in gangster movies, Edward G. Robinson was asked to give his thoughts about the trend in a *Los Angeles Times* interview.

"Violence has always been a prevalent element in drama and all the performing arts, even ballet," he said. "I guess it's paradoxical to say that violence is entertaining, but it's practically impossible to create meaningful conflict without it. Besides, we all get a vicarious kick out of the violence we see on the screen. We live a great repression and this is one way to vent our feelings, to unwind by seeing violence depicted. My concern with this whole question is from the assertion that the gangster pictures of the 1930s were the first step toward the alleged glamorization of violence to pictures like *Bonnie and Clyde*. There is no place in motion picture history that we can point our finger to and say 'Violence started here' because violence is a fact of life, and therefore of

film—and it was a starring part. Playing Lancey Howard, the suave, wily old gentleman cardsharp in *The Cincinnati Kid*, he brought sharply to life a thoughtfully etched and finely honed portrait of The Man as author Richard Jessup had created him in his novel, and once again acted a part originally destined for Spencer Tracy. Wearing an immaculate suit, sporting a carefully barbered white goatee, lighting expensive cigars incessantly, Robinson battles Steve McQueen (in the title role), studying his young opponent through a stoic mask and through nothing more than slits where his weary, wary eyes should be. In one of the most suspenseful showdowns ever filmed, in a lengthy game of stud poker, The Kid, holding a full house, has to decide whether The Man holds a straight flush, and The Man must choose the exact moment to make the wrong move, as he is fond of saying, at the right time.

In *The Cincinnati Kid*, Robinson again worked with Joan Blondell—for the first time since *Bullets or Ballots* nearly thirty years before. He was then to remain off the screen for almost three years, although he had a small

Reminiscing with Joan Blondell about the old Warner Bros. days on the set of THE CINCINNATI KID (1965)

Publicity pose for THE CINCINNATI KID

With a very small portion of the fabled Robinson art collection

drama, and has been an integral part of films since the beginning."

Robinson was seen in cameo roles in 1968 in two Italian-made pictures with a similar theme—the perfect crime. He was the mastermind in both *The Biggest Bundle of Them All* (in which he was asked by a gangster friend, Vittorio De Sica, to set up the big platinum heist, which he did—through the use of visual aids: the "Madison Avenue touch," as he, as Professor Samuels, noted)—and in *Grand Slam* (where he was the architect and financier of an intricate diamond theft to be executed by younger, more agile confederates—all hand-picked specialists—during Carnaval in Rio de Janeiro).

His other two 1968-made films have had only spotty European release; and were sold directly to television in the United States. He was the brains behind another seemingly perfect bank robbery in an Italian-Spanish coproduction, *Uno scacco tutto matto (Mad Checkmate)*, and he was involved in the theft of Michelangelo's *Pieta* in *Operation St. Peter's* for an Italian-French-German motion picture combine.

His role in *Never a Dull Moment*, for the Walt Disney organization, was somewhat larger. Robinson was Leo Smooth, urbane arch-gangster, who has devised an ingenious art theft from the Los Angeles County Museum (where, ironically, many of his own personal paintings were on permanent loan). The robbery is foiled by an at-liberty actor (Dick Van Dyke) who has

stumbled onto the plans by error and who institutes a zany chase throughout the gallery.

In June 1968, Robinson was seriously injured in an automobile accident when his car hit a tree. "I must have fallen asleep," he told reporters when he was able. His hospitalization forced him to relinquish to Jose Ferrer the scheduled role of Hassan Bey, a Turkish war lord, in a film variously entitled *Cervantes* and *The Young Rebel* (Horst Buchholz played the lead), but the loss of the part was of not much consequence since the picture was poorly distributed and passed virtually unnoticed.

Robinson celebrated his 75th birthday in the company of close to 20,000 people at a Madison Square Garden salute which was tied in with the annual Hanukkah Festival in 1968, and he witnessed the world premiere of a new ballet dedicated to him.

In films, Robinson has a brief part in *Mackenna's Gold*, a big, rambling, seemingly out-of-hand western, which was produced by Carl Foreman. The actor appeared as a blind old prospector who is the only link to the exact location of the fabulous gold lode the rest of the disparate cast is seeking in the heart of Apache country. And in television, he starred, in April 1969, in a two-hour pilot film called "U.M.C." (for University Medical Center), which became a series during the 1969-70 season without him. He played an old doctor who is given a heart transplant by his close friend and protege, the skilled young house surgeon (Richard Bradford in the feature; Chad Everett in the weekly series).

In late 1970, he appeared briefly as a friendly piano dealer who sells one of the instruments to the wife of Edvard Grieg in the elaborate musical, *Song of Norway*, and he was seen on television in two dramatic roles which were aired in the span of ten days. In the first, "The Old Man Who Cried Wolf," on the ABC *Movie of the Week* anthology, Robinson was an aged gentleman who witnesses the murder of an old friend (played by old friend Sam Jaffe) but cannot convince the authorities or even his own family that a crime had been committed. Possibly because his was the only truly developed role in the teleplay, Robinson acted circles around the rest of the cast, and *Variety* called him "a tower of acting strength," while *The Hollywood Reporter* noted: "Robinson's performance is strong and moving." Percy Shain, television critic for *The Boston Globe*, felt that "Edward G. Robinson gave movies made for TV a boost with his outstanding performance," and Anthony LaCamera, who reviews television for the *Boston Record American*, decided: "Edward G. Robin-

With Efrem Zimbalist, Jr., on the set of TV's *The FBI*

son deserves an award for his tremendous performance in 'The Old Man Who Cried Wolf.'"

Said Robinson later: "I've gotten so much mail on *The Old Man Who Cried Wolf*, and they absolutely objected to the ending, saying 'Why did you have to die?' I say, people do die for their courage, determination and the things they see that the rest of the world doesn't see."

On the NBC series, *Bracken's World*, Robinson starred as a Hemingway-like character in a story entitled "The Mary Tree," which revolved around the documentary filming of the life of a famed author whose daughter suddenly appears to debunk the image he had so carefully built up over the years. Edward G. Robinson Jr. played a brief role in the episode and spoke a few lines. "We shot it in seven days," Robinson recalled, "which doesn't exactly give you too much rehearsal time. At least if your role is the lead, you have a chance to look at the script before you start and you have time for a conference with the writer and the producer and can suggest changes and discuss values and work on the relationships of the characters." Coincidentally, Robinson was appearing simultaneously on a competing program, *The Tom Jones Show*, doing a few dramatic readings.

On the eve of these aforementioned excursions into television in late 1970, Robinson looked forward to the beginning of a more active career in the medium. After complaining, with a chuckle, about television commer-

On the set of MACKENNA'S GOLD (1969)

At a testimonial dinner for old boss Jack L. Warner (third from right) in November 1969, joined by Bette Davis, Mervyn LeRoy, Rosalind Russell and new studio head Ted Ashley

Robinsons fil and pere in a publicity pose for "The Mary Tree" episode of NBC's *Bracken's World* in 1970

cials, and admitting that "the only one I look at is that Maxwell House Coffee spot which I did [in the late 1950s]," he told Kay Gardella of the New York *Daily News*: "Where I hesitated before, I wouldn't hesitate now to take on a TV role. I think they can do some wonderful things now. One always begins again, and I'm hopelessly in love with spring."

And, to *The Boston Globe's* Percy Shain he confided: "For many years I had turned up my nose to television. I feared I would have to make too many compromises. But I finally said to myself, 'Look, you have to make compromises in everything you do. At this stage of your life, what do you have to lose?' So I decided to get my feet wet. I tried making the pilot of *Medical Center*. Not bad, I said. So I decided to make the big plunge, do a Movie of the Week, to see if I could stand the gaff. Well, we worked on it for ten days, and when I say 'work,' I mean it. We worked days and nights, long hours. It was a little too much, I thought, but we got it done."

Robinson's last television appearance was in a 1971 episode of Rod Sterling's *Night Gallery* entitled "The Messiah on Mott Street."

When Edward G. Robinson was honored by the Masquers after sixty years of acting in the theater, on

With old friend and co-star Sam Jaffe on the set of Robinson's television movie, THE OLD MAN WHO CRIED WOLF (1970)

radio and in films, he spoke of himself as an actor and what it means to be one. "An audience identifies with the actor of flesh and blood, and heartbeat," he said, "as no reader or beholder can identify with even the most artful paragraphs in books, or the most inspired paintings. There, says the watcher, but for some small difference in time, or costume, or inflection, or gait, go I. And so the actor becomes the catalyst: he brings to bright ignition that spark in every human being that longs for the miracle of transformation."

He continued: "Every night the actor bears the stigmata which his imagination inflicts upon him and bleeds from a thousand words. I don't know that I have bled very much. If I have I feel no debility from that loss, perhaps because it has been more than balanced by my satisfactions. Now, in the twilight of my long days of acting, I feel invigorated, proud of the calling of player. I am sure it was not in vain. If mummer I was, it was not mere mummer, no more than any actor is mere, no more than any person who gives of himself to the enrichment of other is mere. Only to that degree will I look back."

Robinson's final two roles were in the little-seen Israeli-made *Neither by Day Nor by Night* and in

With *Laugh-In*'s inimitable Gladys Ormphby (aka Ruth Buzzi) in 1971

In his farewell screen role as Sol Roth in SOYLENT GREEN (1972)

Raymond Serra wrote and starred (as Edward G. Robinson) in the Broadway play MANNY (1979)

MGM's sci-fi *Soylent Green* in which a beautifully played death scene was to be his valedictory performance. In January 1973, the Academy of Motion Picture Arts and Sciences voted Edward G. Robinson a special Oscar in recognition of his body of work. He was very ill at the time and the statuette was presented him at his hospital bedside in advance of Oscar night. The Oscar was inscribed

TO EDWARD G. ROBINSON

Who achieved greatness as a player,
A patron of the arts and a dedicated
citizen . . .
In sum, a Renaissance Man.

FROM HIS FRIENDS IN THE INDUSTRY HE LOVES.

Edward G. Robinson died on January 26, 1973. His wife Jane officially accepted his Academy Award the following March at the Oscar ceremonies.

Just over a year after Edward G. Robinson's death, his only son, Edward G. Robinson, Jr., who in his 1957 autobiography, *My Father, My Son*, chronicled his trouble-plagued life, also died. He was forty.

Robinson continues to be remembered for the film legacy he left. That he was a star was confirmed in two theatrical works—one lovingly invoking his name, the other lovingly recalling his life. In late 1973, a play called *Edward G., Like the Film Star* by John Harvey Flint was staged by the Folger Library Theatre Group in Washington, D.C., and then played briefly in London during the 1973-74 season. (Beyond the title, it had nothing to do with Edward G. Robinson himself.)

In the spring of 1978, character actor Raymond Serra starred as Edward G. Robinson in a play he wrote called *Manny*, spanning the actor's life from 1927 until his death. Frances Helm took the role of Gladys and Loren Hayes was Eddie, Jr. *Manny* played for thirty-one performances at the Century Theatre in New York and then toured the country.

(*Facing page*) Robinson in 1971

THE FILMS

ARMS AND THE WOMAN: Robinson in his very first screen role (to the right of the player gesturing)

ARMS AND THE WOMAN

1916   Pathe-Gold Rooster Plays

Produced by Astra Film Corporation; Director, George Fitzmaurice; Scenario, Ouida Bergere; Photography, A.C. Miller; Art director, Anton Grot. 5 reels

Rozika (*Mary Nash*), David Fravoe (*Lumsden Hare*), Captain Halliday (*H. Cooper Cliffe*), Marcus (*Robert Broderick*), Marcus' Wife (*Rosalind Ivan*), Carl (*Carl Harbaugh*), Factory worker (*Edward G. Robinson*), Bit (*Susanne Willa*)

Edward G. Robinson, just establishing himself on the stage, made his movie debut in a tiny role as an anarchist in this filmed-in-New York drama, written by noted silent screen scenarist Ouida Bergere (later Mrs. Basil Rathbone). It follows the fortunes of a young Hungarian girl named Rozika who has emigrated to America with her brother Carl and has found work singing in a New York dive. When Carl accidentally kills a man during a brawl and has to go into hiding—he is given shelter by an anarchist group—Rozika loses her job and has to sing in the streets. She soon attracts the attention of wealthy steel manufacturer, David Fravoe. They marry and he makes her into an opera star. With the outbreak of the war in Europe, she tries to stop her husband from selling munitions to the allies and even becomes involved with the anarchist brotherhood that has given shelter to her brother. Carl, meanwhile, has been pressed by the anarchists into a plot to destroy Fravoe's munitions factory. Rozika learns of it and tries too late to warn her husband. The factory is bombed, Fravoe is wounded by a gunshot, and Carl dies in the fire he himself started.

"*Arms and the Woman* included several documentary sequences, which would be fascinating today, if only the film had been preserved," screen historian and archivist Kevin Brownlow has written. Brownlow also has noted that the film had to have been considerably altered for showing in Great Britain, an enemy of Hungary at the time. Names and nationalities were altered (Rozika became an Italian girl named Lucia; Carl was not her brother but an Austrian who came over on the boat with her; Fravoe got an Anglo-Saxon name, Trevor). Even the pacifist elements were eliminated. It remains noteworthy, however, because of the documentary-like photography of Arthur Miller who captured New York of the time, for the performance of Mary Nash who enjoyed a distinguished career well into the talkie era, and for the film debut of Edward G. Robinson—who wasn't to make another movie for seven years.

CRITICAL VIEW

"It is a smashing dramatic with frequent passages of extraordinarily fine story and story exposition and comes to a really sensational finish with a fairly hair-raising series of dramatic events. In this finale there must be a thousand feet of thrilling chases, gun fights, killings and finally a fire which burns several acres of munition factory . . . The whole feature is uncommonly interesting, not to say absorbing."—*Variety*

THE BRIGHT SHAWL

1923   Inspiration Pictures/Associated First National

Producer, Charles H. Duell; Director, John S. Robertson; Screenplay, Edmund Goulding; Based on the novel by Joseph

THE BRIGHT SHAWL: Robinson in beard with Richard Barthelmess (left), Andre de Beranger (top hat), Margaret Seddon and Mary Astor

THE BRIGHT SHAWL: Robinson, Mary Astor, Margaret Seddon, Luis Alberni and Andre de Beranger

Hergesheimer; Photography, George Folsey; Art director, Everett Shin; Editor, William Hamilton. 8 reels

Charles Abbott (*Richard Barthelmess*), La Clavel (*Dorothy Gish*), La Pilar (*Jetta Goudal*), Captain Caspar de Vaca (*William Powell*), Narcissa Escobar (*Mary Astor*), Andres Escobar (*Andre de Beranger*), Domingo Escobar (*Edward G. Robinson*), Carmenita Escobar (*Margaret Seddon*), Captain Cesar y Santacilla (*Anders Randolf*), Vincente Escobar (*Luis Alberni*), Jaime Quintara (*George Humbert*).

Between plays on Broadway, Robinson, very early in 1923, was engaged by Richard Barthelmess's company, Inspiration Pictures, for another film, his second. He went to Havana with a company that included Barthelmess, Dorothy Gish, William Powell (his fourth movie), Mary Astor and Jetta Goudal to film Joseph Hergesheimer's popular novel about an American soldier of fortune named Charles Abbott in Spanish-oppressed Cuba of the 1850s. There Abbott falls in love with his Cuban friend's sister, Narcissa, while capturing the eye of La Clavel, a dancer who is the idol of Havana. Robinson, at 30, played Mary Astor's father! La Clavel, however, is the mistress of the infamous Spanish despot, Captain Santacilla. Abbott, asked to obtain valuable information about the Spaniards, makes a play for La Clavel and is decoyed to her home where he and Santacilla have a desperate struggle. La Clavel springs at Santacilla with a knife and in the melee is stabbed. Dying, she gives Abbott her bloodstained bright shawl as a token of her love. The shawl is later stolen by a spy, La Pilar, who, while wearing it one night, kills Vincente Escobar, a young Cuban patriot and another of Narcissa's brothers. In protest, Abbott duels the Spanish authority in the person of the evil Captain Caspar de Vaca and is badly wounded. He regains consciousness aboard a ship bound for the United States, being nursed by Narcissa and her mother. He also discovers a note from de Vaca explaining that the Spanish authorities so admired his courage that they decided to free him and return him to his own country with all his belongings including the bright shawl.

CRITICAL VIEWS

"*The Bright Shawl* is a pretty play of distinct atmospheric charm, the tale of Havana intrigue with Cuban strugglers of liberty on one side and soldiers of Spanish oppression on the other. Well acted."—*Photoplay*

"There is plenty of interesting local color in the production, as the exterior scenes were all made in Havana. The picture is an elaborate one, with fascinating costumes. There is good acting by the members of the well-chosen cast, but the story is rather aimless."—*The New York Times*

"The deal was a trip to Havana where those great cigars were made. That was the only silent part I ever played[!]. I swore off after that because I didn't particularly like it, and I felt that the stage held more of a future for me."—Edward G. Robinson

THE HOLE IN THE WALL

1929   Paramount

Supervisor, Monta Bell; Director, Robert Florey; Screenplay, Pierre Collings; Based on the play by Fred Jackson; Photography, George Folsey; Editor, Morton Blumenstock. 7 reels

Jean Oliver (*Claudette Colbert*), "The Fox" (*Edward G. Robinson*), Gordon Grant (*David Newell*), Madame Mystera (*Nellie Savage*), Goofy (*Donald Meek*), Jim (*Alan Brooks*), Mrs. Ramsay (*Louise Closser Hale*), Mrs. Carslake (*Katherine Emmet*), Marcia (*Marcia Kango*), Dogface (*Barry Macollum*), Inspector (*George MacQuarrie*), Mrs. Lyons (*Helen Crane*), Dancers (*Gamby-Hall Girls*)

THE HOLE IN THE WALL: With Claudette Colbert

At the Astoria Studios in New York, Edward G. Robinson made his talkie debut and Claudette Colbert made hers (this was just her second film) as, respectively, an arch criminal known as "The Fox" and the woman he becomes involved with who was wrongly sent to prison and now seeks revenge. In the film (based on Fred Jackson's 1920 play starring Martha Hedman, John Halliday, and William Sampson in the role equivalent to Robinson's), Colbert, as Jean Oliver, seeks retribution from a Mrs. Ramsay, who had her jailed on a false theft charge rather than have her as a daughter-in-law. After doing time, Jean falls in with a band of phony spiritualists, headed by a man known as The Fox. Posing as a fortune teller named Madame Mystera, a member of the group who has just been killed in an accident, Jean plans to kidnap the woman's young granddaughter, tutor her in the fine art of stealing and then expose her to her grandmother. The plans hit a temporary snag when The Fox falls in love with Jean, but the single-mindedness of her purpose leaves no time to reciprocate his amorous advances. Nor does Jean have time for Gordon Grant, a newspaper reporter who loves her and whom she had secretly loved since their school days.

Not long after kidnapping the young girl, Jean is in her "reading" room, "The Hole in the Wall," busily

THE HOLE IN THE WALL: With Claudette Colbert

THE HOLE IN THE WALL: With Claudette Colbert and player

studying her crystal ball at the behest of Mrs. Ramsey, who, of course, has failed to recognize the thickly-veiled phony "gypsy." While Jean is occupied, the dastardy Fox absconds with the already once-abducted girl as ransom against his love for Jean who has spurned him. The Fox has one of his accomplices take the girl to a railway dock, but, in the process of tying her to a pillar, the hood tumbles into the water and drowns, leaving the bound girl to the oncoming tide. Meanwhile, through the work of reporter Gordon Grant, the police close in on the gypsy parlor, not realizing it is Jean who is posing as Madame Mystera. The Fox intervenes and strikes a bargain with the police—the disclosure of the young girl's whereabouts for the freedom of Jean and a letter from Mrs. Ramsey absolving her of her earlier crime, so that she might marry the reporter.

CRITICAL VIEWS

"[It] is a queer combination of senseless drama and some excellent pictorial direction . . . This production was directed by Robert Florey, who is unfortunate in having such a silly yarn to film, especially considering he has also had to direct the dialogue . . . Another unfortunate feature of this production is that the able Claudette Colbert was called upon to act in it. So was Edward G. Robinson. Both are competent so far as their lines and the action permit."—Mordaunt Hall, *The New York Times*

"I must admit I thought *The Hole in the Wall* was going to be the stinker of all times, and I certainly did not accept the invitation to go to the preview. Claudette went, and she sent me a wire: 'We weren't too bad, baby. We weren't too bad. Love, Claudette.' I take her word for it. I've never seen the film."—Edward G. Robinson in his autobiography, *All My Yesterdays*

NIGHT RIDE

1930   Universal

A Carl Laemmle Presentation; Director, John S. Robertson; Screenplay, Edward T. Lowe, Jr.; Based on a story by Henry La Cossitt; Dialogue by Tom Reed, Edward T. Lowe, Jr.; Titles, Charles Logue; Photography, Alvin Wyckoff; Sound, C. Roy Hunter; Editors, Milton Carruth, A. Ross. 6 reels

Joe Rooker (*Joseph Schildkraut*), Ruth Kearns (*Barbara Kent*), Tony Garotta (*Edward G. Robinson*), Bob O'Leary

(*Harry Stubbs*), Capt. O'Donnell (*DeWitt Jennings*), Blondie (*Ralph Welles*), Mac (*Hal Price*), Ed (*George Ovey*)

Along with his good friend from the stage, Joseph Schildkraut, Edward G. Robinson went to the West Coast to make his first film in Hollywood, continuing in the gangster mode, still being a year or so and several films away from *Little Caesar*, playing here a racketeer whose nemesis is a reporter named Joe Rooker. Rooker, only hours after his wedding to Ruth Kearns, is called out to cover the story of a double murder during a bank robbery. He finds the butts of a special brand of cigarettes at the crime scene, traces them to gangster Tony Garotta, and feels certain he can prove that Garotta pulled the trigger. Garotta, meanwhile, has successfully eluded the police and goes gunning for Rooker, kidnapping him and taking a fellow reporter along as a second hostage, intending to kill them after a one-way night ride, and then make his escape. During the ride, he brags to Rooker that he has bombed the house where Ruth is staying with her mother. They are, in fact, at the hospital where the mother was taken after drinking too much at her daughter's wedding. Rooker presumes they are dead, but is powerless at the moment to avenge the supposed murders.

Before Garotta can make good on his threat to do away with the two reporters, however, he runs into a police roadblock and is captured. Rooker gets the exclusive story to his paper and learns that his wife and mother-in-law are safe. He returns to Ruth and they begin their belated honeymoon.

CRITICAL VIEWS

"A thrilling tale . . . While the series of events are faintly reminiscent of recent films depicting gangsters, they nevertheless are highly diverting . . . Edward G. Robinson is excellent as Tony Garotta."—Mordaunt Hall, *The New York Times*

"Edward G. Robinson is a finished and polished actor, ideal for the character he enacts."—*Variety*

A LADY TO LOVE

1930   Metro-Goldwyn-Mayer

Producer-Director, Victor Seastrom; Screenplay, Sidney Howard; Based on his play *They Knew What They Wanted*;

NIGHT RIDE: Robinson (left) with Joseph Schildkraut (dark jacket and light trousers)

Photography, Merritt B. Gerstad; Sound, Douglas Shearer; Editors, Conrad A. Nervig, Leslie Wilder. 92 minutes

Lena Schultz (*Vilma Banky*), Tony (*Edward G. Robinson*), Buck (*Robert Ames*), Postman (*Richard Carle*), Father McKee (*Lloyd Ingraham*), Doctor (*Anderson Lawler*), Ah Gee (*Gum Chin*), Angelo (*Henry Armetta*), Giorgio (*George Davis*)

Following his portrait of Tony Garotta in *Night Ride*, Edward G. Robinson was contacted by Irving Thalberg, who dangled an MGM contract in front of him. Not ready to make a commitment, Robinson agreed to do one film for the studio and then decide on his future. (Ultimately, he turned down Thalberg and didn't make another MGM picture for seven years.) The one he did do for Thalberg was a sound remake— Paramount had filmed it previously with Pola Negri and Jean Hersholt under the title *The Secret Hour*—of one of the great plays of its day, Sidney Howard's 1925 *They Knew What They Wanted*. Robinson played the middle-

A LADY TO LOVE: With Vilma Banky and Robert Ames

aged, crippled Italian vineyard owner, and Vilma Banky (billed ahead of him) was the young, attractive mail-order bride who is shocked to find him so much older than her but marries him anyway and then ends up falling in love with his hired hand, portrayed by Robert Ames, whose photo the vintner had used to lure her in the first place. Robinson's top-notch reviews encouraged Thalberg to pursue him for the studio with greater zeal, but the actor decided to return to the stage instead—after fulfilling a promise to Carl Laemmle for a couple of pictures at Universal.

(Robinson also starred with Banley in the German-language version filmed simultaneously. In this, Joseph Schildkraut took over Robert Ames' role as Buck, the hired hand.

They Knew What They Wanted was filmed once again in 1940—this time under its true title—with Garson Kanin directing Carole Lombard and Charles Laughton in the Banky-Robinson roles. Contemporary audiences are more familiar with the story as Frank Loesser's Broadway musical, *The Most Happy Fella*.

CRITICAL VIEWS

"[It has] at least one performance, that of Edward G. Robinson, arising out of the mist of only fair direction, and a striving by the other players toward realism that just misses being excellent . . . As Tony, Mr. Robinson is capital. His happiness at discovering Lena and his joy at her willingness to remain . . . are both ably portrayed with sufficient touches of pathos and imagination to bring him definitely forward as a player of no mean dramatic ability. The picture lacks mobility, but the range of acting, as offered by Mr. Robinson . . . is most gratifying."—Mordaunt Hall, *The New York Times*

". . . a somewhat effortful and highly seasoned performance by J. G. Robinson [sic] as the crippled, love-sick Italian, Tony."—Quinn Martin, *New York World*

"Mr. Robinson is the life of the picture as the Italian grape-grower in search of a wife . . . It is not a conventionally romantic role, but that of a man bubbling over with romance and Latin lovableness. It is hard to imagine it better acted."—*Cinema*

"Thalberg sent me the script of *A Lady to Love*. It was sensitive and intelligent and beautifully written—and not unfamiliar. It turned out to be Sidney Howard's own screenplay of *They Knew What They Wanted*, a resounding New York hit that had starred darling Pauline Lord and immensely talented Richard Bennett. It was to star me and Vilma Banky—I mean Vilma Banky and me. I really mean Vilma Banky *with* Edward G. Robinson . . . It did not take long to realize that Miss Banky was seriously out of her depth."—Edward G. Robinson

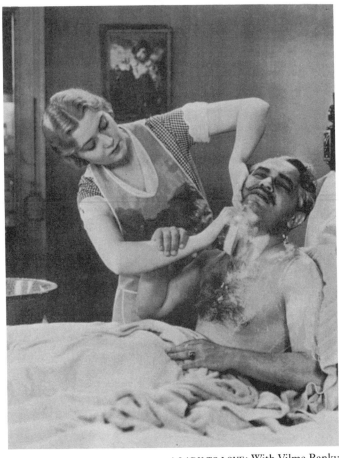

A LADY TO LOVE: With Vilma Banky

A LADY TO LOVE

calls to inform him that the heist is now in progress. At the robbery site, Fingers has hidden himself in the building's locker room, then after blowing open the safe, he escapes and hides out in an apartment, opposite one owned by a cop. The double-crossed Cobra tracks him down and arrives on the scene just as the cops get there. During a shootout, Cobra is killed and Connie and Fingers are sent up the river.

CRITICAL VIEWS

"Competent acting by the principals in *Outside the Law* . . . fails to atone for a flow of incredible incidents. This is another crook yarn in which the criminals are for a time clever enough to pull the wool over the eyes of the slow-witted police. In the end, however, the law has its way, which is something in favor of this picture . . . Edward G. Robinson imparts a good deal of strength to his interpretation of Collins."—Mordaunt Hall, *The New York Times*

OUTSIDE THE LAW

1930   Universal

Presented by Carl Laemmle; Producer, Carl Laemmle, Jr. Associate producer, E.M. Asher; Director, Tod Browning; Screenplay, Tod Browning and Garrett Fort; Photography, Roy Overbaugh; Art director, William R. Schmidt; Synchronization and Score, David Broekman; Sound, C. Roy Hunter; Supervising editor, Maurice Pivar; Editor, Milton Carruth. 76 minutes

Cobra Collins (*Edward G. Robinson*), Connie Madden (*Mary Nolan*), "Fingers" O'Dell (*Owen Moore*), Jake (*Edwin Sturgis*), Humpy (*John George*), The Kid (*Delmar Watson*), Police Chief Kennedy (*DeWitt Jennings*), Captain Fred O'Reilly (*Rockliffe Fellowes*), District Attorney (*Frank Burke*), Assistant (*Sidney Bracy*), Onlooker Outside Bank (*Rose Plummer*), Judy (Maid) (*Louise Beavers*), Stage Manager (*Mathew Betz*), Cigar Clerk (*Charles Rogers*), Messenger (*James Leong*), Sergeant (*Rodney Hildebrand*)

Robinson returned to Hollywood for a two picture deal with Universal. The first, another gangster part, was *Outside the Law*, co-written and directed by Tod Browning. He plays a gang leader named Cobra Colins who learns about an upcoming $500,000 bank heist to be pulled off in his territory by one Fingers O'Dell, and he wants to be cut in on it 50-50. Fingers' moll, Connie, tries to bluff Cobra by telling him that the robbery is scheduled for next week, but one of Cobra's henchmen

OUTSIDE THE LAW

OUTSIDE THE LAW: With Mary Nolan and Owen Moore

OUTSIDE THE LAW: With Mary Nolan

"My experience with *Outside the Law* was a mirror image of *A Lady to Love*. Replace Victor Seastom with Tod Browning, replace Vilma Banky with Mary Nolan, and it was the same agony all over again."—Edward G. Robinson

OUTSIDE THE LAW

EAST IS WEST

1930   Universal

Presented by Carl Laemmle; Associate producer, E.M. Asher; Director, Monta Bell; Screenplay and additional dialogue, Tom Reed; Adaptation, Winnifred Eaton Reeve; Based on the play by Samuel Shipman and John Hymer; Photography, Jerry Ash; Music, Heinz Roemheld; Sound, C. Roy Hunter; Special effects photography, Frank H. Booth; Supervising Editor, Maurice Pivar; Editor, Fred Allen. 75 minutes

Ming Toy (*Lupe Velez*), Billy Benson (*Lewis Ayres*), Charlie Yong (*Edward G. Robinson*), Lo Sang Kee (*E. Alyn Warren*), Hop Toy (*Tetsu Komai*), Mr. Benson (*Henry Kolker*), Mrs. Benson (*Mary Forbes*), Thomas (*Edgar Norton*), Dr. Fredericks (*Charles Middleton*)

For this light-hearted Carl Laemmle presentation, Edward G. Robinson (3rd-billed) donned Oriental makeup for the first time, but not the last, to play what can best be described as a loveable chop suey king in San Francisco, who is pressed into service to keep an affable American socialite (played by Lew Ayres) from marrying a saucy young Chinese girl (played by filmdom's future "Mexican Spitfire," Lupe Velez). Actually, Robinson was on his way back to New York when Laemmle sent him a frantic wire and increasing offers of money to come back West to save a picture (filmed earlier in 1922 with Constance Talmadge and Warner Oland) that Jean Hersholt had just made and was laughed off the screen in previews when he tried to mix a Chinese dialect with his Danish accent.

In the reshot version, Robinson took the role of Charlie Yong. In the film, the American, Billy Benson, it seems had saved the girl, Ming Toy, from being sold at auction in China. Later, in America where she has been taken by a kindly Chinese patriarch, Ming Toy's vivaciousness gets her into assorted difficulties with a waterfront missionary society, and the immigration service comes looking for her. To save her from deportation, she is "sold" to Charlie Yong, the chop suey king. Billy Benson once again appears on the scene and kidnaps Ming Toy, hoping to marry her. Charlie Yong realizes the potential repercussion of Billy's social position as heir to a family fortune and discourages the union. Ming Toy eventually, however, learns that she really is not Chinese but was taken from a murdered missionary as a baby and raised by a local family. With this revela-

EAST IS WEST

tion, Charlie Yong allows her to go to Billy with his blessings.

CRITICAL VIEWS

"E.G. Robinson appears in this first talker [!] as Charlie Yong, the chop suey 'king' of San Francisco's Chinatown, and provides most of the entertainment with his amusing characterization of an egocentric half-caste . . . Both Mr. Robinson and Miss Velez liven the rambling narrative with many amusing moments, but their

EAST IS WEST: With Charles Middleton

task is a heavy and thankless one."—Mordaunt Hall, *The New York Times*

"Edward G. Robinson, as the suey king, is allowed too much footage for mugging and repetitious action."— *Variety*

"It was easier to enjoy the takeoff that George Burns and Gracie Allen did on *East Is West* with Gracie playing Lupe and George playing me. It was one of their favorite movies."—Edward G. Robinson

THE WIDOW FROM CHICAGO

1930   A First National & Vitaphone Production

Director, Edward Cline; Story and screenplay, Earl Baldwin; Photography, Sol Polito; Music director, Erno Rapee; Sound, Clifford A. Ruberg; Editor, Edward Schroeder. 64 minutes

Polly Henderson (*Alice White*), Swifty Dorgan (*Neil Hamilton*), Dominic (*Edward G. Robinson*), Slug O'Donnell (*Frank McHugh*), Chris Johnston (*Lee Shumway*), Mullins (*Brooks Benedict*), Det. Lt. Finnegan (*John Elliott*), Cora (*Dorothy Mathews*), Mazie (*Ann Cornwall*), Capt. Davis (*E.H. Calvert*), Helen (*Betty Francisco*), Jimmy Henderson (*Harold Goodwin*), Desk Man (*Mike Donlin*), Patrolman (*Robert Homans*), Johnston's Henchman (*Al Hill*), Neighbor Woman (*Mary Foy*), Sgt. Dunn (*Allan Cavan*)

EAST IS WEST: With Henry Kolker, Lew Ayres and Lupe Velez

Now under a long-term contract from Jack Warner, Robinson—again billed third—fell back into the gangster mode as yet another Italian-named underworld kingpin. The run-of-the-mill plot: Veteran New York cop Lieutenant Finnegan and detective Jimmy Henderson, following a tip, board an inbound train hoping to nab Swifty Dorgan, who has come East to "do a job" for Dominic, a notorious vice baron. Swifty is apparently killed trying to escape the two, but a news story is planted that he has eluded the police. Jimmy assumes Swifty's identity and joins Dominic's gang, none of whom actually had met Swifty. One day as Jimmy waits for a gangland car to pick him up, his sister Polly sees him gunned down in a doorway. Determined to avenge his death, Polly poses as Swifty's widow from Chicago and lands a job in Dominic's nightclub.

Later the real Swifty shows up at the club, and Polly has to persuade him to play dumb. Soon, he has fallen in love with her and thinks of quitting the rackets. When Dominic and his men attempt to hold up a rival club, a detective tries to gun down Swifty, but is shot by

Polly and the gang makes its getaway. Back at his office, Dominic comforts Polly and tells her that he has killed several cops in the past—including Jimmy Henderson. As Dominic completes the account of his various slayings, he notices that the phone is off the hook (Polly had arranged it so that detectives could hear his confession) and he tries to flee. Using Polly as as shield, he makes his move, but Swifty arrives and he and Dominic have a shootout. Dominic finally surrenders and Polly and Swifty leave together.

CRITICAL VIEWS

"The endless variety of Edward G. Robinson's particular world of make believe is demonstrated once again in *The Widow From Chicago*, which presents him as an agreeably despicable gang leader in the metropolitan beer racket . . . Mr. Robinson gives an interesting and authentic characterization as Dominic, a resourceful and intelligent underworld power. It is not his fault that he is made to provide a denouement by falling in the most puerile of traps."—Mordaunt Hall, *The New York Times*

"Mr. Robinson plays the underworld king in the best Nick Scarsi manner, and, as usual, presents a vivid and striking portrait of a coldly malignant killer."—*New York Herald Tribune*

"Edward G. Robinson's gang leader is the poorest such characterization he has turned in . . . Some of the

THE WIDOW FROM CHICAGO: With Alice White

things Robinson has to say sound all out of proportion. Miss White's exaggerated eye-rolling is just as bad. Neil Hamilton is miscast."—*Variety*

"I would prefer to forget the first picture I made under my new and highly rewarding Warner Brothers contract. It is a good thing that the contract was rewarding because the picture certainly was not . . . The director, Eddie Cline, had a very minimum sense of the uses of the English language. Nice man, Cline, and I liked him, but I liked my mother better, and I wouldn't let *her* direct a picture."—Edward G. Robinson

THE WIDOW FROM CHICAGO: With Neil Hamilton and Alice White

THE WIDOW FROM CHICAGO: With Neil Hamilton and Alice White

LITTLE CAESAR

1931   A First National & Vitaphone Production

Producer, Hal B. Wallis; Director, Mervyn LeRoy, Screenplay, Francis Edwards Faragoh and (uncredited) Robert N. Lee, Darryl F. Zanuck, Robert Lord; Based on the novel by William R. Burnett; Photography, Tony Gaudio; Art director, Anton Grot; Music, Erno Rapee; Music director, Leo Forbstein; Editor, Ray Curtiss. 77 minutes

Cesare Bandello (Rico) (*Edward G. Robinson*), Joe Massara (*Douglas Fairbanks Jr.*), Olga Strassoff (*Glenda Farrell*), "Big Boy" (*Sidney Blackmer*), Lt. Tom Flaherty (*Thomas Jackson*), Sam Vettori (*Stanley Fields*), Otero (*George E. Stone*), "Diamond" Pete Montana (*Ralph Ince*), Tony Passa (*William Collier Jr.*), Arnie Lorch (*Maurice Black*), DeVoss (*Armand Kaliz*), Commissioner McClure (*Landers Stevens*), Peppi (*Noel Madison*), Ritz Colonna (*Nick Bela*), Kid Bean (*Ben Hendricks, Jr*), Ma Magdalena (*Lucille La Verne*), Mrs. Passa (*Ferike Boros*), A Guest (*Gladys Lloyd*)

Edward G. Robinson was summoned by Hal Wallis in late summer 1930 to read for the part of Otero, one of the underlings of Cesare Bandello, the Little Caesar of W.R. Burnett's novel. Not at all impressed, Robinson reportedly insisted "The only part I will consider playing is Little Caesar." Not only that but he had the audacity to outline script changes with him in the lead. He was reminded by Wallis that, according to his studio contract, he had no script approval and could be suspended for refusing a part. Wallis would take up the matter with Jack Warner. Meanwhile, director Mervyn LeRoy has tested another actor the title role and he was not satisfied. Warner recollected in his book, *My First 100 Years in Hollywood*, that the other actor was Clark Gable, "the guy with the big ears." Mervyn LeRoy later recalled he had wanted Gable for the part of Joe Massara, the role taken by Douglas Fairbanks, Jr. Changes, of course, were ultimately made in the script, and Edward G. Robinson went on to create the characterization that would forever change the face and form of the gangster film, and the film itself a cinema milestone.

Cesare Bandello, known as Rico, is a small-time hood anxious to move on the bigger things, and with his pal Joe Massara, manages to worm his way into bigtime racketeer Sam Vettori's gang. Rico works his way up from bodyguard and triggerman to Vettori's hard-as-nails right-hand man. Vettori and his mob meanwhile,

LITTLE CAESAR

have been engaged in a running battle with the cops, led by Lt. Tom Flaherty, and the pressures of having to deal not only with Flaherty and his men but also with rival gangs take their toll on Vettori. "Sam, you're getting soft," Rico tells him, "You're getting so you can dish it out but you can't take it." Rico soon deposes Vettori as the gang's leader and rapidly claws his way to the top of the underworld. Now the kingpin, he offers his pal Joe Massara a top spot, but Joe has fallen for a dish named Olga Strassoff and decides to go straight. When Rico

threatens to kill the girl, Joe turns state's evidence to save himself and Olga. Soon increasingly alone after his gang overthrows him because of his penchant for cold-blooded murder, Rico turns on Joe but finds he is unable to pull the trigger.

Finding that he has been blackballed in the rackets for his ruthlessness, Rico sinks into the gutter and is eventually reduced to living in flop-houses. He is lured out by Lt. Flaherty who wants to close the case on Rico, and in a violent shootout, Little Caesar is gunned down,

67

LITTLE CAESAR

LITTLE CAESAR

gasping with his final breath the now classic fadeout line, "mother of mercy . . . can this be the end of Rico?"

Over the years, *Little Caesar*, which spawned the entire Warner Bros. gangster cycle of the Thirties, was reissued time and again with the studio's follow-up gangster smash, *The Public Enemy*, the film that made a star of James Cagney. The film earned an Academy Award nomination for Best Adaptation for writers Francis Faragoh and Robert N. Lee (they lost to Howard Estabrook for *Cimarron*). Meanwhile, after *Little Caesar*, while waiting for Warners to come up with another script for him, Robinson returned to the stage in New York for the last time for over two decades.

CRITICAL VIEWS

"The production is ordinary and would rank as just one more gangster film but for two things. One is the excellence of Mr. Burnett's creditable and compact story. The other is Edward G. Robinson's wonderfully effective performance. Little Caesar becomes at Mr. Robinson's hands a figure out of Greek epic tragedy, a cold, ignorant, merciless killer, driven on and on by an insatiable lust for power, the plaything of a force greater than himself."—Mordaunt Hall, *The New York Times*

"With less adroit handling, *Little Caesar* might easily

have been no more than a fair program picture and its central character merely a reflection of its many forerunners. Instead, actor Edward G. Robinson has made his role the supreme embodiment of a type. He is helped by Mervyn LeRoy's fine directing and by the fact that W. R. Burnett's story was comprehensive, telling the whole of a gangster's life . . . Actor Robinson makes *Little Caesar* far more complete than author Burnett saw him—a gangster of Greek tragedy, destroyed by the fates within him. The only miscast character is Douglas Fairbanks, Jr., as a tough Italian thug."—*Time*

"For a performance as Little Caesar, no director could ask for more than E. G. Robinson's contribution. Here, no matter what he has to say, he's entirely convincing, because of the lines he speaks and the way he speaks them."—*Variety*

LITTLE CAESAR: With Douglas Fairbanks, Jr.

LITTLE CAESAR: With George E. Stone (far left), Noel Madison (with tommygun) and Douglas Fairbanks, Jr. (second from right)

SMART MONEY

1931   A First National & Vitaphone Production

Director, Alfred E. Green; Screenplay, Kubec Glasmon, John Bright; Based on an original story by Lucien Hubbard and Joseph Jackson; Photography, Robert Kurrle; Makeup, Perc Westmore; Music director, Leo Forbstein; Editor, Jack Killifer. 83 minutes

Nick (The Barber) Venizelos (*Edward G. Robinson*), Jack (*James Cagney*), Irene Graham (*Evalyn Knapp*), Sleepy Sam (*Ralf Harolde*), Marie (*Noel Francis*), District Attorney's Girl (*Margaret Livingston*), The Greek Barber (*Maurice Black*), Sport Williams (*Boris Karloff*), District Attorney Black (*Morgan Wallace*), Salesman-Gambler (*Billy House*), Alexander Amenoppopolus (*Paul Porcasi*), Lola (*Polly Walters*), Hickory Short (*Ben Taggart*), Cigar Stand Clerk (*Gladys Lloyd*), Back-To-Back Schultz (*Clark Burroughs*), Two-Time Phil (*Edwin Argus*), Snake Eyes (*John Larkin*), Dealer Barnes (*Walter Percival*), Small Town Girl (*Mae Madison*), A Suicide (*Allan Lane*), Matron (*Eulalie Jensen*), Desk Clerk (*Charles Lane*), Reporter (*Edward Hearn*), Tom, Customer (*Eddie Kane*), George, Porter (*Clinton Rosemond*), Machine-Gunner (*Charles O'Malley*), Joe, Barber Customer (*Gus Leonard*), Cigar Stand Clerk (*Wallace MacDonald*), Dwarf On Train (*John George*)

Encouraged by the success of both Edward G. Robinson in *Little Caesar* and James Cagney in *The Public Enemy*, Warners naturally decided to team its two tough-guy stars—for the only time. Oddly, instead of tailoring a big-scale gangster epic for the pair, the studio handed the two a modest little crime drama that gave Robinson a flamboyant part and Cagney a relatively colorless one, playing a couple of con-men who run a crooked gambling joint. Robinson is Nick Venizelos, a neighborhood barber with two weaknesses: gambling and blondes; Cagney is his brash young protegé, Jack. Yearning to try his skills in a big-time poker game, Nick buys his way into a high-stakes game in a swank Manhattan hotel and wins big, only to be cheated out of his money by Marie, a cigar counter girl who happens to be in league with a hood named Sleepy Sam. Vowing revenge, Nick bides his time and resumes his back room gambling operation with Jack. Eventually staked to another big game, Nick beats Sleepy Sam and steals Marie from him. (Look closely and you'll spot a pre-*Frankenstein* Boris Karloff as one of the gamblers, Sport Williams, with whom Nick would rather not play.)

SMART MONEY: With James Cagney

70

SMART MONEY: With Billy House (3rd from left), Boris Karloff, Harry Semels, James Cagney and Maurice Black

SMART MONEY: With James Cagney

SMART MONEY: With Charlotte Merriam and Noel Francis

71

Moving up in the gambling world, Nick finds himself the target of the District Attorney, and when a dame called Irene comes into Nick's life, Jack becomes convinced that she's a D.A. plant. Nick's head is turned though, and soon he is proposing marriage. Jack soon finds Irene planting incriminating evidence in Nick's coat and he confronts her. He is wrestling with her when Nick shows up, misunderstands the situation, gets into a fight with Jack and accidentally kills him. Nick is sent up the river, but Irene is at the station and promises to wait for him. It appears that Nick is ready to gamble on anything.

CRITICAL VIEWS

". . . it is fast moving and fairly interesting . . . Mr. Robinson gets all that is humanly possible out of the part of Nick the Barber, who, aside from his penchant for gambling, also has a weakness for blondes, canaries and meticulously polished fingernails . . . [He] leaves no stone unturned to attract the spectator's attention."—Mordaunt Hall, *The New York Times*

"In an effort to vary, however slightly, the frayed formula for underworld pictures, Warner Brothers stumbled into the environment of illegal gambling, a field so fertile it is hard to see how it had hitherto been neglected. Nick is played by Edward G. Robinson, an actor with the face of a depraved cherub and a voice which makes everything he says seem violently profane."—*Time*

FIVE STAR FINAL: With Ona Munson

FIVE STAR FINAL: With George E. Stone

FIVE STAR FINAL

1931   A First National & Vitaphone Production

Producer, Hal B. Wallis; Director, Mervyn LeRoy; Screenplay, Robert Lord; Based on the play by Louis Weitzenkorn; Additional dialogue, Byron Morgan; Photography, Sol Polito; Art director, Jack Okey; Music director, Leo Forbstein; Editor, Frank Ware. 89 minutes

Joseph Randall (*Edward G. Robinson*), Michael Townsend (*H.B. Warner*), Jenny Townsend (*Marion Marsh*), Phillip Weeks (*Anthony Bushell*), Nancy (Vorhees) Townsend (*Frances Starr*), Kitty Carmody (*Ona Munson*), Ziggie Feinstein (*George E. Stone*), Bernard Hinchecliffe (*Oscar Apfel*), Robert French (*Purnell Pratt*), Miss Taylor (*Aline MacMahon*), T. Vernon Isopod (*Boris Karloff*), Brannegan (*Robert Elliott*), Miss Edwards (*Gladys Lloyd*), Goldberg (*Harold Waldridge*), Mrs. Weeks (*Evelyn Hall*), Mr. Weeks (*David Tor-*

FIVE STAR FINAL: With Boris Karloff

FIVE STAR FINAL: With Oscar Apfel

rence), Telephone Operator (*Polly Walters*), Reporter (*James Burtis*), Schwartz (*Frank Darien*)

Aside from gangster movies, newspaper yarns were considered sure-fire hits, thanks to the runaway success of the Hecht-MacArthur play and recent movie of *The Front Page*, and who better in the eyes of producer Hal Wallis and director Mervyn LeRoy to play a tough newspaper editor than Edward G. Robinson, chomping on a cigar and barking orders. In his first starring role as a good guy, Robinson, then, was cast as pugnacious Joe Randall, editor of a sleazy tabloid and surrounded by a rogues gallery of Warner Bros. players. To build up the paper's circulation, Randall's publisher Hinchecliffe has persuaded him to dig up a twenty year old scandal involving Nancy Voorhees, a woman who shot her lover and later bore his child, who is now grown (Marian Marsh) and engaged to be married. Nancy herself is now married to Michael Townsend, who gave up his social position to wed her soon after she was cleared by the police. On the eve of daughter Jenny's wedding to Phillip Weeks, one of Randall's reporters, who is actually a defrocked preacher (in the person of Boris Karloff), manages to get a photo of her by deceit and the paper prepares to rehash the story. Nancy contacts Randall and begs him not to ruin her daughter's future, but to the editor, news is news. The story breaks, and the parents kill themselves.

The paper's circulation skyrockets with sensational headlines, but Randall suddenly gains a sense of conscience and tells off his boss in some of the strongest language the movie censors of the time would allow, and he quits the rag. Storming through the city room, he announces to the stunned reporters, "I'm not working here anymore. No, Hinchecliffe has to get himself a new head butcher. I've had ten years of filth and blood, I'm splashed with it, drenched with it! I've had all I can stand! Plenty of it! Take your . . . killings to Hinchecliffe with my compliments! And tell him to shove it up his . . . !" (That's tough dialogue for an early '30s movie.) Returning to his office to clean out his desk, Randall finds Jenny there with a gun, waiting to shoot him, but when he explains his new sensibility, she calms down and they walk out together.

The dialogue fairly crackled in this filming of the 1930 play (Arthur Byron was Randall on the stage) and Robinson had wonderful support from the likes of Aline MacMahon as his flip secretary, Ona Munson as the city room tootsie, Karloff as a slimy reporter, Purnell Pratt as a hard-nosed circulation manager, George E. Stone as a crum-bum of a hanger-on, even Robinson's wife Gladys Lloyd as the endearing Miss Edwards. *Five Star Final* was nominated as Best Picture of the Year (it lost to *Grand Hotel*) and was to be remade in 1936 as *Two Against the World* with Humphrey Bogart in Robinson's role and the setting changed from a newspaper to a radio station.

CRITICAL VIEWS

"Edward G. Robinson . . . gives another strong performance as the editor of a muckraking tabloid on the pictorial translation of Louis Weitzenkorn's play . . . It is a picture which in the matter of production and acting takes its place beside the film of *Front Page* . . . With a big cigar in the corner of his mouth most of the time, Edward G. Robinson as Randall, the editor of the New York *Gazette*, makes the most of every line."—Mordaunt Hall, *The New York Times*

"As Randall, Mr. Edward G. Robinson succeeds in the best way an actor can—he succeeds, that is, in endowing the character he is playing with a definite personality. Randall is a far finer man than the people for whom he works, but familiarity with the methods of cheap newspapers has given him a protective armor of cynicism."—*The London Times*

"I loved Randall because he wasn't a gangster. I suspect he was conceived as an Anglo-Saxon. To look at me nobody would believe it, but I enjoyed doing him. He made sense, and thus I'm able to day that *Five Star Final* is one of my favorite films."—Edward G. Robinson

THE HATCHET MAN

1932   A First National & Vitaphone Production

Producer, Hal B. Wallis; Director, William A. Wellman; Screenplay, J. Grubb Alexander; Based on the play *The Honorable Mr. Wong* by Achmed Abdullah and David Belasco; Photography, Sid Hickox; Art director, Anton Grot; Music director, Leo Forbstein; Editor, Owen Marks. 74 minutes

Wong Low Get (*Edward G. Robinson*), Toya San (*Loretta Young*), Nag Hong Fah (*Dudley Digges*), Harry En Hai (*Leslie Fenton*), Yu Chang (*Edmund Breese*), Long Sen Yat (*Tully Marshall*), Charley Kee (*Noel N. Madison*), Madame Si-Si (*Blanche Frederici*), Sun Yat Ming (*J. Carrol Naish*), Miss Ling (*Toshia Mori*), Li Hop Fat (*Charles Middleton*), Malone (*Ralph Ince*), Chung Ho (*Otto Yamaoka*), Wah Li (*Evelyn Selbie*), Soo Lat (*E. Alyn Warren*), Foo Ming (*Eddie Piel*), Fung Loo (*Willie Fung*), Fan Yi (*Gladys Lloyd*), Sing Girl (*Anna Chang*), Tong Member (*James Leong*)

Once more donning Oriental makeup, Robinson plays the hatchet man of a Chinese tong in San Francisco. He marries the daughter of the man he is forced to kill—his boyhood friend—only to discover that she is unfaithful. In this atmospheric drama, based on an unproduced play, Wong Low Get (played by a Rumanian Jew named Edward G. Robinson) has become a powerful figure in San Francisco's Chinatown years after the forced assassination and his friend's now-grown daughter Toya San (enacted sweetly but perfunctorily by Loretta Young) dutifully marries Wong, although she secretly loves the evil, handsome Harry En Hai, a half-caste she first met at a dance hall.

Tong wars rage again in San Francisco, although Wong pleads for restraint. However, when his confidential clerk is murdered, he throws his support to group leader Chung Ho, who unburies the avenging hatchet. Chung Ho eloquently wins over the loyalty of the opposing tong, except Malone, the white leader, whom Wong then kills. Returning home, he finds Toya in the arms of Harry En Hai. Despite her explanations, Wong banishes both of them from his house, but word gets out and he is shunned by his friends for this scandalous act. Wong sells his shops and becomes a farmer. Later he learns that Harry En Hai has been deported to China for selling drugs, taking Toya with him. Following them overseas, Wong traces Toya to the Hanghow Sing House where she is virtually a slave. Informing the owner that Toya is his wife, Wong kills Harry En Hai with his honorable hatchet, then gathers up Toya and leaves with her, unmolested.

THE HATCHET MAN: With Loretta Young

THE HATCHET MAN: With Leslie Fenton and Loretta Young

THE HATCHET MAN

CRITICAL VIEWS

"It's a ruddy affair, this *Hatchet Man* . . . Although Wong, played by Mr. Robinson, is clad most of the time in Chinese silks, his voice, like the voices of others in this tale, is decidedly American, something which is accounted for through the years the characters have spent over here. All the same, Mr. Robinson is a better barber, gambler, gangster and tabloid writer than he is a Chinese Hatchet Man."—Mordaunt Hall, *The New York Times*

"Mild gang stuff in Oriental trappings with a Chinese twist, resting solely on Robinson for its love interest does not intrigue and is often slow. Dynamic action or high voltage drama now connected with the scowling Edward, and implied in the film's title, is missing . . .

[His] performance is emphatic and as sinister as usual in this type of story, though the marriage offers the opportunity to soften him up a little."—*Variety*

". . . one of my most horrible memories."—Edward G. Robinson

TWO SECONDS

1932   A First National & Vitaphone Picture

Supervised by Hal B. Wallis; Director, Mervyn LeRoy; Screenplay, Harvey Thew; Based on the play by Elliott Lester; Photography, Sol Polito; Art director, Anton Grot; Music director, Leo Forbstein; Editor, Terrill Morse. 68 minutes

John Allen (*Edward G. Robinson*), Bud Clark (*Preston Foster*), Shirley Day (*Vivienne Osborne*), Tony (*J. Carrol Naish*), Bookie (*Guy Kibbee*), Annie (*Adrienne Dore*), Judge (*Frederick Burton*), Lizzie (*Dorothea Wolbert*), The Doctor (*Edward McWade*), The Warden (*Berton Churchill*), A College Boy (*William Janney*), Reporter (*Lew Brice*), Reporter (*Franklin Parker*), Reporter (*Frederick Howard*), Mrs. Smith (*Helen Phillips*), Fat Girl (*June Gittleson*), Tart (*Jill Dennett*), Tart (*Luana Walters*), Justice of the Peace (*Otto Hoffman*), Doctor (*Harry Beresford*), Masher (*John Kelly*), Masher (*Matt McHugh*), Executioner (*Harry Woods*), Woman (*Gladys Lloyd*)

This filming of Elliott Lester's 1931 Broadway play that starred Edward Pawley—the title refers to the space of time it takes for a man to die in the electric chair once the switch is thrown—reunited Edward G. Robinson with Mervyn LeRoy for the last time for nearly a decade. To costar with Robinson, LeRoy engaged Preston Foster to repeat his stage role as the pal of the lead, a convicted murder named John Allen who insists that he is dying for the wrong crime. In the last two seconds of his life, he recalls the events leading him to the electric chair. John Allen and Bud Clark are riveters working on a skyscraper girder. Allen is rather sour on life, but Bud is reveling that he has just cashed in at the races. That night the two have dates, but Allen is not interested, and after work he wanders off to a dance hall where he meets Shirley Day. The two begin seeing each other quite regularly, and one night when he gets drunk, she takes him to a justice of the peace and they get married.

While Allen is at work, Bud discovers that Shirley is two-timing him with Tony, proprietor of the dance hall. Learning the truth from his pal, Allen gets angry and swings at him while they are high on a girder. Bud loses his balance and falls to his death. Allen goes to pieces. Shirley taunts him, stating that she had to borrow money from Tony to pay for rent and food. Allen resolves to avenge his friend's death himself, hiding away his few dollars until he has enough to bet on the races. When he wins a fairly big stake, he takes only enough to pay off his debts; then he goes looking for Shirley and finds her with Tony. After stuffing the money that she had borrowed from Tony into Tony's hand, Allen pulls a gun and shoots her.

Back in the deathhouse, Allen repeats that if he had been sentenced for Bud's death, that would have been fair, but it is a miscarriage of justice for him to die for killing Shirley.

CRITICAL VIEWS

"Edward G. Robinson contributes a remarkably force-

TWO SECONDS: With Vivienne Osborne

TWO SECONDS: With J. Carrol Naish and Vivienne Osborne

ful portrayal in the picture version of Elliott Lester's play . . . When Mr. Robinson depicts the nerve-wracked condition of Allen or delivers a heated talk to the judge who sentences him, his acting is unusually impressive."—Mordaunt Hall, *The New York Times*

"With *Two Seconds* . . . the distinguished screen career of Edward G. Robinson encounters a temporary lapse.

TWO SECONDS: With Vivienne Osborne

With the excellent Mervyn LeRoy as director, and with several experienced players to support him, Mr. Robinson, whose Little Caesar still stands as his finest screen portrayal, moves indifferently, and at times almost amateurishly, through a picture of incredibly meagre purpose . . . I had no idea that Mr. Robinson, whose flair for choosing good parts for himself is well known, could be caught so empty handed and that he would ever allow himself to indulge in such overacting as he does here."—William Boehnel, *New York World-Telegram*

TIGER SHARK

1932   A First National & Vitaphone Picture

Supervised by Ray Griffith; Director, Howard Hawks; Screenplay, Wells Root; Based on the story "Tuna" by Houston Branch; Photography, Tony Gaudio; Art director, Jack Okey; Music director, Leo Forbstein; Assistant director, Robert Rosson; Editor, Thomas Pratt. 80 minutes

Mike Mascarena (*Edward G. Robinson*), Quita (*Zita Johann*), Pipes Boley (*Richard Arlen*), Lady Barber (*Leila Bennett*), Engineer (*Vince Barnett*), The Man (*J. Carrol Naish*), Manuel (*William Ricciardi*), Doctor (*Edwin Maxwell*)

Working for the first time with Howard Hawks, known in the business as a real man's director, Edward G. Robinson turns in an especially strong portrayal as a crippled tuna fisherman who marries a girl with whom his best friend later falls in love. On the seas he is the master; still he cannot fathom how he came to be involved in a romantic triangle. Captain Mike Mascarena lost a hand to a shark some years earlier while rescuing a buddy, Pipes Boley. Mike's tough exterior masks a complex that women laugh at him because of his hook and that he will not be allowed in heaven when he dies because he is not whole. On one cruise, old Manuel, a member of Mike's crew, is killed, leaving an orphan his daughter, Quita. When Mike comes ashore, he looks her up, saving the girl from suicide. Eventually he asks her to marry him, and out of gratitude for his kindness, she feels she cannot refuse.

Pipes resents the marriage, thinking Quita to be a gold-digger, but Mike is so happy with married life that he fails to notice Pipes and Quita falling in love. On the next voyage out, Pipes falls ill and is sent ashore. Mike has him taken to his home where Quita nurses him back

TWO SECONDS

TIGER SHARK: With J. Carrol Naish and Zita Johann

TIGER SHARK: With Zita Johann

TIGER SHARK: With Richard Arlen and Zita Johann

to health. Pipes wants to leave before things between him and Quita get out of hand, but she won't let him go. It isn't long before Mike happens in on them while they are embracing. Instantly, the friendship turns to hate, and Mike forces both of them onto his ship. At sea, Mike knocks Pipes unconscious and tosses him into an open boat. He drives a harpoon into the craft intending to sink it. He hurls another into a maneating shark, but as the shark swims away, the harpoon rope catches around Mike's foot and he is dragged overboard. His crew rescues Pipes but fails to reach Mike in time. Pulled aboard, he dies in Quita's arms.

TIGER SHARK: With Zita Johann

79

SILVER DOLLAR: With Aline MacMahon

SILVER DOLLAR: With Bebe Daniels

"This fisherman is portrayed splendidly by Edward G. Robinson, who makes the character both sympathetic and fearsome according to what is happening."—Mordaunt Hall, *The New York Times*

"Mr. Robinson gives a fine, finished performance as Mike, blending love and hatred in exactly the right manner."—William Boehnel, *New York World-Telegram* "I adored *Tiger Shark* because I admired Howard Hawks, and I think the reason I admired him is because he let me chew the scenery."—Edward G. Robinson

SILVER DOLLAR

1932   A First National & Vitaphone Picture

Director, Alfred E. Green; Screenplay, Carl Erickson; Based on the biography of H.A.W. Tabor by David Karsner; Photography, James Van Trees; Art director, Anton Grot; Music director, Leo Forbstein; Editor, George Marks. 84 minutes

Yates Martin (*Edward G. Robinson*), Lily Owens (*Bebe Daniels*), Sarah Martin (*Aline MacMahon*), Poker Annie (*Jobyna Howland*), Mine Foreman (*DeWitt Jennings*), Col. Stanton (*Robert Warwick*), Hamlin (*Russell Simpson*), Adams (*Harry Holman*), Jenkins (*Charles Middleton*), Gelsey (*John Marston*), Mrs. Adams (*Marjorie Gateson*), Pres. Chester A. Arthur (*Emmett Corrigan*), Miner (*Wade Boteler*), Miner (*William Le Maire*), Mark (*David Durand*), Rische (*Lee Kohlmar*), Mrs. Hamlin (*Teresa Conover*), Secretary (*Leon Waycoff [Ames]*), Emma Abbott (*Virginia Edwards*), Hook (*Christian Rub*), General Grant (*Walter Rogers*), William Jennings Bryan (*Niles Welch*), and: (*Wilfred Lucas, Alice Wetherfield, Herman Bing, Bonita Granville, Walter Long, Willard Robertson, Frederick Burton, Charles Coleman*).

In *Silver Dollar*, Robinson had his first biographical role—that of H.A.W. Tabor, the Colorado silver-mining senator of the 19th century—although in the highly fictionalized film, Tabor is called Yates Martin. Yates is a Kansas farmer who gets caught up in the Colorado gold rush and, with his wife Sarah, opens a general store in one of the boom towns. He goes broke, however, extending credit to the miners, who pay him with shares in their mines. As Yates and his wife are about to shut the doors of their store and return to Kansas and farming, two miners come in with bags of silver. Becoming wealthy almost overnight, Yates soon becomes the town's leading figure and gets into politics,

SILVER DOLLAR: With Bebe Daniels and Emmett Corrigan

being elected in turn mayor, postmaster, sheriff and eventually lieutenant governor. He has, in fact, so much money, he is literally throwing it away. He buys a mansion in Denver, erects a big opera house, donates land for a post office, and is the first to give charity on any occasion.

Yates soon meets Lily, a beautiful woman who delights in diamonds and pearls, and adores the limelight—a complete contrast to his wife Sarah. The resulting scandal when Yates leaves Sarah for Lily nearly ruins his chances for the U.S. Senate, but he manages to win a vacant seat. He weds Lily in Washington with the President and senators in attendance. Returning to Denver, Yates continues his reckless spending, and when silver is demonetized due to the gold standard, he is ruined. Now destitute and alone, he visits the Grand Opera House which he had once built. There he is found dying of heart failure.

CRITICAL VIEWS

"The role of Tabor, who in this offering is called Yates Martin, is especially well-suited to Mr. Robinson's talent. His characterization is compelling and convincing, and he succeeds admirably in delivering the complex nature of the man who, in the film, is invariably more fortunate than clever. [He] makes the most of Martin's egoism and of his confidence in the power of wealth he derives from silver mines."—Mordaunt Hall, *The New York Times*

SILVER DOLLAR: With Bonita Granville

"Directed and written with proper vigor and quite brilliantly played by Edward G. Robinson, the film presents what is perhaps a fairly neglected period in the national life with raciness and authenticity."—Richard Watts, Jr., *New York Herald-Tribune*

"The picture provides Edward G. Robinson with one of the most vibrant of all the lively parts he has portrayed.

81

And needless to say, he creates a character rich and full and colorful, vivid in all its dimensions. It is an achievement, perhaps the finest in all his cinematic career, at least comparable to any."—Regina Crewe, *New York American*

THE LITTLE GIANT

1933 A First National & Vitaphone Picture

Supervised by Ray Griffith; Director, Roy Del Ruth; Screenplay, Robert Lord and Wilson Mizner; Based on an original story by Lord; Photography, Sid Hickox; Art director, Robert Haas; Music director, Leo Forbstein; Editor, George Marks. 74 minutes

James Francis "Bugs" Ahearn (*Edward G. Robinson*), Polly Cass (*Helen Vinson*), Ruth Wayburn (*Mary Astor*), John Stanley (*Kenneth Thomson*), Al Daniels (*Russell Hopton*), Edith Merriam (*Shirley Grey*), Gordon Cass (*Donald Dillaway*), Mrs. Cass (*Louise Mackintosh*), Donald Hadley Cass (*Berton Churchill*), Frankie (*Helen Mann*), Voice of Radio Announcer (*Selmer Jackson*), Butch Zanwutoski (*Dewey Robinson*), (Ed) Tim (*John Kelly*), Butler (*Sidney Bracy*), Joe Milano's Hoods (*Bob Perry, Adrian Morris*), Waiter (*Rolfe Sedan*), Charteris (*Charles Coleman*), Guest (*Bill Elliott*), Ingleby (*Leonard Carey*), Maid (*Nora Cecil*), Investment Clerks (*Lester Dorr, Lorin Raker*), Detective (*Guy Usher*), D.A. (*John Marston*), Pulido (*Harry Tenbrook*)

In this amiable spoof of Robinson's gangster roles, he is cast as a beer baron who, sensing the inevitable end of Prohibition, decides to crash high society. This was, in fact, Robinson's first out-and-out chance to play comedy on the screen, and he proved to be more than merely adept, although the film's not half as funny as his later *A Slight Case of Murder*. He's "Bugs" Ahearn here, bootlegger extraordinaire, but he wants something better—he wants respect. With his pal, Al Daniels, he signs in at a swanky West Coast hotel and joins a polo club. He is ignored, though, by the best citizens, and is about to give up in disgust when Polly Cass, whom he believes to be a wealthy society girl, falls from her horse. Bugs helps her up and takes her home. She invites him to stay for tea, where he is ribbed about his manners—until Polly's brother Gordon discovers that Bugs is a millionaire; then the entire family adopts him.

Bugs inquires about renting a house so that he can entertain properly, and Ruth Wayburn, a society girl whose father died broke, leases him hers. Bugs in return

THE LITTLE GIANT: With Helen Vinson

engages Ruth as his social secretary. It's not long before the Cass family and their horsy set make Bugs' house their headquarters. Ruth knows they are frauds but she cannot convince Bugs, who becomes engaged to Polly. Shortly thereafter, Polly's father sells Bugs some phony stocks. The District Attorney, it seems, is after Mr. Cass because of a stock deal in which he was involved, but Bugs persuades the D.A. to give him a few days to return the money. Bugs then sends for his boys from Chicago to strong-arm the people who sold him the fraudulent stocks and get his money back. He then goes to the Cass' house, retrieves his money from Polly's father and forcibly takes back the engagement ring he'd given her. He then walks out and returns to Ruth, who welcomes him with open arms and a ring-poised finger.

CRITICAL VIEWS

"Edward G. Robinson, as the prime player, reveals himself as no mean comedian, and yesterday afternoon, the audience roared when the gangster, who is known here as Bugs Ahearn, tackles a French menu and when he turns up at an informal afternoon party in full regalia . . . [He] is alert and forceful even in this light affair."—Mordaunt Hall, *The New York Times*

"*The Little Giant* is an amusing bit of fluff which gives Mr. Robinson a chance to reveal unsuspected comedy talents."—Marguerite Tazelaar, *New York Herald-Tribune*

THE LITTLE GIANT: With Russell Hopton and Mary Astor

"This fast moving and thoroughly entertaining picture shows Mr. Robinson at his best and is one of the really worthwhile films that have come along during the last few weeks . . . [He] is excellent as the erstwhile racketeer."—William Boehnel, *New York World-Telegram*

"*Little Giant*—with that little giant of an actor, Eddie Robinson, the two of us rather sadly doing a bad picture together, knowing it, telling each other, 'It might be funny.' It was. Sort of. But there was something wrong about Edward G. Robinson taking pratfalls from a polo pony."—Mary Astor in her autobiography, *A Life on Film* (1971)

I LOVED A WOMAN

1933   A First National & Vitaphone Picture

Supervised by Henry Blanke; Director, Alfred E. Green; Screenplay, Charles Kenyon and Sidney Sutherland; Based on the book by David Karsner; Photography, James Van Trees; Art director, Robert Haas; Gowns, Earl Luick; Music director, Leo Forbstein; Editor, Bert Levy. 90 minutes

Laura McDonald (*Kay Francis*), John Hayden (*Edward G. Robinson*), Martha Lane Hayden (*Genevieve Tobin*), Shuster (*J. Farrell MacDonald*), Sanborn (*Henry Kolker*), Charles Lane (*Robert Barrat*), Henry (*George Blackwood*), Davenport (*Murray Kinnell*), Larkin (*Robert McWade*), Oliver (*Walter*

I LOVED A WOMAN: With Kay Francis

I LOVED A WOMAN: With Kay Francis

I LOVED A WOMAN: With Genevieve Tobin

I LOVED A WOMAN: With Kay Francis

Like *Silver Dollar*, this melodrama was directed by Alfred E. Green, came from a book by David Karsner, and provided Edward G. Robinson with two leading ladies (along with the standard Warner Bros. roster of sterling players). This time, rather than being a wealthy senator from Colorado he is a meat magnate in Chicago (the profession was "in" apparently in 1933—several months afterwards, Paul Muni played a meat magnate in the same studio's *The World Changes*). Taking over from his father, idealistic John Hayden (Robinson) is attracted by Martha Lane, daughter of his biggest competitor. Only after marrying her however does John discover her to be nothing but a social climber, and begins to suffer her unmerciful taunting when his business takes a downturn. One evening at the opera, he meets Laura McDonald, a beautiful young singer, and offers to finance her musical education abroad. John asks for a divorce so he can marry Laura, but shrewish Martha refuses. Then too, Laura pleads that marriage would interfere with her career, but she and John continue meeting secretly. Her success in the music world and her ambition to even greater glory encourages John to become a mogul in his business, and his sense of values undergoes a change.

During the Spanish American War, he outbids his rivals and secures major Army contracts. Then he supplies the Army with tainted beef. Colonel Teddy Roosevelt charges him with the deaths of a number of soldiers and threatens to have him prosecuted. When Roosevelt becomes President, John is tried for manslaughter but acquitted. Martha, in the meantime, has hired detectives to follow John and Laura, but they report back that Laura has been seeing other men. John is told and reluctantly leaves Laura whom he still loves. As years pass, John undertakes increasingly bigger business gambles and efforts to match the rising peaks of Laura's career. Indicted for fraud when his company faces bankruptcy, he flees to Greece. A broken man, deserted by his friends, John is alone until Laura learns of his plight. She begs Martha to go to him, but Martha refuses. So Laura goes to John herself, offering him the comfort he needs.

In his autobiography, Edward G. Robinson talked about getting involved with script changes—extensive in this case. "I admit now, with some dismay," he wrote, "that from that picture forward I achieved a lousy reputation with writers; I was always arguing about scripts, but so were Bette Davis and Bogie and Jimmy Cagney and—I am certain, over at MGM—

Crawford and Gable and, I'm told, at Universal, so distinguished a literary figure as Deanna Durbin."

CRITICAL VIEWS

"Edward G. Robinson's latest picture . . . is a worthy offering, even though it is open to the accusation of being anti-climactic. It is concerned with the crimes of Chicago meat-packers both during the Spanish American War and the World Wars, and in it, Mr. Robinson has an excellent opportunity for a definite characterization, of which, if need hardly be said, this efficient actor takes full advantage . . . [His] portrayal rivals his splendid interpretation in *Silver Dollar*."—Mordaunt Hall, *The New York Times*

"A careful and conscious account of the life of a zestful American character, effectively acted by Edward G. Robinson."—Marguerite Tazelaar, *New York Herald-Tribune*

"Mr. Robinson is never so admirable as in portraying what may be described as a ruthless rise to power, and thus he has another personal success on his hands." —John S. Cohen, Jr., *New York Sun*

"A dull and lifeless picture, with virile Edward G. Robinson badly miscast."—*New York American*

DARK HAZARD

1934   A First National & Vitaphone Picture

Supervised by Robert Lord; Director, Alfred E. Green; Screenplay, Ralph Block and Brown Holmes; Based on the novel by William R. Burnett; Photography, Sol Polito; Art director, Robert Haas; Musical director, Leo Forbstein; Editor, Herbert Levy. 72 minutes

Jim "Buck" Turner (*Edward G. Robinson*), Marge Mayhew (*Genevieve Tobin*), Valerie (*Glenda Farrell*), Tex (*Robert Barrat*), Joe (*Gordon Westcott*), George Mayhew (*Hobart Cavanaugh*), Pres Barrow (*George Meeker*), Schultz (*Henry B. Walthall*), Bright (*Sidney Toler*), Mrs. Mayhew (*Emma Dunn*), Fallen (*Willard Robertson*), Miss Dolby (*Barbara Rogers*), Plummer (*William V. Mong*)

Teamed again with one of the two leading ladies from his last film, Genevieve Tobin, and house director Alfred E. Green, and working from a novel by the man who wrote *Little Caesar*, Robinson made this nearly for-

DARK HAZZARD: With Glenda Farrell

DARK HAZZARD: With Glenda Farrell

gotten—and in fact forgettable—programmer about a gambler and a racing dog (the title character). He's an inveterate high-roller who, to stay close to the betting scene, takes a job as cashier at a small-town Ohio racetrack. There he meets Marge Mayhew at a boarding house run by her mother, who has been trying to marry her off to Pres Barrow, one of the town's leading citizens. Jim Turner (Robinson), however, sweeps her off

DARK HAZZARD: With Genevieve Tobin

DARK HAZZARD: With Dark Hazzard

her feet and she marries him on condition that he give up gambling. Jim finds the gambling bug hard to shake, and eventually he finds work managing a California dog track. Enter an old flame, Valerie Wilson, who turns up at the track one day. When she pops in at Jim's home somewhat intoxicated not long afterwards, Marge is angered and locks Jim out. Resentful, he goes off with Valerie to gamble and wins big. Remorseful, he comes back to Marge and promises again to quit gambling, but she walks out on him.

Jim knocks around the country for a few years and then decides to patch things up with Marge, who takes him in but admits she is now in love with Pres Barrow who has been courting her again. Lured back to the track when the dog races come to town, Jim spots Dark Hazard, one of the dogs he bred in California. Dark Hazard is injured in a race and is about to be put to sleep when Jim ups and buys him. But Marge will not let Jim keep him in the house. The last straw for Jim is when he comes home one night and finds Marge in Pres Barrow's arms. He and Pres fight, but then Jim comes to accept the true situation at home and leaves with Dark Hazard, who begins racing again and brings Jim back into the big dough—but Jim just can't stop despite his killings at the track, and he finally goes broke at the gaming table.

"Try not to see it on TV," Robinson wrote in his autobiography. "I loathed it."

Three years after its release, *Dark Hazard* was remade by Warners as a quickie "B" under the title *Wine, Women and Horses* with Barton MacLane, Ann Sheridan, Dick Purcell and Peggy Bates in the roles played by Robinson, Glenda Farrell, Hobart Cavanaugh and Genevieve Tobin, respectively.

CRITICAL VIEWS

"Again the combination of Edward G. Robinson and W. R. Burnett results in that singular emotional quality which was the touchstone of *Little Caesar*. While the latter was a far more sensational and melodramatic piece, the star's performance in *Dark Hazard* is just as true to type and as poignantly drawn . . . It is the contrast in Mr. Robinson's characters which give them much of their fascination. His heroes are never completely heroic and his villains are never altogether unsympathetic."—Marguerite Tazelaar, *New York Herald-Tribune*

"It's an unusual portrayal for Robinson, despite the fact that he's cast as a gambler. A big shot for a few moments, a bum most of the time, he's always dominated by those around him and near him, instead of, as in his past pictures, being the head man."—*Variety*

"Edward G. Robinson adds one more portrait to his

THE MAN WITH TWO FACES: With Mae Clarke

gallery of quaint likable misfits."—John S. Cohen, Jr., *New York Sun*

"Jim Turner, the hunch gambler, spills himself noisily on the screen in Edward G. Robinson's familiar style of alternately sly and snarling moods. Mr. Robinson provides a hearty cartoon character which is admirably suited to the unexpected guffaw and the well-timed hook to the chin."—Andre D. Sennwald, *The New York Times*

THE MAN WITH TWO FACES

1934   A First National & Vitaphone Picture

Supervised by Robert Lord; Director, Archie Mayo; Screenplay, Tom Reed and Niven Busch; Based on the play *The Dark Tower* by George S. Kaufman and Alexander Woollcott; Photography, Tony Gaudio; Art director, John Hughes; Music director, Leo Forbstein; Editor, William Holmes. 72 minutes

Damon Wells (*Edward G. Robinson*), Jessica Wells (*Mary Astor*), Ben Weston (*Ricardo Cortez*), Daphne Martin (*Mae Clarke*), Dr. Kendall (*Arthur Byron*), Stanley Vance (*Louis Calhern*), Barry Jones (*John Eldredge*), Patsy Dowling (*Dorothy Tree*), Inspector Crane (*Henry O'Neill*), William Curtis (*David Landau*), Hattie (*Emily Fitzroy*), Peabody (*Virginia Sale*), Martha Temple (*Margaret Dale*), Morgue Keeper (*Arthur Aylesworth*), Debutante (*Mary Russell*), Matron (*Mrs.*

Wilfred North), Mr. Jones (*Howard Hickman*), Mrs. Jones (*Maude Turner Gordon*), Call Boy (*Dick Winslow*), Doorman (*Frank Darien*), Driver (*Bert Moorhouse*), Bell Boy (*Ray Cooke*), Newsboy (*Jack McHugh*), Lieutenant of Detectives (*Douglas Cosgrove*), Detective (*Wade Boteler*), Weeks (*Guy Usher*), Rewrite Man (*Milton Kibbee*), Editor (*Joseph Crehan*)

In the screen adaptation of George S. Kaufman and Alexander Woollcott's 1933 play about actors, *The Dark Tower* (Warners changed the title for the screen so as not to confuse this film with Robinson's previous one, *Dark Hazard*), Edward G. Robinson took the role that British actor Basil Sydney had played on Broadway, and Mary Astor, Ricardo Cortez and Mae Clarke had the roles Margalo Gillmore, William Harrigan and Leona Maricle had played. The movie is little shown even on television, and film historian William K. Everson feels that "In a way it's easy why: the play has no special reputation, it's not one of the more dynamic Robinson vehicles, and most especially, it has such distasteful plot elements (and this is not said critically) that it doesn't have the 'fun' aspects of the average old Warner film. The dialogue is good, often vicious and/or cynical, but it doesn't have the sparkle or the virility of a *Five Star Final*."

THE MAN WITH TWO FACES: With Louis Calhern and Mary Astor

This melodrama (a change of pace for playwrights Kaufman and Woollcott) focuses on brilliant, egotistical New York stage actor and director Damon Wells and his sister Jessica, a top star of the day until a mysterious mental and physical breakdown interrupts her career. It is discovered that she is under the Svengali-like influ-

THE MAN WITH TWO FACES:
With Louis Calhern

THE MAN WITH TWO FACES: With Margaret Dale and Emily Fitzroy

ence of her husband, Stanley Vance. When Vance strangely vanishes, Jessica regains her health and soon stages a theatrical comeback. Then Vance returns—he had been in prison—and Jessica agains begins to break down. Shortly thereafter, Vance is found murdered in the closet of a hotel suite where he was attempting to make a deal with a theatrical producer named Chautard.

Chautard has disappeared, leaving no trace. The police are completely baffled and soon give up the case—except for one detective, who soon discovers that Vance had murdered his former wife for her money and had been involved in other criminal activities. A false moustache the detective finds in a Gideon Bible in the murder room convinces him that Chautard is really an actor. Recalling seeing a play, *The Dark Tower*, many years before which had a character similar to Chautard in the cast, he begins to haunt the theaters on Broadway, especially the dressing room of Damon Wells. Wells starts to get uneasy when, one night, the detective hands him the false moustache, advises him to be more careful in the future, and suggests that the world was well rid of a scoundrel like Chautard. He tells Wells he's officially giving up the case. The only person knowing of the crime is Ben Weston, a theatrical producer, who loves Jessica, and it was in Weston's office that Wells had changed into his Chautard character.

The British remake of the film in 1943 under its original title (*The Dark Tower*) substituted a circus background for the theater. Ben Lyon, David Farrar, Anne Crawford and Herbert Lom had the roles equivalent to Robinson, Cortez, Astor and Calhern.

CRITICAL VIEWS

"Mr. Robinson, as the self-confessed best actor in America and the self-appointed executioner of a first-class knave, maintains a comic mood successfully, which is a considerable help to the story."—Andre D. Sennwald, *The New York Times*

"Edward G. Robinson's impression of Jessica's brother is a suave bit of acting, done in the best tradition of good actors impersonating good actors."—William Boehnel, *New York World-Telegram*

"Edward G. Robinson, who is nothing if not versatile, is seen in the role of Damon Wells, the excellent and slightly egotistical actor. The role gives Robinson plenty of opportunity to exercise his recognized bent for character work and disguise."—Regina Crewe, *New York American*

"I liked it not only because Mary Astor was to play opposite me but also because I'd be able to use a putty nose, a set of whiskers, false eyebrows, and a French accent. Archie Mayo was the director, a man out of the Mervyn LeRoy school, and the script, almost too faithful to Kaufman and Woollcott, was not too bad."—Edward G. Robinson

THE WHOLE TOWN'S TALKING: With Jean Arthur

THE WHOLE TOWN'S TALKING

1935   Columbia Pictures

Producer, Lester Cowan; Director, John Ford; Screenplay, Jo Swerling and Robert Riskin; Based on the novel by William R. Burnett; Photography, Joseph August; Editor, Viola Lawrence. 95 minutes

Arthur Ferguson Jones/Killer Mannion (*Edward G. Robinson*), Wilhelmina "Bill" Clark (*Jean Arthur*), Healy (*Wallace Ford*), District Attorney Spencer (*Arthur Byron*), Det. Sgt. Mike Boyle (*Arthur Hohl*), Hoyt (*Donald Meek*), J. G. Carpenter (*Paul Harvey*), "Slugs" Martin (*Edward Brophy*), Seaver (*Etienne Girardot*), Det. Sgt. Pat Howe (*James Donlan*), Warden (*J. Farrell MacDonald*), Aunt Agatha (*Effie Ellsler*), Police Lt. Mac (*Robert Emmett O'Connor*), Man-

THE WHOLE TOWN'S TALKING

nion's Henchmen (*John Wray, Joseph Sauers (Sawyer)*), Russell (*Frank Sheridan*), President of the Chamber of Commerce (*Clarence Hummel Wilson*), Ribber (*Ralph M. Remley*), Seaver's Private Secretary (*Virginia Pine*), Mayor (*Ferdinand Munier*), Radio Man (*Cornelius Keefe*), Reporter at Dock (*Francis Ford*), Bit Girl (*Lucille Ball*), Detective

THE WHOLE TOWN'S TALKING: With Etienne Girardot and office staff

THE WHOLE TOWN'S TALKING: With Jean Arthur

(*Robert E. Homans*), Sob Sister (*Grace Hayle*), Convict (*Walter Long*), Traffic Cop (*Ben Taggart*), Gangster (*Al Hill*), Bit Man (*Gordon DeMain*), City Official (*Sam Flint*), Reporter (*Emmett Vogan*), Secretary (*Bess Flowers*), Landlady (*Mary Gordon*), Guard (*Tom London*), Bit Man (*Charles King*)

After turning down Jack Warner's next assignment for him, *Upper World*, Robinson got into a protracted battle with the studio, frustrated by his wish to be loaned out to other studios like some of his fellow contract players-cum-stars. Ultimately, Warner Bros. saw things his way and loaned him to Columbia for what was to be a refreshing change of pace and the chance to work for the first time with director John Ford (his only other Ford film wouldn't come for another 30 years). In this gangster spoof, based on yet another W.R. Burnett novel, Robinson has the dual role of a milquetoast hardware clerk, Arthur Jones, and the notorious escaped con, Killer Mannion, who is an exact look-alike. While having lunch with "Bill" Clark, a pretty girl in the office he's gotten up enough gumption to ask out, Arthur is suddenly surrounded by the police and arrested. His more than passing resemblance to Public Enemy No. 1, who had earlier in the day broken out of prison, is the reason, but Arthur is able to prove his identity, although the publicity suddenly makes him famous. Returning home, he finds Mannion in his room, and he is forced to surrender to his "guest" the special identity papers given him by the police should he be picked up again. Mannion plans on using the documents to further his schemes.

After Bill is kidnapped by Mannion's gang when she comes calling on Arthur and mistakes Mannion for him, the police decide to place Jones in a jail for his own safekeeping. Actually it is Mannion whom the police have locked up—part of his scheme to settle an old score with Slugs Martin, a former gang member who doublecrossed him. Plotting to have Arthur killed and identified as an escaped convict, Mannion then sends his meek double to the bank with a bundle, supposedly containing stolen money. The plan goes awry, however, and Mannion is gunned down by his own gang, mistaking their boss for Arthur. Collecting both the reward money and his new found courage, Arthur asks Bill to marry him.

The Whole Town's Talking (called *Passport to Fame* during production) was Edward G. Robinson's first picture to play at Radio City Music Hall in New York and was an unqualified smash that doubtless did not go unnoticed back at Warner Bros. Where it did go unnoticed was at the Academy of Motion Picture Arts and Sciences.

CRITICAL VIEWS

"Pungently written, wittily produced and topped off with a splendid dual performance by Edward G. Robinson, it may be handsomely recommended as the best of the new year's screen comedies . . . Mr. Robinson, while he succeeds in being unbelievably down-trodden in the wistful little man who looks like Public Enemy No. 1, has not forgotten how to play Little Caesar, and he stifles the laugh in your throat when he is being Killer Mannion . . . With a splendid narrative like this, he returns with a rush to the front line of film players." —Andre D. Sennwald, *The New York Times*

"After a number of recent cinema adventures in a minor key, Edward G. Robinson returns to the days of his Hollywood glory in a lively and satisfying combination of farce and melodrama . . . The work manages to supply a one-man carnival for its star, and, with Mr. Robinson taking every advantage of its side-show possibilities, you have the opportunity to enjoy good acting and to have the soul-satisfying pleasure of watching the shrewd and resourceful performer on one of the happiest times of his life."—Richard Watts, Jr., *New York Herald-Tribune*

"The best thing Mr. Robinson has done since the unforgettable *Little Caesar* . . . [He] is twin star of the picture, for he portrays both clerk and killer, and delivers two separate and distinct characterizations which never once overlap or intrude one upon another. No one need be told how thrilling [he] can impersonate an underworlding, and his Killer Mannion ranks with the finest of these conceptions . . . The entire piece is a field day for Robinson."—Regina Crewe, *New York American*

"Robinson will derive a heap of benefits from this assignment. It hands him some dazzling moments of acting . . . notably his characterization of the submerged, overpolite and indecisive office worker is human and believable. Always having been a swell actor, because he makes you believe him in various roles, this picture is a great break for him."—*Variety*

BARBARY COAST

1935   United Artists

Producer, Samuel Goldwyn; Director, Howard Hawks; Screenplay, Ben Hecht and Charles MacArthur; Photography, Ray June; Art director, Richard Day; Costume designer, Omar Kiam; Musical director, Alfred Newman; Assistant director, Walter Mayo; Editor, Edward Curtiss. 91 minutes

Mary Rutledge (Swan) (*Miriam Hopkins*), Louis Chamalis (*Edward G. Robinson*), Jim Carmichael (*Joel McCrea*), Old Atrocity (*Walter Brennan*), Col. Marcus Aurelius Cobb

(*Frank Craven*), Knuckles Jacoby (*Brian Donlevy*), Peebles (*Otto Hoffman*), Wigham (*Rollo Lloyd*), Sawbuck McTavish (*Donald Meek*), Sandy Ferguson (*Roger Gray*), Oakie (*Clyde Cook*), Jed Slocum (*Harry Carey*), Judge Harper (*J. M. Kerrigan*), Bronco (*Matt McHugh*), Ah Wing (*Wong Chung*), Sheriff (*Russ Powell*), Ship's Captain (*Fredrik Vogeding*), First Mate (*Dave Wengren*), McCready, The Second Mate (*Anders Van Haden*), Pilot (*Jules Cowles*), Steward (*Cyril Thornton*), Drunk (*Clarence Wertz*), Lookout (*Harry Semels*), Helmsman (*Theodore Lorch*), Bit Sailors (*Olin Francis, Larry Fisher*), Lead Line Sailor (*George Simpson*), Bit Passengers (*Bert Sprotte, Claude Payton, Frank Benson, Bob Stevenson*), Sailor (thrown out of saloon) (*David Niven*), Bill (*Edward Gargan*), Fish Peddler (*Herman Bing*), Ringsider (*Tom London*), Gamblers (*Heinie Conklin, Charles West, Constantine Romanoff, Art Miles, Sammy Finn*)

Edward G. Robinson continued on loan-out when Samuel Goldwyn made a deal with Jack Warner for the actor's services to play the colorful San Francisco gangland kingpin, Louis Chamalis, in the boisterous, sumptuously made (per Goldwyn standards) romantic saga, *Barbary Coast*. Goldwyn, it seems, had heard about a novel of that name by Herbert Asbury, and snapped it up sight unseen, thinking it was a rip-roaring Gold Rush tale, and made certain that everybody in Hollywood knew it. Instead it turned out to be a record of the San Francisco underworld of the late 19th century, and, according to *Harrison's Reports* (a respected industry trade paper from the earliest days of movies through the

BARBARY COAST: With Edward Gargan and Walter Brennan

BARBARY COAST: With Miriam Hopkins

BARBARY COAST: With Brian Donlevy

1950s), "one of the filthiest, vilest, most degrading books that has ever been chosen for the screen." Never one to shy away from publicity, positive as well as negative, Goldwyn simply kept the title, tossed out the story, and had Ben Hecht and Charles MacArthur concoct a lusty, action-filled Gold Rush drama for two of his stars, Gary Cooper and Anna Sten. Filming with this pair began under William Wyler's direction in late May 1934, but Goldwyn, ever on top of every production personally, was dissatisfied. He sent Hecht and MacArthur back to the typewriter, shifted Cooper and Sten to another project, reassigned Wyler, and subsequently began all over again with director Howard Hawks, Robinson, and two other Goldwyn stars, Miriam Hopkins and Joel McCrea in the first of their four Goldwyn films together. (And look for David Niven in what amounts to a bit in one of his earliest film roles.)

Louis Chamalis, the most powerful man in San Francisco of the 1850s, owns, among other properties, a gaudy gambling palace, the Bella Donna Club, into which sashays Mary Rutledge, known as Swan. She had come West to marry only to discover that her fiancé had died, and now she's looking for work. Chamalis sizes her up, thinks she's his kind of woman, and puts her in charge of his crooked roulette wheel. But when a miner loses last year's digging at the wheel and is killed when he protests, she crosses Chamalis by intervening on behalf of Col. Marcus Cobb, the verbose newspaper editor (he had shown Swan a kindness when she first came to town) who wants to print the true story of the miner's murder, despite Chamalis' threat to demolish his presses.

Riding in the gold fields one day, Swan meets Jim Carmichael, a poetry-spouting Easterner who has just struck it rich, and they instantly hit it off. Then Carmichael discovers what she does for a living when he happens into Chamalis' place and, disillusioned, he recklessly gambles away his money and, to pay off the house, is put to work cleaning Chamalis' spittoons. Violence soon breaks out at the hands of Chamalis' henchmen, and editor Cobb is killed for printing an expose of the town boss and his crooked dealings. Chamalis, now having to protect himself from a vigilante committee that wants to close him down, learns that Swan has let Carmichael win back his money at the table, and orders him killed, but the two manage to escape together, hoping to reach a ship laying at anchor in the bay. When Carmichael is shot by one of Chamalis' men, Swan promises to go back to her boss if Carmichael is allowed to go. Chamalis knows he's been beaten and decides to send Swan back to Carmichael. (Many later carped that the character had too rapid a change of heart and was too gracious in defeat.) Then he turns and finds himself facing the vigilantes with drawn guns and walks off to meet his fate.

The sole Academy Award nomination for *Barbary Coast* went to cinematographer Ray June. The Oscar, however, was won by Hal Mohr for *A Midsummer Night's Dream*, from Robinson's home studio, to which he next returned (after having a number of unkind things to say about Miriam Hopkins, repeated over a span of several pages in his autobiography) to wrap up his initial Warners contract. Goldwyn's film later was leased to an independent distributor in the 1940s along with others from his vault and was reissued with a juicier title, *Port of Wickedness*, although on TV it's back to its original title under the control of the Goldwyn company.

CRITICAL VIEWS

"In Chamalis, Edward G. Robinson has again found a character that suits him from the top of his black thatch to his laquered toes. He hasn't been able to get his teeth into such a juicy role since his appearance on the screen in *Little Caesar*, and he gives us this Barbary Coast dictator with a relish."—Kate Cameron, New York *Daily News*

"A gaudy, gripping melodrama of guns and gold . . . made colorful by the histrionics of Edward G. Robinson, played out against a background of San Francisco's rough and tumble glitter in the days of Forty-Nine. It's a thoroughly satisfying entertainment and you'd better mark it 'must' . . . Robinson dominates every instant of the drama with a superlative conception of the sinister spoilsman . . . and he manages, with ineffable artistry, to be so appealing a rogue that one regrets to see his final desserts meted out with such inexorable justice."—Regina Crewe, *New York American*

"Edward G. Robinson is an effective Chamalis although the gangster pictures have made his snarl overly familiar."—Andre D. Sennwald, *The New York Times*

BULLETS OR BALLOTS

1936   A First National & Vitaphone Picture

Associate producer, Louis F. Edelman; director, William Keighley; Screenplay, Seton I. Miller; Based on a story by Miller and Martin Mooney; Photography, Hal Mohr; Art

BARBARY COAST: With Miriam Hopkins

BARBARY COAST advertisement under the re-release title PORT OF WICKEDNESS

BULLETS OR BALLOTS: With Humphrey Bogart and Barton MacLane

director, Carl Jules Weyl; Music, Heinz Roemheld; Special effects, Fred Jackman, Jr. and Warren E. Lynch; Sound, Oliver S. Garretson; Editor, Jack Killifer. 81 minutes

Johnny Blake (*Edward G. Robinson*), Lee Morgan (*Joan Blondell*), Al Kruger (*Barton MacLane*), Nick "Bugs" Fenner (*Humphrey Bogart*), Captain Dan McLaren (*Joseph King*), Herman (*Frank McHugh*), Ed Driscoll (*Richard (Dick) Purcell*), Wires (*George E. Stone*), Nellie LaFleur (*Louise Beavers*), Grand Jury Spokesman (*Joseph Crehan*), Bryant (*Henry O'Neill*), Thorndyke (*Gilbert Emery*), Hollister (*Henry Kolker*), Caldwell (*Herbert Rawlinson*), Specialty (*Rosalind Marquis*), Vinci (*Norman Willis*), Gatley (*Frank Faylen*), Old Lady (*Alice Lyndon*), Ticket Seller (*Victoria Vinton*), Announcer's Voice (*Addison Richards*), Second Kid (*Harry Watson*), Third Kid (*Jerry Madden*), First Man (*Herman Marks*), Second Man (*Benny, The Gouge*), Proprietor (*Ray Brown*), First Man (*Al Hill*), Second Man (*Dutch Schlickenmeyer*), Truck Driver (*Eddie Shubert*), First Man (*George Lloyd*), Second Man (*Jack Gardner*), Third Man (*Saul (Sol) Gorss*), Actor Impersonating Kruger (*Max Wagner*), Judge (*Ed Stanley*), Jury Foreman (*Milton Kibbee*), Crail (*William Pawley*), Cigar Clerk (*Jack Goodrich*), First Beauty Attendant (*Alma Lloyd*), Kelly (*Ralph M. Remley*), Bank Secretaries (*Anne Nagel, Gordon (Bill) Elliott*), Kruger's Secretary (*Carlyle Moore Jr.*), Mary (*Virginia Dabney*)

Back on his home lot to wrap up his first contract after a couple of loan-outs, and not having been seen in a Warners film in nearly two years, Robinson was reported to have been handed the role of Duke Mantee in *The Petrified Forest*, but Leslie Howard, who had starred with Humphrey Bogart in it on Broadway, balked at doing the movie without Bogart. Instead, Robinson was given the good guy lead as a tough but honest cop in *Bullets or Ballots*. Bogart was assigned the bad guy role. It was the first of five times Robinson worked with Bogart (Robinson—along with Paul Muni, Warners' top star—killed contract player Bogey in the first four; in the fifth, Bogey—now the studio's top star—bumped off Robinson, who was ending his Warner contract).

Robinson is Johnny Blake, former detective and head of New York's famous strong-arm squad (a character vaguely based on real-life cop Johnny Broderick), has been forced by political pressure back to a beat in the Bronx. Resigned to his fate, he marks time until his friend Capt. Dan McLaren is made commissioner, but when he is promoted, and Blake goes to him expecting to be reinstated, he is discharged. Later, when the two meet, Blake knocks the police commissioner down. This act convinces tough Al Kruger, the city's rackets boss, that Blake and McLaren are through, and he puts Blake on his payroll. Right away, Blake butts heads with Kruger's chief henchman "Bugs" Fenner, who's

BULLETS OR BALLOTS: With Humphrey Bogart

BULLETS OR BALLOTS: With Humphrey Bogart and George E. Stone

convinced Blake is working undercover for the police. Bugs, a hothead, not long afterwards has a falling out with his boss, Kruger, and kills him. Blake, meanwhile, has taken over the numbers game for the syndicate and undercuts Kruger's moll, Lee Morgan, who has been operating the rackets in Harlem. Impressed, the mob bosses, a triumverate of politically ambitious businessmen, send for Blake and give him Kruger's job—the one Bugs had killed for.

Having learned the identities of the men behind the rackets, Blaked sets up a police raid on the gang's headquarters. Bugs, in the meantime, has learned positively that Blake is working undercover and forces Lee to lead him to Blake's apartment. In a shootout there, Bugs is killed and Blake badly wounded. Learning the truth, Lee comes to his rescue and finds him staggering on the sidewalk, satchel in hand. She drives him to the gang leaders' office and there he leads a police raid before collapsing and dying in Lee's arms.

CRITICAL VIEWS

"The Brothers Warner who have been making crime pay (cinematically, of course) ever since they produced *Little Caesar* have turned out another crackling underworld melodrama in *Bullets or Ballots* . . . [with] a crisp, cohesive and fast-moving script which has been capitally served by such Warner crime experts as Edward G. Robinson, Humphrey Bogart, Barton MacLane and Joan Blondell. Although Mr. Robinson's detective, Johnny Blake, figures in some wild-eyed

melodrama as the film races along, the character at least has been taken from life . . . It is a top-notch performance, his best in fact since *Little Caesar*."—Frank S. Nugent, *The New York Times*

"The role of Johnny Blake . . . is a natural for Edward G. Robinson, and it is a tribute to [his] art that he tosses his studio differences into the ashcan and throws himself wholeheartedly into the part for a performance unequalled since his Little Caesar."—Douglas Gilbert, *New York World-Telegram*

BULLETS OR BALLOTS: With Joan Blondell

"Mr. Robinson emerges from milquetoast roles to bring all the forcefulness, the dynamic power of his vivid histrionicism to beat in a piercing, pungent portrait such as only he can conceive and execute . . . He dominates the drama with the sheer strength of his characterization. Never for an instant does he lose control. He knows this man and limns him in clear, incisive colors. The character has its shades and moods and vagaries. Mr. Robinson registers each with keen, accurate artistry of a super-craftsman in the theatre."—Regina Crewe, *New York American*

"Edward G. Robinson bows out of his Warner contract in this picture by one of his most virile he-man characterizations . . . a tough but honest dick."—*Variety*

"I agreed to do it after some minimal (I wanted maximal, but settled for minimal) changes were made because there were only three more pictures left on my Warners contract, and to tell you the truth, I didn't know whether to be glad or sorry. A contract is a straightjacket; it's also an assured income."—Edward G. Robinson

THUNDER IN THE CITY

1937   Atlantic Films/Columbia Pictures

Producers, Alexander Esway and Akos Tolnay; Director, Marion Gering; Screenplay, Akos Tolnay, Aben Kandel, Walter Hackett and Robert Sherwood; Photography, Arthur Gilks; Editor, Arthur Hilton. 76 minutes

Dan Armstrong (*Edward G. Robinson*), Lady Patricia (*Luli Deste*), The Duke of Glenavon (*Nigel Bruce*), The Duchess of Glenavon (*Constance Collier*), Henry Graham Manningdale (*Ralph Richardson*), Lady Challoner (*Annie Esmond*), Sir Peter Challoner (*Arthur Wontner*), Dolly (*Elizabth Inglis*), James (*Cyril Raymond*), Edna (*Nancy Burne*), Bill (*Billy Bray*), Snyderling (*James Carew*), Millie (*Everley Gregg*), Casey (*Elliott Nugent*), Reporter (*Terence De Marney*), Frank (*Roland Drew*)

THUNDER IN THE CITY: With Luli Deste and Nigel Bruce

With Jack Warner's apparent blessings, Edward G. Robinson went off to London to make a film for an independent distributor who not only paid the actor a generous salary but also lined up a supporting cast that included Nigel Bruce, Constance Collier, Ralph Richardson, and an up and coming actress named Luli Deste—whose promise was never realized. According to Robinson, who had his doubts about the flat, rather silly script he was handed, it was he who brought a new writer to the project. "I'd run across a gentleman I'd known on Broadway," Robinson wrote in his autobiography, *All My Yesterdays*. "He was a very tall gentleman, and his name was Robert Sherwood. He was in London for reasons unknown—maybe something to do with FDR and the British government—but apparently time was not ripe for his negotiations, so he was at loose ends. Twenty minutes after we met and had a cup of tea, he was no longer at loose ends—he was engaged to rewrite *Thunder in the City*."

The plot, Sherwood notwithstanding, was no great shakes, having to deal with an American salesman, a go-getter who's a bit too high pressure for his employers. He is shipped off to his company's London offices to observe how English business is able to flourish with more sedate methods, and is taken under the wing of a couple of impoverished distant relatives. He finds his way into London society, falls for the pretty daughter of a Duke and Duchess, who think him to be well-to-do. He impresses his hosts with a grand scheme for a miracle metal called Magnelite, and steals the girl away from her wealthy fiancé, and comes back to America with her, a hero to his company.

The title, perhaps, misled moviegoers of the day, and

THUNDER IN THE CITY: With Constance Collier

Robinson's name alone had to carry the film. It wasn't widely seen at the time and has since, for all practical purposes, vanished. What it produced for him, however, was the beginnings of his fabled art collection, based on his prowlings through London galleries. A handsome contract was hammered out with Jack Warner on his arrival back in Hollywood.

"The British are having a bit of good wholesome fun at their own expense in *Thunder in the City* . . . whether you have fun, too, will depend largely on how you feel about the Edward G. Robinson brand of Napoleonics . . . Our Robinson reflex is normal: we cringe at the rasping voice, genuflect when the great man pounds the table, feel involuntary tears when he stands before hysterically admiring or dramatically hostile throngs to make his grand gesture of success or renunciation grander than success, but all the time we are emotionally thinking: Please, for goodness sake, somebody give him a tricornered hat."—Bosley Crowther, *The New York Times*

"Edward G. Robinson is brilliantly comic in *Thunder in the City* as he was sinisterly forbidding in his memorable gangster roles."—Howard Barnes, *New York Herald-Tribune*

"What [Sherwood] did was turn it into a satire—tongue-in-cheek—transform idiot comedy into subtle wit. He really did wonders with the script—but not enough. It was a flop, and I apologized to Bob a thousand times for mixing him up in it."—Edward G. Robinson

THUNDER IN THE CITY: With Nigel Bruce and Ralph Richardson

KID GALAHAD

1937   Warner Bros.-First National

Associate producer, Samuel Bischoff; Director, Michael Curtiz; Screenplay, Seton I. Miller; Based on the novel by Francis Wallace; Dialogue director, Irving Rapper; Photography, Tony Gaudio; Art director, Carl Jules Weyl; Gowns, Orry-Kelly; Music, Heinz Roemheld and Max Steiner; Orchestrations, Hugo Friedhofer; Song "The Moon Is in Tears Tonight" by M. K. Jerome and Jack Scholl; Special effects, James Gibbons and Edwin B. DuPar; Sound, Charles Lang; Editor, George Amy. 101 minutes

Nick Donati (*Edward G. Robinson*), Louise (Fluff) Phillips (*Bette Davis*), Turkey Morgan (*Humphrey Bogart*), Kid Ward Guisenberry (*Wayne Morris*), Marie Donati (*Jane Bryan*), Silver Jackson (*Harry Carey*), Chuck McGraw (*William Haade*), Mrs. Donati (*Soledad Jiminez*), Joe Taylor (*Joe Cunningham*), Buzz Stevens (*Ben Welden*), Editor Brady (*Joseph Crehan*), Redhead at Party (*Veda Ann Borg*), Barney (*Frank Faylen*), Gunman (*Harland Tucker*), Sam McGraw (*Bob Evans*), Jim Burke (*Hank Hankinson*), Tim O'Brien (*Bob Nestell*), Den-

KID GALAHAD: With Bette Davis

baugh (*Jack Kranz*), Referee (*George Blake*), Second (*Charlie Sullivan*), Girl on Phone (*Joyce Compton*), Louie (Pianist) (*Eddie Foster*), Barber (*George Humbert*), Ring Announcer (*Emmett Vogan*), Ringsider (*Stan Jolley*), Reporters at Press Conference (*Harry Harvey, Horace McMahon, John Shelton*), Reporters (*Don Brodie, Milton Kibbee*), Reporter at Dinner

KID GALAHAD: With Wayne Morris and Bette Davis

Edward G. Robinson's tough fight manager, Nick Donati, was his first role under his new, improved contract that allowed him to work not just for Warner Bros. but elsewhere when projects that interested him came along. *Kid Galahad* not only teamed him with Bogart again but also matched him up with Bette Davis for the only time. Nick Donati has just lost his best fighter—and most of his dough—in a bout in which his boy had sold out to crooked Turkey Morgan, Donati's rival. With what's left of his bankroll, Nick throws a bash in his hotel suite, with his girlfriend Fluff Phillips as hostess. Helping serve drinks is a bellhop, Ward Guisenberry. When Ward knocks down Chuck McGraw, Turkey's star attraction who has insulted Fluff, Nick spots a new ring diamond in the rough. Fluff dubs him Kid Galahad for his gallant behavior. With Fluff and trainer Silver Jackson, Nick and The Kid go out to Nick's country place to train, and there the potential fighter meets and falls for Nick's sister Marie.

After knocking out McGraw's brother in his first fight, The Kid goes on a barnstorming tour to gain experience, mostly by KOs, before Nick lines up the big one for him—McGraw himself for the champion-

KID GALAHAD: With Harry Carey, Humphrey Bogart and William Haade

KID GALAHAD: With Bette Davis

boy when the latter falls in love with his sister."—Howard Barnes, *New York Herald-Tribune*

"Assisted no little by the comforting presence of Edward G. Robinson, Bette Davis and Harry Carey in his corner, young Wayne Morris, the Warners' latest astronomical discovery, comes through with a natural and easy performance in *Kid Galahad* . . . It is a promising debut for a new star [ed.: Morris already had made a half-dozen B movies for the studio] and a good little picture as well."—Frank S. Nugent, *The New York Times*

KID GALAHAD: With Harry Carey (partially hidden), Wayne Morris, Humphrey Bogart and William Haade

ship. However Nick knows that the Kid can slug but can't box. He guarantees that the Kid will lose, and bets on McGraw. Turkey warns Nick that if there is any funny business, there'll be a killing. The Kid takes a savage beating until Fluff and Marie plead with Nick to save him. Nick relents and changes his ring instructions. The Kid wins by a knockout, and a double-crossed Turkey comes gunning for Nick in the Kid's dressing room. In the shootout, Turkey is killed and Nick mortally wounded. The Kid meanwhile is crowned World Champ.

In the title role of *Kid Galahad* (renamed *The Battling Bellhop* for television) was a young up-and-comer, Wayne Morris. His role was played in the remake in 1962 by Elvis Presley, with Gig Young in Robinson's role. In between these two versions was a Grade B edition from Warners in 1941, *The Wagons Roll at Night*, reset in a circus background, with Bogart in the lead this time, and Eddie Albert as a rube who wants to become a top-notch lion tamer.

CRITICAL VIEWS

"Robinson has here his best role since the Little Caesar days, that of Nick Donati, a racketeering fight promoter who insists on being the brains of the boy he handles."—Rose Pelswick, *New York Journal-American*

"The stars of the photoplay are Edward G. Robinson and Bette Davis, and they contribute steady impersonations that add immeasurably to its power. The power is at its nervous best in the part of a manager who grooms a nobody for the world's championship but turns on the

THE LAST GANGSTER

1937   Metro-Goldwyn-Mayer

Producer, J.J. Cohn; Director, Edward Ludwig; Screenplay, John Lee Mahin; Based on an original story by William A. Wellman and Robert Carson; Photography, William Daniels; Art directors, Cedric Gibbons and Daniel Cathcart; Set decorator, Edwin B. Willis; Music, Edward Ward; Editor, Ben Lewis. 81 minutes

Joe Krozac (*Edward G. Robinson*), Paul North, Sr. (*James Stewart*), Talya Krozac (*Rose Stradner*), Curly (*Lionel Stander*), Paul North, Jr. (*Douglas Scott*), Casper (*John Carra-*

dine), San Francisco Editor (*Sidney Blackmer*), Fats Garvey (*Edward Brophy*), Frankie "Acey" Kile (*Alan Baxter*), Warden (*Grant Mitchell*), Sid Gorman (*Frank Conroy*), Shea (*Moroni Olsen*), Wilson (*Ivan Miller*), Broderick (*Willard Robertson*), Gloria (*Louise Beavers*), Billy Ernst (*Donald Barry*), Bottles Bailey (*Ben Welden*), Limpy (*Horace McMahon*), Brockett (*Edward Pawley*), Red (*John Kelly*), Boys (*David Leo Tillotson, Jim Kehner, Billy Smith, Reggie Streeter*), Boy (*Dick Holland*), Editor (*Pierre Watkin*), Reporter (*Douglas McPhail*), Editor (*Cy Kendall*), Reporter (*Ernest Wood*), First Reporter (*Phillip Terry*), Office Boy (*William Benedict*), Boston Editor (*Frederick Burton*), Train Guard (*Lee Phelps*), Jo Krozac (*Larry Simms*), Turnkey (*Wade Boteler*), Mike Kile (*Walter Miller*), Hoods (*Victor Adams, George Magrill, Jerry Jerome*)

On the MGM lot after seven years (Thalberg, who had tried in vain to entice him there earlier, was now dead), Robinson has the title role as an aging gangster determined to reclaim his turf that rival mobsters have split up. Viennese actress Rose Stradner was the young bride

THE LAST GANGSTER: With Lionel Stander and Rose Stradner

THE LAST GANGSTER: With James Stewart, Douglas Scott and Rose Stradner

he has brought back from Europe and a gangling, mustached Jimmy Stewart, himself just on the brink of stardom, was a good-hearted reporter fired for writing sympathetic articles about him. When racketeer Joe Krozac gets hunted down by the police after a mob rubout, and is sent up the river on an income tax rap, Paul North, a newspaperman, becomes close with Joe's

wife Talya and their young son. Soon Paul persuades her to get a divorce and marry him.

Ten years later, Joe gets out of prison and begins tracking down Talya for deserting him and taking their son. One of his old henchmen, Curly, persuades him to come East and head up the gang again, but it's a setup. The gang grabs Joe and tries to make him tell where he had hidden a large cache before being sent off to prison. Curly then has Joe's son kidnapped and beaten in front of him. Joe finally discloses the whereabouts of the money. Then he and the boy escape when the gang members rush out to retrieve the loot. Joe wants revenge, not just on the gang, but also on Paul, now a respected newspaper editor, and Talya, for taking his son. However, when Joe sees the happy environment the couple has created for the boy, he changes his mind. Not long afterwards, Joe gets into a shootout with Acey Kile, an old racketeer rival he had once tried to kill. In the suddenly sentimental ending, he dies holding a merit badge his son had earned in school.

CRITICAL VIEWS

"Had Warners been doing it, it would have read: 'Mr. Edward G. Robinson in "The Life of the Last Gangster."' . . . Mr. Robinson's crime lord is a natural family man with a warped desire to create a Public Enemy No. One, Jr. [His] snarls and menace and brooding hate eminently qualify him to be not only 'The Last' but the very first gangster of filmdom. Mr. Robinson, in brief, is the gang cycle by himself. We refuse to believe that *The Last Gangster* is really his epitaph . . . [He] plays it

with an assurance born of long practice."—Frank S. Nugent, *The New York Times*

"It is eminently fitting that Edward G. Robinson should be the hero of what we fervently hope is the last Hollywood gangster film, *The Last Gangster*. A lot of water has flowed under the bridge since *Little Caesar* but Mr. Robinson has breasted the tides to make his impersonation of a 1937 thug as persuasive as was his portrait of a killer in that earlier classic of rats and rackets. In the new offering, he creates a bitterly effective impersonation of a beaten hoodlum, which should put a definite period after the cycle of public enemy melodramas. Just as in *Little Caesar*, the film pivots surely around [his] performance. Accept his highly psychological projection of Joe Krozak and you'll find *The Last Gangster* a sociological thriller . . . [He] does a showy job with the role of Krozak, keeping the thug human, recognizable and pathological."—Howard Barnes, *New York Herald-Tribune*

"I had always known that MGM films had a very special hallmark on them, discounting my bad experience with *A Lady to Love*, but I'm prone to think now that a great deal of that was my own fault . . . And so I made *The Last Gangster* at Metro and found that it was politically the most schizophrenic of lots."—Edward G. Robinson

THE LAST GANGSTER: With Alan Baxter, Moroni Olsen and Lionel Stander

A SLIGHT CASE OF MURDER

1938   Warner Bros.-First National

Producer, Hal B. Wallis; Associate producer, Sam Bischoff; Director, Lloyd Bacon; Screenplay, Earl Baldwin and Joseph Schrank; Based on the play by Damon Runyon and Howard Lindsay; Photography, Sid Hickox; Art director, Max

A SLIGHT CASE OF MURDER: With Paul Harvey and Jane Bryan

A SLIGHT CASE OF MURDER: With Ruth Donnelly

Parker; Music director, Leo Forbstein; Music and lyrics, M.K. Jerome and Jack Scholl; Editor, James Gibbons. 85 minutes

Remy Marco (*Edward G. Robinson*), Mary Marco (*Jane Bryan*), Mike (*Allen Jenkins*), Nora Marco (*Ruth Donnelly*), Dick Whitewood (*Willard Parker*), Post (*John Litel*), Lefty (*Edward Brophy*), Ritter (*Eric Stanley*), Giusseppe (*Harold Huber*), Mr. Whitewood (*Paul Harvey*), Douglas Fairbanks Rosenbloom (*Bobby Jordan*), Innocence (*Joseph Downing*), Mrs. Cagle (*Margaret Hamilton*), Ex-Jockey Kirk (*George E. Stone*), Sad Sam (*Bert Hanlon*), Remy's Secretary (Myrtle) (*Jean Benedict*), The Singer (*Harry Seymour*), Loretta (*Betty Compson*), No Nose Cohen (*Joe Caits*), Little Dutch (*George Lloyd*), Blackhead Gallagher (*John Harmon*), A Stranger (*Harry Tenbrook*), Champ (*Duke York*), Champ's Manager (*Pat Daly*), Radio Commentator (*John Hiestand*), Speakeasy Proprietor (*Bert Roach*), Pessimistic Patron (*Harry Cody*), First Policeman (*Ben Hendricks*), Second Policeman (*Ralph Dunn*), Third Policeman (*Wade Boteler*), Nurses (*Myrtle Stedman, Loia Cheaney*), French Teacher (*Isabel La Mal*), Factory Foreman (Tony) (*Alan Bridge*), Freckle-Faced Kid (*Tommy Bupp*), Orphanage Singing Teacher (*Anne O'Neal*), Jim (*Al Herman*), Freddie (*John Harron*), Bartender (*Jack Mower*), Beer Salesman (*Elliott Sullivan*)

Refashioning the 1935 play by Damon Runyon and Howard Lindsay into a vehicle for Edward G. Robinson, Warners gave its star one of his most satisfying light roles—a gangster spoof that was a great deal more entertaining and twice as funny as *The Little Giant* a couple of years before. Robinson was a beer baron looking for post-Prohibition greener pastures, surrounded by an assortment of amusing toughs essayed by the studio's famed group of stock players. He's tough guy Remy Marco, who calls his mob together and informs them that he's going legitimate because the repeal of Prohibition has knocked the bottom out of the bootlegging business. No more police blotter stuff, he tells them; from now on it's the social register. Marco it seems is a right guy—for a beer runner—but his beer tastes terrible. How would he know; he's never tasted it, but the public has, and can't stomach it.

Marco's also a good family man, who wants to do right by his daughter. She's fallen for Dick Whitewood, a rich man's son, but refuses to marry him until he gets a job. The best he can do is become a motorcycle cop. An ambush of Marco backfires, and the four would-be killers end up shooting each other. Marco discovers them in his daughter's bedroom together with their half-million dollar racetrack haul. Mary's boyfriend arrives on the scene and Marco, to help the young cop attain some glory, gets him to shoot the dead gangsters all over again. And for good measure, he accidentally kills another hood who's been hiding out in the room.

In the heat of the excitement, Marco gets a taste of his own beer and realizes he's got to give the drinking public a better product—with the $500,000 he lifted from the guys who bumped each other off. He ends up saving his business while losing his daughter to a cop.

In the somewhat musicalized, not nearly as funny 1952 color remake, *Stop, You're Killing Me!*, Broderick Crawford inherited Robinson's role and Claire Trevor was his wife, Nora.

CRITICAL VIEWS

"One of the funniest and most satisfying farces which has come out of Hollywood in some time. For Mr. Robinson, the show is a major dispensation. After *The Last Gangster*, it was fairly obvious that straight variations on the Little Caesar role has been exhausted. *A Slight Case of Murder* gives him a burlesque underworld big-shot to portray and he handles the assignment with comical efficiency. As a prohibition needled-beer baron who turns square but forgets to stop needling his beer, he realizes a nice blend of ruthlessness and clowning . . . Little Caesar has died hard but his passing shouldn't grieve Mr. Robinson unduly if he can get

A SLIGHT CASE OF MURDER: With Margaret Hamilton and Bobby Jordan

room of the Saratoga house his boss has rented for the season . . . For a Runyonesque panel, the casting director had the marvelous good fortune to find Edward G. Robinson and Ruth Donnelly to play Mr. and Mrs. Marco . . ."—Frank S. Nugent, *The New York Times*

"I returned to Warners to make *A Slight Case of Murder*, from a play by Damon Runyon and Howard Lindsay. I had absolutely no fault to find with the script because it was beautifully constructed and written and it was very funny."—Edward G. Robinson

A SLIGHT CASE OF MURDER: With Ruth Donnelly and Jane Bryan

more scripts like this one."—Howard Barnes, *New York Herald-Tribune*

"We haven't laughed so much since Remy Marco's Mike found four parties shot to death in the back bed-

THE AMAZING DR. CLITTERHOUSE

1938   Warner Bros.-First National

Associate producer, Robert Lord; Director, Anatole Litvak; Screenplay, John Wexley and John Huston; Based on the play by Barre Lyndon; Photography, Tony Gaudio; Art director, Carl Jules Weyl; Wardrobe, Milo Anderson; Music, Max Steiner; Sound, C.A. Riggs; Editor, Warren Low. 87 minutes

Dr. Clitterhouse (*Edward G. Robinson*), Jo Keller (*Claire Trevor*), Rocks Valentine (*Humphrey Bogart*), Nurse Randolph (*Gale Page*), Inspector Lane (*Donald Crisp*), Okay

THE AMAZING DR. CLITTERHOUSE: With Maxie Rosenbloom, Claire Trevor and Humphrey Bogart

104

(*Allen Jenkins*), Grant (*Thurston Hall*), Prosecuting Attorney (*John Litel*), Judge (*Henry O'Neill*), Butch (*Maxie Rosenbloom*), Rabbit (*Curt Bois*), Pal (*Bert Hanlon*), Tug (*Ward Bond*), Popus (*Vladimir Sokoloff*), Candy (*Billy Wayne*), Lieut. Johnson (*Robert Homans*), Watchman (*William Haade*), Connors (*Thomas Jackson*), Sergeant (*Edward Gargan*), Mrs. Ganswoort (*Winifred Harris*), Dr. Ames (*Eric Stanley*), Nurse Donor (*Loia Cheaney*), Capt. MacLevy (*Wade Boteler*), Mrs. Jefferson (*Libby Taylor*), Patrolman (*Edgar Dearing*), Chemist (*Sidney Bracy*), Foreman of Jury (*Irving Bacon*), Woman Juror (*Vera Lewis*), Bailiff (*Bruce Mitchell*), Bit Guests (*William Worthington, Ed Mortimer*), Bit Policemen (*Ray Dawe, Bob Reeves*), Bit Guest (*Larry Steers*)

Thanks to the adaptation by John Wexley and young John Huston of Barre Lyndon's 1937 Broadway play, Edward G. Robinson got the chance to explore another facet of the gangster character he had virtually patented. At the same time he played a good guy in one of the more unusual crime films. As a dedicated doctor named Clitterhouse who becomes, at least for a time, a gangster to research a book he's writing on crime, Robinson reteamed with Humphrey Bogart, who played a notorious safecracker who is Clitterhouse's underworld mentor then nemesis. The movie also had Claire Trevor as a fence working with the good doctor and Donald Crisp as a relentless police inspector—plus of course that matchless roster of Warner contract players.

Not long after joining the underworld, Dr. Clitterhouse has become a successful jewel thief, involved with Rocks Valentine's gang, and masterminds a number of heists. Rocks begins to resent Clitterhouse's attempts to take over leadership of the gang, and is jealous as well because of lady fence Jo Keller's wavering affections. Rocks is in love with the dame himself. Clitterhouse, who has been taking meticulous notes as a "criminal," decides ultimately that his research is complete, but he plans one last great job. He is determined to break away from the gang not only because he finds Jo falling in love with him but also because he fears he is beginning to like criminal life. Quitting is not so easy, he learns. When Rocks demands that the doctor stay on with the gang, Clitterhouse realizes that the one facet of the criminal mind he has not researched is the act of murder. He poisons Rocks and coolly studies his reactions as the gang leader dies. When Inspector Lane closes in and rounds up Rocks's boys, Clitterhouse is put on trial. The doctor—rather implausibly—pleads insanity as his defense but claims he was sane during the crimes. He is acquitted. It seems the jury was convinced that any man who insists he is insane at one point and sane at another must be in fact insane.

CRITICAL VIEWS

"As a primary fault in an otherwise smooth and satisfying melodrama, we have Edward G. Robinson being *The Amazing Dr. Clitterhouse*. Mr. Robinson plays him well enough, but hardly as effective as Cedric Hardwicke did in the play . . . Little Caesar keeps coming through the dignified veneer. It is easier to think of him as a criminal masquerading as a physician than as a medico fronting as a gang lord . . . he never quite succeeds in shaking the role free from the shadowy public enemies, numbers one to ten, which have been the larger part of his past."—Frank S. Nugent, *The New York Times*

"A deft and amusing job of screen transcription has been done with *The Amazing Dr. Clitterhouse* . . . Edward G. Robinson would not have been my choice for the Clitterhouse role, but he performs the assignment capably. Perhaps it is because he has been so clearly identified with gangster roles that he has trouble in underlining the Jekyll and Hyde quality which Cedric Hardwicke accomplished so suavely in the drama. In any case, he never fails to give the picture dramatic punch when it requires it, whether he is calmly stealing or murdering, or testing the reflexes of his henchmen in the very act of lawbreaking."—Howard Barnes, *New York Herald-Tribune*

I AM THE LAW

1938   Columbia Pictures

Producer, Everett Riskin; Director, Alexander Hall; Screenplay, Jo Swerling; Based on magazine articles by Fred Allhoff; Photography, Henry Freulich; Music director, Morris Stoloff; Editor, Viola Lawrence. 83 minutes

John Lindsay (*Edward G. Robinson*), Jerry Lindsay (*Barbara O'Neil*), Paul Ferguson (*John Beal*), Frankie Ballou (*Wendy Barrie*), Eugene Ferguson (*Otto Kruger*), Tom Ross (*Arthur Loft*), Eddie Girard (*Marc Lawrence*), Berry (*Douglas Wood*), Moss Kitchell (*Robert Middlemass*), Inspector Gleason (*Ivan Miller*), Leander (*Charles Halton*), J.W. Butler (*Louis Jean Heydt*), Brophy (*Emory Parnell*), Cronin (*Joseph Downing*), Martin (*Theodore Von Eltz*), Prisoner (*Horace McMahon*), Governor (*Frederick Burton*), Roberts (*Lucien Littlefield*), Witnesses (*Ed Keane, Robert Cummings, Sr., Harvey Clark, James Flavin*), Mrs. Butler (*Fay Helm*), Students (*Kane Richmond, James Bush, Anthony Nace*), Professor Perkins (*Walter Soderling*), Graduate Law Students (*Scott Colton, (Steve) Gaylord Pendleton*), Witness (*Harry Bradley*), Austin (*Ed Fether-*

I AM THE LAW: With John Beal and Barbara O'Neil

stone), Bartender (*Bud Jamison*), Girard's Girl (*Iris Meredith*), Student (*Robert McWade Jr.*), Police Sergeant (*Lee Shumway*), Secretary (*Bess Flowers*), Policemen (*Bud Wiser, Lane Chandler*), Photographers (*Reginald Simpson, Cyril Ring*)

Firmly on the right side of the law in this brief excursion away from the Warner Bros. backlot, Edward G. Robinson is John Lindsay, a big city law professor who is hired by the District Attorney as special prosecutor to clean out the mob. At the urging of prominent civic leader Eugene Ferguson, Lindsay hires Ferguson's son Paul, one of the students of the professor-turned-racketbuster, as his top aide. Newspaper columnist Frankie Ballou draws Lindsay's attention to an underworld figure, who is promptly gunned down after telling Lindsay what he knows about the rackets. Suspicious of Frankie, Lindsay does some investigating and finds that she is on Eugene Ferguson's payroll. Lindsay's job keep frustrating him, and soon the townsfolk get impatient with his efforts and he is fired by the D.A.

I AM THE LAW: With Wendy Barrie

Lindsay, however, proves a bulldog, a difficult man to get rid of. He moves his staff—composed primarily of former students—into his home and works with funds borrowed from loan sharks. By pitting gang members against one another, he and Paul find out about Paul's father and his complicity in the rackets. Ready at last to expose the mob, Lindsay, with a force of handpicked cops, herds all the criminal elements in town into a circus tent where they are forced to watch actual films of an electrocution. Then Ferguson is

I AM THE LAW: With Barbara O'Neil

I AM THE LAW: With Arthur Loft, Ivan Miller (chief in background), Wendy Barrie and player

shown a special reel where he is consorting with known criminals, and Frankie is shown a filmed record of a murder she had committed.

Frankie confesses and the elder Ferguson signs a paper leaving his fortune to crime control efforts. He then borrow's Lindsay's car—knowing that one of his henchmen had planted a bomb in it.

CRITICAL VIEWS

"That the motion picture pays more attention to a racketbuster than racket busting is obviously due to the fact that this particular crusading prosecutor is none other than Edward G. Robinson. It seems evident that he is determined to make filmgoers forget that he was once the archetype of the genius gangster. Here he plays a law professor who bucks crooked politics and a blonde gun moll as well as menacing racketeers. It is my hunch, though, that he is still not at home in heroic roles. In *I Am the Law*, he is at his best when he is mussing up three thugs to show his staff how yellow they really are. He delivers a number of speeches about law and order crisply if not very convincingly, dances the 'Big Apple' to lead on the blonde, and acts extremely executive. It's still hard for me to keep in mind that he is a cleaner-upper rather than Little Caesar."—Howard Barnes, *New York Herald-Tribune*

"It isn't so much that we feel Mr. Robinson is limited in his screen roles since the night he died, clutching dramatically at his throat, behind a billboard in Chicago; it's just that he strains the imagination a little trying to play both ends of the criminological scale, so to speak, against—or let us say, for the amusement of—the mid-

dle . . . The fact that [he] seems slightly miscast, however, is no reflection on *I Am the Law*, which is still the liveliest melodrama in town."—Bosley Crowther, *The New York Times*

"The film was clearly a potboiler, but at least I was on the right side of the law for once and survived; up to now, it seemed to me, I had died in every picture."—Edward G. Robinson

CONFESSIONS OF A NAZI SPY

1939   Warner Bros.-First National

Associate producer, Robert Lord; Director, Anatole Litvak; Screenplay, Milton Krims and John Wexley; Based on the series of articles, "Storm Over America," by Leon G. Turrou and his book *The Nazi Spy Conspiracy*; Photography, Sol Polito; Art director, Carl Jules Weyl; Music director, Leo Forbstein; Sound, C.A. Riggs; Editor, Owen Marks. 102 minutes

Ed Renard (*Edward G. Robinson*), Kurt Schneider (aka Harold Mitchell) (*Francis Lederer*), Franz Schlanger (*George Sanders*), Dr. Karl Kassel (*Paul Lukas*), D.A. Kellogg (*Henry O'Neill*), Erika Wolff (*Lya Lys*), Mrs. Schneider (*Grace Stafford*), Scotland Yard Man (*James Stephenson*), Dr. Krogman (*Sig Rumann*), Fred Phillips (*Fred Tozere*), Hilda Kleinhauer (*Dorothy Tree*), Lisa Kassel (*Celia Sibelius*), Werner Renz (*Joe Sawyer*), Hintze (*Lionel Royce*), Wildebrandt (*Henry Victor*), Max Heldorf (*Hans Von Twardowsky*), Captain Richter (*Fredrik Vogeding*), Klauber (*George Rosener*), Wilhelm Straubel (*Robert O. Davis*, [*Rudolph Anders*]), Johann Westphal (*John Voigt*, [*Paul Ander*]), Gruetzwald (*Willy Kaufman*), Capt. Von Eichen (*William Vaughn*, [*Von Brincken*]), McDonald (*Jack Mower*), Harrison (*Robert Emmett Keane*), Mrs. MacLaughlin (*Eily Malyon*), Staunton (*Frank Mayo*), Postman McGregor (*Alec Craig*), Kassel's Nurse (*Jean Brooks*), Kranz (*Lucien Prival*), U.S. District Court Judge (*Frederick Burton*), American Legionnaire (*Ward Bond*), U.S. Intelligence (*Charles Trowbridge*), Army Hospital Clerk (*John Ridgely*), Hotel Clerk (*Emmett Vogan*), FBI Man (*Edward Keane*), Goebbels (*Martin Kosleck*), Customs Official (*Selmer Jackson*), Nazi Agent (*Egon Brecher*), Narrator (*John Deering*), FBI Men (*John Hamilton, William Gould*), German Ship Captain (*Hans Schumm*), Naval Courier (*Gaylord (Steve) Pendleton*), Customer (*Regis Toomey*), U.S. Embassy Official (*Edwin Stanley*), Air Force Officer (*Max Hoffman, Jr.*)

Awaiting Edward G. Robinson at Warners on his return was a project he had urged the studio to option for him,

CONFESSIONS OF A NAZI SPY:
With Paul Lukas

CONFESSIONS OF A NAZI SPY: With Frank Mayo and Lya Lys

a semi-documentary account of Nazi espionage based on Leon Turrou's controversial book of the time. It was Hollywood's first important film about the Nazis in America. Robinson here is a dedicated FBI agent obsessed with cracking a Nazi spy ring. He worked once again with Anatole Litvak, saluted by Robinson in his autobiography as "surely one of the most urbane, sophisticated, haut monde anti-Nazis ever known—and one of the most talented." At the time shooting began, in late 1938, this "yanked from the headlines" exposé pre-dated the war but turned the unwelcomed spotlight on pro-Nazi groups flourishing throughout the country. The German-American Bund, among others, tried to have the production suppressed. The German Consul in Los Angeles threatened reprisals from his government. "Even some of our powerful Hollywood executives," Jack Warner revealed in his autobiography, *My First 100 Years in Hollywood*, "were furious with me for going ahead on the film."

G-Man Ed Renard is called on to investigate Nazi activities in the United States after a letter is intercepted by British Intelligence from a German-American named Schneider, detailing plans to kidnap an American Air Force general. Schneider, who has strong Nazi sympathies and has been recruited to obtain Allied military secrets, is painstakingly tracked down, apprehended and interrogated by Renard, and is persuaded to divulge the names of the Nazi spy ring leaders in the United States. Among them: Erika Wolff, posing as a German hairdresser aboard a transatlantic liner; Dr. Kassel, head of the local bund in the New York area; Schlanger, the liaison officer in German Intelligence; and Hilda, Erika's American-based accomplice. Through Renard's unceasing efforts, virtually throughout the western world, and with the cooperation of various international police agencies, the spy network is closed down.

Confessions of a Nazi Spy was named Best Picture of the Year by the National Board of Review of Motion Pictures. It beat out *Wuthering Heights*, *Stagecoach* and *Ninotchka*. (*Gone With the Wind* ended up on the Board's 1940 list.) Both Francis Lederer and Paul Lukas were also cited by the Board.

CRITICAL VIEWS

"It is one of Robinson's finest roles, one which he plays with neither bluster not ranting heroics, but with a quiet and authoritative conviction."—*New York Journal-American*

"Edward G. Robinson is eloquently persuasive as the

CONFESSIONS OF A NAZI SPY: With Max Hoffman, Jr., Joe Sawyer and Frank Mayo

investigator of spy ring doings."—Howard Barnes, *New York Herald-Tribune*

"As melodrama, the film isn't bad at all. Anatole Litvak has paced it well, and key performances of Edward (G-man) Robinson as the Federal Man, Mr. Lederer as the weak link in the Nazi spy network, and Mr. Lukas as the propaganda agent are thoroughly satisfactory."— Frank S. Nugent, *The New York Times*

". . . it was less than an artistic triumph due to the fact that the participating actors, including myself, were too familiar to be taken seriously. Three beautiful actors, Paul Lukas, Francis Lederer and George Sanders, playing Nazis, were just about as believable as myself as a G-man. The picture suffered from the familiarity of the cast and the inevitability of the denouement; nobody, obviously, was going to outdo G-man Edward G. Robinson, and by no stretch of the imagination could the Nazis win."—Edward G. Robinson

CONFESSIONS OF A NAZI SPY: With Francis Lederer

BLACKMAIL

1939   Metro-Goldwyn-Mayer

Producer, John Considine, Jr.; Director, H.C. Potter; Screenplay, David Hertz and William Ludwig; Based on a story by Endre Bohem and Dorothy Yost; Photography, Clyde De Vinna; Editor, Howard O'Neill. 81 minutes

BLACKMAIL: With Gene Lockhart

John Ingram (*Edward G. Robinson*), Helen Ingram (*Ruth Hussey*), William Ramey (*Gene Lockhart*), Hank Ingram (*Bobs Watson*), Moose McCarthy (*Guinn Williams*), Diggs (*John Wray*), Rawlins (*Arthur Hohl*), Sarah (*Esther Dale*), Anderson (*Joe Whitehead*), Blaine (*Joseph Crehan*), Warden Miller (*Victor Kilian*), Kearney (*Gil Perkins*), 1st Workman (*Mitchell Lewis*), 2nd Workman (*Ted Oliver*), 3rd Workman (*Lew Harvey*), Sunny (*Willie Best*), Driver (*Art Miles*), Desk Sergeant (*Robert Middlemass*), Weber (*Ivan Miller*), Desk Clerk (*Hal K. Dawson*), Local Trooper (*Philip Morris*), 1st Deputy (*Charles Middleton*), 3rd Deputy (*Trevor Bardette*), Colored Prisoner (*Everett Brown*), Juan (*Ed Montoya*), Pedro (*Joe Dominguez*), Boss Brown (*Eddy Chandler*), Guard (*Lee Phelps*), Sheriff (*Cy Kendall*), Police Sergeant (*Wade Boteler*), Oil Worker (*Harry Fleischmann*)

Back at MGM again, between assignments on his home lot, Robinson somehow got involved in and dressed up what, without him, would have been a 'B' programmer. He played a hapless individual who is bounced in and out of prison, with some chain gang sequences that had been done to death over the years since Paul Muni had done the screen's definitive ones. Incarcerated for a crime he did not commit, a convict named John Harrington escapes from a Southern chain gang and assumes the identity of John Ingram, building a lucrative, if dangerous, business of putting out oil fires. Helen, his wife, knows of his past, but furthers his ambitions and bears him a son, Hank. A newsreel photograph reveals Ingram's identity to William Ramey, who had framed him. Down on his luck, Ramey offers to clear Ingram for $25,000. Ingram gives Ramey part of the money in cash and signs a note for the balance. The insidious Ramey, however, destroys the confession and turns Ingram over to the police. Ingram is sent back to prison and Ramey escapes with a mortgage on Ingram's oil property. Learning that Ramey holds the note, that Helen and young Hank have been forced out of their home, and that his business is being ruined, Ingram is driven to desperation. With the aid of his former foreman, Moose McCarthy, he once again breaks out of prison and goes after Ramey, who has skipped town after trying to negotiate the sale of a rich oil well that has come in on Ingram's former property

Desperate to lure Ramey back to exact revenge, Ingram conceives the idea of firing Ramey's well. Ramey turns up to find that Moose and his crew are unsuccessful at extinguishing the blaze. Ingram then manages to get Ramey onto the field near the well and extracts from him a confession that Moose and the men overhear. Reconciled at last with Helen and their son, whom he had located in a shanty town to which they had been forced to move, Ingram caps his well and saves the property that is now again his.

CRITICAL VIEWS

"The greater part of the film paints the villainy and inhuman treatment that exists in chain gangs. It is not a

BLACKMAIL: With Ruth Hussey

BLACKMAIL: With Guinn (Big Boy) Williams and Ruth Hussey

pretty picture: it becomes a fairly real one, though, as Mr. Robinson and his unfortunate comrades conduct it, but even with an exciting escape and the ultimate atonement of justice, *Blackmail* proves little more than the fact that Mr. Robinson is a sturdy villain."—Robert W. Dana, *New York Herald-Tribune*

"In his day, Edward G. Robinson has been one of the screen's greatest criminals. There was a time, in fact, during the height of the vogue, when he was said to be widely imitated in the underworld. What a sad thing it

111

BLACKMAIL: With Charles Middleton and Ruth Hussey

is, then, to see this distinguished inhabitant of the Rogues' Gallery, this Napoleon of crime, this indomitably amoral spirit who belongs with the Borgias, feebly trying to go straight in *Blackmail*."—Bosley Crowther, *The New York Times*

". . . two handsome and intense young writers, William Ludwig and David Hertz . . . worked like fiends and came up with a reasonable facsimile of a good script. They could do no better because I was on payroll and the shooting date could not be set ahead because the precise terms of my agreement with MGM spelled out exactly when I was to be returned to Warners. Accordingly, we did one of those pictures that pleased few, entertained many, and somehow got its money back and made a few shekels for the stockholders."—Edward G. Robinson

DR. EHRLICH'S MAGIC BULLET

1940   Warner Bros.-First National

Producers, Jack L. Warner and Hal B. Wallis; Associate producer, Wolfgang Reinhardt; Director, William Dieterle; Screenplay, John Huston, Heinz Herald and Norman Burnside; Story, Norman Burnside; Based on biographical material in the possession of Dr. Ehrlich's family; Photography, James Wong Howe; Art director, Carl Jules Weyl; Music, Max Steiner; Music director, Leo Forbstein; Special microscopic effects, Robert Burks; Sound, Robert E. Lee; Editor, Warren Low. 103 minutes

Dr. Paul Ehrlich (*Edward G. Robinson*), Heidi Ehrlich (*Ruth Gordon*), Dr. Emil Von Behring (*Otto Kruger*), Minister Althoff (*Donald Crisp*), Dr. Hans Wolfert (*Sig Rumann*), Franziska Spever (*Maria Ouspenskaya*), Dr. Lantz (*Henry O'Neill*), Dr. Morgenroth (*Edward Norris*), Judge (*Harry Davenport*), Professor Hartman (*Montagu Love*), Dr. Robert Koch (*Albert Basserman*), Dr. Kunze (*Louis Jean Heydt*), Mittelmeyer (*Donald Meek*), Speidler (*Douglas Wood*), Becker (*Irving Bacon*), Sensenbrenner (*Charles Halton*), Miss Marquardt (*Hermine Sterler*), Brockdorf (*Louis Calhern*), Hirsch (*John Hamilton*), Defense Attorney (*Paul Harvey*), Old Doctor (*Frank Reicher*), Kadereit (*Torben Meyer*), Dr. Kraus (*Theodore Von Eltz*), Dr. Bertheim (*Louis Arco*), Dr. Hata (*Wilfred Hari*), Dr. Bucher (*John Hendrick*), Marianne Ehrlich (*Ann E. Todd*), Steffi Ehrlich (*Rolla Stewart*), Hans Weigart (*Ernst Hausman*), Male Nurse (*Stuart Holmes*), Arab Man (*Frank Lackteen*), Arab Woman (*Elaine Renshaw*), Assistant (*Herbert Anderson*), Martl (*Egon Brecher*), Koerner (*Robert Strange*), Haupt (*Cliff Clark*), Kellner (*Wolfgang Zilzer [Paul Andor]*)

DR. EHRLICH'S MAGIC BULLET

As the famed German bacteriologist Paul Ehrlich (1845-1915), Edward G. Robinson had what was to be his personal favorite role. Doubtless it's the type of part Paul Muni would have been expected to play and add to his gallery of Warner biographical figures. But he and the studio had come to a parting of the ways over his increasing demands. Jack Warner quite naturally turned to his other "class act," the distinguished Mr. Robinson. In his characterization of the dedicated physician who pioneered modern immunology and chemotherapy, a bearded Robinson, working for the first time with William Dieterle (Warners' director of its great biographies, primarily with Muni) and with legendary cinematographer James Wong Howe, crafted one of the screen's memorable roles in one of the all-time great medical films.

The screenplay by John Huston and cohorts follows Paul Ehrlich, a doctor in the staid Berlin Hospital, in his seemingly endless round of dubious experiments that eventually lead him to the discovery of formula 606—the "magic bullet" that is a cure for syphillis. It caused a number of deaths because it was released prematurely, and Ehrlich had to stand trial but was vindicated. "In the end," as Robinson himself noted, "he died with the final plea for truth and justice in science."

Oddly, *Dr. Ehrlich's Magic Bullet* was snubbed by the Academy of Motion Picture Arts and Sciences, except for a nomination for Best Original Screenplay by Huston, Herald and Burnside. There was nothing for Robinson, or Ruth Gordon (in a then-rare screen role) as his wife, or Maria Ouspenskaya as the philanthropist Franziska Spever, who bankrolled Ehrlich after the German government cut off his funds, or Otto Kruger as his old colleague who had faith in Ehrlich's experiments from the beginning and stepped forward at his trial to reaffirm his support, or Donald Crisp as the health minister who regrettably had to separate the government from Ehrlich's experiments. And not even a nomination to Dieterle or James Wong Howe or Max Steiner for his score.

CRITICAL VIEWS

"We have to go . . . [to] *The Story of Louis Pasteur* to match it in its line, combing out new synonyms for 'great' to classify Edward G. Robinson's performance . . . There is a perfect delineation of the man by Mr. Robinson. It is a rounded gem of a portraiture, completely free from the devastating self-consciousness that plagues so many actors when they are forced to wear a beard, almost electric in its attractiveness, astonish-

DR. EHRLICH'S MAGIC BULLET: With Otto Kruger

DR. EHRLICH'S MAGIC BULLET: With Ruth Gordon and Otto Kruger

DR. EHRLICH'S MAGIC BULLET: With Maria Ouspenskaya

BROTHER ORCHID: With Humphrey Bogart and Paul Guilfoyle

ingly apart from the manneristic screen behavior of Little Caesar."—Frank S. Nugent, *The New York Times*

"The most dramatic and moving medical film I have ever seen . . . due in no small degree to the brilliant portrayal of Dr. Ehrlich by Edward G. Robinson. Aided by superb make-up, the erstwhile player of gangster roles gives a modulated and understanding performance which is in the first rank of biographical portraits."—Howard Barnes, *New York Herald-Tribune*

"Edward G. Robinson's portrayal of the famed Dr. Ehrlich is one of the most distinguished performances in the star's lengthy film career."—*Variety*

"Among all the plays and the films in which I've appeared, I'm proudest of my role in *Dr. Ehrlich's Magic Bullet* . . . It was, I think, one of the most distinguished performances I've ever given. I say that not only because the critics said it and my mail and the box office said it, but most of all because that inner voice, that inner self, that captious critic Emanuel Goldenberg said it."—Edward G. Robinson

BROTHER ORCHID

1940   Warner Bros.-First National

Executive Producer, Hal B. Wallis; Associate producer, Mark Hellinger; Director, Lloyd Bacon; Screenplay, Earl Baldwin; Based on the *Collier's* magazine story by Richard Connell; Photography, Tony Gaudio; Art director, Max Parker; Music, Heinz Roemheld; Orchestrations, Ray Heindorf; Gowns, Howard Shoup; Makeup, Perc Westmore; Montages, Don Siegel and Robert Burks; Sound, C.A. Riggs; Special effects, Byron Haskin, Willard Van Enger and Edwin B. DuPar; Editor, William Holmes. 91 minutes

Little John Sarto (*Edward G. Robinson*), Flo Addams (*Ann Sothern*), Jack Buck (*Humphrey Bogart*), Clarence Fletcher (*Ralph Bellamy*), Brother Superior (*Donald Crisp*), Willie (The Knife) Corson (*Allen Jenkins*), Brother Wren (*Charles D. Brown*), Brother Goodwin (*Cecil Kellaway*), Brother MacEwen (*Joseph Crehan*), Brother MacDonald (*Wilfred Lucas*), Philadelphia Powell (*Morgan Conway*), Mugsy O'Day (*Richard Lane*), Texas Pearson (*John Ridgely*), Buffalo Burns (*Dick Wessel*), Curley Matthews (*Tom Tyler*), French Frank (*Paul Phillips*), Al Muller (*Don Rowan*), Pattonsville Supt. (*Granville Bates*), Fifi (*Nanette Vallon*), Red Martin (*Paul Guilfoyle*), Turkey Malone (*Tim Ryan*), Handsome Harry Edwards (*Joe Caits*), Dopey Perkins (*Pat Gleason*), Joseph (*Tommy Baker*), Tim O'Hara (*G. Pat Collins*), Mr. Pigeon (*John Qualen*), Englishman (*Leonard Mudie*), Englishman

BROTHER ORCHID: With Ann Sothern

(*Charles Coleman*), Meadows (*Edgar Norton*), Frenchman (*Jean Del Val*), Frenchman (*Armand Kaliz*), Stable Boy (*Charles de Ravenne*), Artist (*Gino Corrado*), Warehouse Manager (*Paul Porcasi*), Casino Attendant (*George Sorel*), Cable Office Clerk (*Georges Renavent*), 1st Reporter (*De Wolfe (William) Hopper*), 2nd Reporter (*George Haywood*), 3rd Reporter (*Creighton Hale*), Mrs. Sweeney (*Mary Gordon*), Supt. of Service (*Frank Faylen*), Policeman (*Lee Phelps*), Janitor (*Sam McDaniel*), Parking Attendant (*James Flavin*)

Returning to screen gangsterdom once again—but in a lighthearted vein, a la *The Little Giant* and *A Slight Case of Murder*, Robinson faced off with Bogart for the last time for a while, in the role of hard-boiled rackets boss Little John Sarto. It was well known that Robinson long had tired of playing gangster roles and made that clear to Warners, and reportedly agreed to do this one only after the studio promised him the lead in its upcoming production of *The Sea Wolf*, based on Jack London's story.

Sarto has been to Europe in search of "class" but has run out of dough and has returned to find that his former associate Jack Buck has taken over the Sarto mob. Organizing a new gang, Sarto muscles into his old territory and begins challenging Buck. But his girlfriend, Flo Addams, who checks hats in a local nightclub, inadvertently sends him into a trap and he is taken for a one-way ride by Buck's henchman. Left for dead, Sarto makes his way to a nearby monastery where he is nursed back to health. He then cynically determines "the joint" would make an ideal hideout. Eventually he adjusts to his new surroundings where he finds a peaceful life, comes to admire the selfless work of the flower-selling Brothers and takes pleasure in growing orchids.

Sarto's idyll is temporarily disturbed when the Brothers inform him that they cannot sell their flowers in town at the market because of a gangland protection racket, headed by Jack Buck. Learning that Flo Addams is planning to marry hick rancher Clarence Fletcher, Sarto calls on Fletcher and his fellow ranchers to help break up the racketeer monopoly and destroy Buck's gang. But first Sarto and his nemesis beat each other to a pulp in a fist fight. In appreciation for Fletcher's aid, he gives Flo and Clarence his blessings, Then as Brother Orchid he returns to the monastery, happy in his new home, which has true class.

CRITICAL VIEWS

"A funnier piece of hard-boiled impudence hasn't been enjoyed hereabouts since Mr. Robinson's Remy Marco found his new home cluttered up with certain parties,

BROTHER ORCHID: With Jean Del Val and Armand Kaliz

BROTHER ORCHID: With Ann Sothern

115

not so tastefully composed, in *A Slight Case of Murder*
. . . Obviously, this is a story which was destined for no
one but Mr. Robinson, and he plays it with all the egotistical but vaguely cautious push that one would expect
from a gangster who found himself in such a spot."—
Bosley Crowther, *The New York Times*

"The gayest variation of the gangster film since *A Slight
Case of Murder*. Midway between straight melodrama
and outright burlesque, it shows one what happens
when a kingpin of the rackets lands in a monastery and
discovers that life can be lived without playing all the
angles. The story is funnier than the treatment given it,
I would say, but even so, the production keeps to a high
level of entertaining nonsense and is frequently hilarious. Edward G. Robinson . . . plays with vigor and
humor the gangster-turned-monk."—Howard Barnes,
New York Herald-Tribune

A DISPATCH FROM REUTERS: With players

A DISPATCH FROM REUTERS

1940   Warner Bros.-First National

Producer, Hal B. Wallis; Associate producer, Henry Blanke;
Director, William Dieterle; Screenplay, Milton Krims; Story,
Valentine Williams and Wolfgang Wilhelm; Photography,
James Wong Howe; Art director, Anton Grot; Music, Max
Steiner; Music director, Leo Forbstein; Sound, C. A. Riggs;
Special effects, Byron Haskin; Editor, Warren Low. 89
minutes

Julius Reuter (*Edward G. Robinson*), Ida Reuter (*Edna Best*),
Max Stargardt (*Eddie Albert*), Franz Geller (*Albert Basser-
man*), Herr Bauer (*Gene Lockhart*), Magnus (*Otto Kruger*),
Delane (*Montagu Love*), Sir Randolph Persham (*Nigel Bruce*),
Carew (*James Stephenson*), Napoleon III (*Walter Kingsford*),
Bruce (*David Bruce*), Grant (*Alec Craig*), Julius Reuter (Boy)
(*Dickie Moore*), Max Stargardt (Boy) (*Billy Dawson*), Herbert
(*Richard Nichols*), Chairman of the Anglo-Irish Tel. Co.
(*Lumsden Hare*), American Ambassador (*Hugh Sothern*),
Reingold (*Egon Brecher*), Stein (*Frank Jaquet*), Von Danstadt
(*Walter O. Stahl*), Josephat Benfey (*Paul Irving*), Chemist
(*Edward McWade*), Lord Palmerston (*Gilbert Emery*), Oppo-
sition Speaker (*Robert Warwick*), Speaker (*Ellis Irving*), Otto
(*Henry Roquemore*), Gauss (*Paul Weigel*), Assistant (*Joseph
Stefani*), Post Office Clerk (*Wolfgang Zilzer, [Paul Andor]*),
Man (*Frederic Mellinger*), Attendant (*Stuart Holmes*), Com-
panion (*Sunny Boyne*), Heinrich (*Ernst Hausman*), Young
Woman (*Grace Stafford*), Actor (*Theodore Von Eltz*), Mem-
bers of Parliament (*Kenneth Hunter, Holmes Herbert, Leonard
Mudie, Lawrence Grant*), Workman (*Pat O'Malley*), News
Vendors (*Cyril Delevanti, Norman Ainsley, Bobby Hale*), Bit
Girl (*Mary Anderson*)

A DISPATCH FROM REUTERS: With Edna Best

Much of the same behind the camera talent and several
of his acting colleagues joined Robinson in his second
biographical screen study—this time, pioneering German newsgatherer Julius Reuter (1816-1899), in a film
produced under the title *The Man From Fleet Street*.
Several critics pointed out the fact that the curly mus-

A DISPATCH FROM REUTERS: With Gene Lockhart

tache applied to his upper lip every morning made Robinson look less a press freedom trailblazer than a monkey-less organ grinder.

The film begins in 1833. Paul Julius, Baron Reuter, is trying to establish his "pigeon post" as an agency for fast transmission of news between European centers not yet linked by the new telegraph system. As that system expands, the use of carrier pigeons becomes virtually obsolete, and Reuter turns to the transmission of news by wire. Soon after leasing the wire linking the station he has set up in Paris with his London office, he comes up with his first scoop—the transmission of Louis Napoleon's speech. The coup established his future, based on his credo of speed, truth and accuracy on which he built the great English newsgathering agency in 1858.

An invaluable aid to Reuter in his work is his wife, Ida, who shows him early in his career that, above all else, his moral obligations to the public must be the guiding factor to a newsman. As his wire service grows, competition developed in the Anglo-Irish Telegraph Company. Reuter successfully meets the challenge with his own cable from Cork to Crookshaven by again scooping the world with news of Abraham Lincoln's

A DISPATCH FROM REUTERS: With Adolph Faylaner, Albert Basserman, Egon Brecher, Frank Jaquet, Gene Lockhart (seated) and Walter O. Stahl

117

assassination, flashing the information before the American ambassador has even learned of it.

CRITICAL VIEWS

"The Warners have given Edward G. Robinson a fat and rewarding role in Reuter, and his performance justifies their good judgement . . . Robinson, with the aid of William Dieterle's thoughtful direction, makes Reuter a compelling figure, one that the Fourth Estate should be happy to extol . . . [Reuters] isn't a great picture by any means, but it shows that screen biography has its own proper role to play in motion picture education."—Robert W. Dana, *New York Herald-Tribune*

"Edward G. Robinson gives a sincere though not always convincing performance in the leading role." —Thomas M. Pryor, *The New York Times*

"Robinson provides an excellent characterization of the resourceful Reuter who, time after time, stakes everything on his aim to 'make the world smaller by quicker transmission of the news.' "—*Variety*

"I was prepared to put on my private walk-out on Hal Wallis and Jack Warner when they came at me, like gangbusters, with two new scripts: *A Dispatch From Reuters* and *The Sea Wolf*. No actor could ask for more—no actor nearing fifty, that is . . . In any pecking order of my preferences, I name *Reuters* as my number-two favorite."—Edward G. Robinson

THE SEA WOLF

1941   Warner Bros.-First National

Producers, Jack L. Warner and Hal B. Wallis; Associate producer, Henry Blanke; Director, Michael Curtiz; Screenplay, Robert Rossen; Based on the novel by Jack London; Photography, Sol Polito; Art director, Anton Grot; Music, Erich Wolfgang Korngold; Special effects, Byron Haskin and H. F. Koenekamp; Editor, George Amy. 100 minutes

Wolf Larsen (*Edward G. Robinson*), George Leach (*John Garfield*), Ruth Webster (*Ida Lupino*), Humphrey Van Weyden (*Alexander Knox*), Dr. Louie Prescott (*Gene Lockhart*), Cooky (*Barry Fitzgerald*), Johnson (*Stanley Ridges*), Svenson (*Francis McDonald*), Young Sailor (*David Bruce*), Harrison (*Howard da Silva*), Smoke (*Frank Lackteen*), Agent (*Ralf Harolde*), Member of Crew (*Louis Mason*), Member of Crew (*Dutch Hendrian*), 1st Detective (*Cliff Clark*), 2nd Detective (*William Gould*), 1st Mate (*Charles Sullivan*), Pickpocket

(*Ernie Adams*), Singer (*Jeane Cowan*), Helmsman (*Wilfred Lucas*), Sailors (*Ethan Laidlaw, George Magrill*)

Scheduled as a vehicle for Paul Muni, this hand-me-down gave Robinson the opportunity to play one of literature's most sadistic sea captains. The Jack London story already had been filmed four times previously and would be done again in 1958 and 1977, as well as be converted into the 1950 Western called *Barricade*. It also would team Robinson with up-and-coming tough guy John Garfield for the only time.

Wolf Larsen is the tyrannical captain of a mysterious ship, *Ghost*, and passes the time tormenting his cabin boy, George Leach, who had signed aboard to escape the police. The malevolent Larsen's *Ghost* comes to the rescue of Humphrey Van Weyden, a writer, and Ruth Webster, a fugitive from justice, who have survived a ferry sinking in San Francisco Bay. To their later regret they are taken aboard.

One day, the crew mutinies and there is an unsuccessful attempt on Larsen's life. Humphrey, Leach and Ruth decide to get off the ship at any cost and put to sea in an open boat. After days of drifting, they sight the *Ghost* apparently sinking, and Leach climbs aboard looking for food and fresh water. When he fails to return, Ruth and Humphrey follow, only to find Larsen sitting in his cabin slowly going blind and Leach locked in the galley where he will soon be trapped by rising water. When Humphrey turns to leave, Larsen levels a gun at him and demands that he remain in the cabin. Promising to stay aboard and go down with the captain, Humphrey is given the key which he passes under the door to Ruth. She then frees Leach and they row away toward an island refuge as the *Ghost* goes down.

CRITICAL VIEWS

"We don't recall that [Larsen] has ever been presented with such scrupulous psychological respect as he is in [this] version of *The Sea Wolf* . . . This time the monstrous sadism is explored, and the mind of the Wolf is exposed as just a bundle of psychoses. With Edward G. Robinson playing him, the exposé is vivid indeed . . . Some of *The Sea Wolf* is too heavily drenched with theatrical villainy, and Mr. Robinson occasionally overacts the part. But on the whole, the slapping and cuffing are done with impressive virility and in a manner distinctive to Warner films."—Bosley Crowther, *The New York Times*

"On the whole, the cast is first rate. Robinson gives to a few moments of overacting as the tyrannical captain of the *Ghost*, but he is generally helpful to the melodra-

THE SEA WOLF: With John Garfield and Ida Lupino

THE SEA WOLF: With Howard Da Silva, Stanley Ridges, Ida Lupino and Gene Lockhart

THE SEA WOLF: With Alexander Knox

matic scheme of things."—A. S. G., *New York Herald-Tribune*

"*The Sea Wolf* is strong adventure drama that will sail a profitable course through theatre boxoffices, with the fair weather aided considerably by the marquee voltage of Edward G. Robinson, John Garfield and Ida Lupino . . . Robinson provides plenty of vigor and two-fisted energy to the actor-proof role of Wolf Larsen and at times is over-directed."—*Variety*

THE SEA WOLF: With John Garfield

MANPOWER: With Marlene Dietrich

MANPOWER: With Marlene Dietrich

"It was pure Jack London, and the character I played, Wolf Larsen, was a Nazi in everything but name . . . John Garfield was one of the best young actors I ever encountered, but his passions about the world were so intense that I feared any day he would have a heart attack."—Edward G. Robinson

MANPOWER

1941   Warner Bros.-First National

Executive producer, Hal B. Wallis; Producer, Mark Hellinger; Director, Raoul Walsh; Screenplay, Richard Macaulay and Jerry Wald; Photography, Ernest Haller; Art director, Max Parker; Music, Adolph Deutsch; Music director, Leo Forbstein; Songs, Frederick Hollander and Frank Loesser; Costumes, Milo Anderson; Makeup, Perc Westmore; Sound, Dolph Thomas; Special effects, Byron Haskin and H. F. Koenekamp; Editor, Ralph Dawson. 105 minutes

Hank McHenry (*Edward G. Robinson*), Fay Duval (*Marlene Dietrich*), Johnny Marshall (*George Raft*), Jumbo Wells (*Alan Hale*), Omaha (*Frank McHugh*), Dolly (*Eve Arden*), Smiley Quinn (*Barton MacLane*), Sidney Whipple (*Walter Catlett*), Scarlett (*Joyce Compton*), Flo (*Lucia Carroll*), Eddie Adams (*Ward Bond*), Pop Duval (*Egon Brecher*), Cully (*Cliff Clark*), Sweeney (*Joseph Crehan*), Al Hurst (*Ben Welden*), Noisy Nash (*Carl Harbaugh*), Marilyn (*Barbara Land*), Polly (*Barbara Pepper*), Wilma (*Dorothy Appleby*), Man (*Roland Drew*), 1st Man (*Eddie Fetherstone*), 2nd Man (*Charles Sherlock*), 3rd Man (*Jeffrey Sayre*), 4th Man (*De Wolfe (William) Hopper*), 5th Man (*Al Herman*), Man At Phone (*Ralph Dunn*), Foreman (*Harry Strang*), Waiter (*Nat Carr*), Bouncer (*John Kelly*), Nurse (*Joan Winfield*), Floor Nurse (*Isabel Withers*), Nurse (*Faye Emerson*), Orderly (*James Flavin*), Clerk (*Chester Clute*), Floorlady (*Nella Walker*), Justice Of The Peace (*Harry Holman*), Mrs. Boyle (*Dorothy Vaughan*), Linemen (*Murray Alper, Dick Wessel*), Chinese Singer (*Beal Wong*), Hat Check Girl (*Jane Randolph*), 1st Detective (*Eddy Chandler*), 2nd Detective (*Lee Phelps*), Bondsman (*Robert Strange*), 1st Drunk (*Dick Elliott*), 2nd Drunk (*Arthur Q. Bryan*), Piano Player (*Harry Seymour*), Bartender (*Joe Devlin*)

Like Robinson's *Tiger Shark* of a decade earlier, *Manpower* tells of a couple of he-men (this time they're power company linesmen rather than tuna fishermen) who are good buddies until a woman comes between them. A reworking of sorts of the studio's 1937 *Slim* with Henry Fonda, Pat O'Brien and Margaret Lindsay, this was Edward G. Robinson's only movie with

Marlene Dietrich (who gets to sing a couple of original songs, "I'm in No Mood for Music Tonight" and "He Lied and I Listened"), and the first of two with George Raft (the other not for 14 years).

While making repairs on storm-damaged lines, Hank McHenry saves his pal Johnny Marshall from being electrocuted on high voltage wires, but suffers an electric shock in one leg that cripples him for life. The two, who room together, are soon to become closely involved with nightclub hostess Fay Duval, after having to tell her of her father's death on a repair assignment. Johnny had previously met Fay, who had been in prison, when he and Pop Duval went to meet her on her release. While Johnny has no use for Fay, Hank idealistically becomes attached to her, thinking that fate has dealt her a raw deal.

As time passes, Hank and Johnny find themselves fighting over Fay, with Johnny thinking she's out to make a chump of his pal. Hank is determined, however and proposes marriage. Fay accepts, although she does not love him. Later, Johnny is injured on the job and Hank insists that he move in with Fay and him until he recuperates. Soon Johnny and Fay realize they're in love with one another, but don't want to hurt Hank. Fay decides to leave, but not long afterwards is caught in a police raid at the club. Johnny bails her out, but doesn't tell Hank. Eventually the truth comes out and Hank flies into a rage. In a savage fight with Johnny on the high poles, Hank falls to his death, and Johnny and Fay are now free to go off together.

CRITICAL VIEWS

"The Warner Brothers, like vulcan, know the pat way to forge a thunderbolt. They simply pick a profession in which the men are notoriously tough and the mortality rate is high, write a story about it in which both features are persistently stressed, choose a couple of aces from their pack of hard-boiled actors, and, with these assorted ingredients, whip together a cinematic depth charge . . . To say that Mr. Raft and Mr. Robinson make excellent 'squirrels' is like saying two and two make four . . . Take it from us, *Manpower* is a tough picture, awfully tough."—Bosley Crowther, *The New York Times*

"The trouble is that *Manpower* has a really bad script. The story itself wanders vaguely around in circles until it settles for that old gag about two pals being estranged by a siren. The wrong guy gets killed, of course, living only long enough to give his blessings to the real lovers . . . Robinson, Raft and Dietrich are no novices at handling conventional screen situations and infusing them with a bit of vitality, but they are stopped in their tracks

MANPOWER: With George Raft and Marlene Dietrich

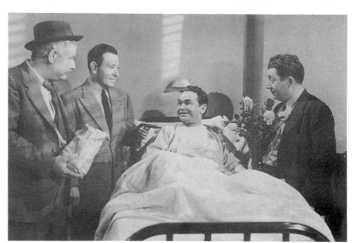

MANPOWER: With Alan Hale, George Raft and Frank McHugh

by the inanities of *Manpower*."—Howard Barnes, *New York Herald-Tribune*

"A lot of it was inane, yet Dietrich and I (I say this in no immodesty but rather as a fact) were a stunning combination, and our joint presence was tough box office. Add George Raft, and you had showmanship casting. Bad—but showmanship. Raft was touchy, difficult, and thoroughly impossible to play with."—Edward G. Robinson

UNHOLY PARTNERS

1941   Metro-Goldwyn-Mayer

Producer, Samuel Marx; Director, Mervyn LeRoy; Screenplay, Earl Baldwin, Bartlett Cormack and Lesser Samuels; Photography, George Barnes; Art director, Cedric Gibbons; Music, David Snell; Sound, Douglas Shearer; Editor, Harold F. Kress. 94 minutes

Bruce Corey (*Edward G. Robinson*), Miss Cronin (*Laraine Day*), Merrill Lambert (*Edward Arnold*), Gail Fenton (*Marsha Hunt*), Tommy Jarvis (*William T. Orr*), Mike Reynolds (*Don Beddoe*), Clyde Fenton (*Charles Dingle*), Inspector Pat Brody (*Robert Homans*), Managing Editor Peck (*Walter Kingsford*), Kaper (*Charles Halton*), Jason Grant (*Clyde Fillmore*), Molyneaux (*Marcel Dalio*), Roger Ordway (*Frank Faylen*), Jerry (*Joseph Downing*), Boy (*William Benedict*), Copy Boy (*Charles B. Smith*), Old Man (*Frank Dawson*), Reporter (*Tom Seidel*), Young Man (*Tom O'Rourke*), Old Timer (*George Ovey*), Colonel Mason (*Emory Parnell*), Rector (*Al Hill*), Stick Man (*Jay Novello*), Circulation Man (*John Dilson*), Barber (*Billy Mann*), Hazel (*Ann Morrison*), Tony (*Lester Sharpe*), Glamour Girl (*June MacCloy*), Pelotti (*Don Costello*), Girl at Party (*Lorraine Krueger*), Girl at Party (*Natalie Thompson*), Mary (*Florine McKinney*), Gorilla (*Charles Jordan*), Operator (*Ann Pennington*), Mechanic (*Lee Phelps*), Circulation Manager (*Lester Dorr*), Newspaper Women (*Gertrude Bennett, Estelle Etterre*), Man Reading Newspaper (*Milton Kibbee*), Gunman (Eddie) (*Elliott Sullivan*), Bartender (*Gino Corrado*), Shiner McGoohan (*Frank Orth*), Reporters (*Walter Sande, Frank Puglia*), Young Reporter (*Tom Neal*)

Another sojourn to MGM allowed Edward G. Robinson to work once again with Mervyn LeRoy (for the fourth and final time), here on a combination newspaper/gangster film set "between the wars." It was produced as *The New York Story*; it was released as *Unholy Partners*. Robinson is Bruce Corey, a reporter back from WWI who wants to publish his own tabloid. Edward Arnold is Merrill Lambert, a gangster who's willing to bankroll him. And so the plot begins. Corey and his star reporter Tommy Jarvis set up the paper in direct opposition to the many interests of Corey's "partner," Lambert, who also happens to be Jarvis' rival for the affections of singer Gail Fenton. Although she professes to hate Lambert, she is constantly seen with him, bewildering Jarvis, who, after some investigation, discovers that Gail's father is paying Lambert protection

UNHOLY PARTNERS: With Edward Arnold and William Orr

UNHOLY PARTNERS: With William Orr

UNHOLY PARTNERS: With Laraine Day

money. Before Corey's tabloid can expose Lambert's racket, Jarvis is kidnapped. Lambert will exchange him for complete control of Corey's paper.

Tensions lead to a bitter argument between the "partners" and Corey is forced to kill Lambert in self defense. He then dictates a confession to his devoted secretary, Miss Cronin, and takes off with a wild pilot on a suicidal transatlantic flight, sponsored by the paper. When news comes back that the plane is lost at sea, Miss Cronin destroys the confession, and the paper continues under her and Jarvis's leadership—after Jarvis returns from his honeymoon with Gail.

CRITICAL VIEWS

"Mervyn LeRoy and three able-bodied scriptwriters have sketched out a hardbitten melodrama of a tabloid editor during the Twenties when 'death and emotions were cheap.' They have brought in Edward G. Robinson to play the editor, and he knows how to make a caustic line flip like the tip of a bull-whip . . . Credit much of the film's intermittent excitement to Mr. Robinson, who still packs more drive than almost any six actors one could name."—Theodore Strauss, *The New York Times*

"Both Robinson and Arnold play the leads with the snarling bravado reminiscent of the gangster style of films. It fact, it all seems like a reissue."—*Variety*

UNHOLY PARTNERS: With Marcel Dalio

123

LARCENY, INC.: With Edward Brophy

LARCENY, INC.: With Broderick Crawford

LARCENY, INC.

1942   Warner Bros.-First National

Producer, Hal B. Wallis; Associate producers, Jack Saper and Jerry Wald; Director, Lloyd Bacon; Screenplay, Everett Freeman and Edwin Gilbert; Based on the play *The Night Before Christmas* by Laura and S. J. Perelman; Photography, Tony Gaudio; Art director, John Hughes; Music, Adolph Deutsch; Editor, Ralph Dawson. 95 minutes

Pressure Maxwell (*Edward G. Robinson*), Denny Costello (*Jane Wyman*), Jug Martin (*Broderick Crawford*), Jeff Randolph (*Jack Carson*), Leo Dexter (*Anthony Quinn*), Weepy Davis (*Edward Brophy*), Homer Bigelow (*Harry Davenport*), Sam Bachrach (*John Qualen*), Mademoiselle Gloria (*Barbara Jo Allen* [*Vera Vague*], Aspinwall (*Grant Mitchell*), Hobart (*Jack C. (Jackie) Gleason*), Oscar Engelhart (*Andrew Tombes*), Smitty (*Joseph Downing*), Mr. Jackson (*George Meeker*), Anton Copoulos (*Fortunio Bonanova*), Warden (*Joseph Crehan*), Florence (*Jean Ames*), McCarthy (*William Davidson*), Buchanan (*Chester Clute*), Mr. Carmichael (*Creighton Hale*), Officer O'Casey (*Emory Parnell*), Umpire (*Joe Devlin*), Convict (*Jimmy O'Gatty*), Another Convict (*Jack Kenney*), Batter (*John Kelly*), Guard (*Eddy Chandler*), Chuck (*Dutch Hendrian*), Muggsy (*William "Bill" Phillips*), Player (*Hank Mann*), Player (*Eddie Foster*), Player (*Cliff Saum*), Player (*Charles Sullivan*), Guard (*James Flavin*), Auto Driver (*Charles Drake*), Woman (*Vera Lewis*), Young man (*Ray Montgomery*), Customer (*Lucien Littlefield*), Secretary (*Grace Stafford*), Man (*Roland Drew*), Customer (*De Wolfe (William) Hopper*), Policeman (*Pat O'Malley*), Bronson (*Fred Kelsey*), Little Girl (*Janice Ohman*), Drunk (*Don Barclay*), Stout Man (*Arthur Q. Bryan*), Metropolitan Mission Leader (*Harry Hayden*), Guard (*Frank Mayo*), Customer (*Jack Mower*)

Wrapping up his million-dollar contract with Warner Bros. before becoming a free-lancer, Edward G. Robinson played a prison parolee in this comedy-melodrama based on a Broadway play of the year before by Laura and S. J. Perelman, looking to go legit on the outside with his ex-con pal Broderick Crawford.

Robinson is Pressure Maxwell and Crawford is Jug Martin. Both are about to be paroled from Sing Sing when they are approached by convicted bank robber Leo Dexter, who invites them to join him on a planned

LARCENY, INC.: With Broderick Crawford, Edward Brophy, Anthony Quinn and Joseph Downing

heist as soon as he gets out. Pressure and Jug decline because of a prior commitment—they're going straight. Pressure's idea of making a living is to get rich quick by opening a dog track. On the outside, though, he and Jug discover that their partner Weepy Davis has lost their slot machines on which their investment had been riding, and soon they are making plans to knock over the bank that Dexter had planned on robbing. Pressure purchases a small luggage shop next door to the bank and plans to drill a tunnel from the store's basement into the vault.

He has his adopted daughter, Denny Costello, run the shop. Denny soon falls for Jeff Randolph, a high voltage luggage salesman, who finds her a pushover for his wares. Pressure, meanwhile, finds that he's become a popular and respected member of the local community and, when the bank authorities offer him a large sum for the shop so they can enlarge their premises, he decides that honesty and the straight life might not be so bad—and he accepts. Just as the deal is going through, Dexter turns up, learns of Pressure and Jug's original scheme and tries to force them to help him with the planned underground heist. However, too much dynamite is used; the shop is blown up and the police arrive to escort Dexter back to Sing Sing. With nobody else aware that the robbery plan was theirs, Pressure, Jug and their cronies are left to start life all over again—as upstanding citizens.

With this movie the Edward G. Robinson epoch at Warners came to a close. He was supposed to have begun an all-star war movie with Humphrey Bogart, George Raft, Sydney Greenstreet, entitled *Heroes With-out Uniforms*. It ultimately was made as *Action in the North Atlantic* with only Bogart from the original stellar lineup. Robinson did return to Warners several times over the years to make a film, but he no longer had ties to any one studio.

CRITICAL VIEWS

"You can't say that Edward G. Robinson doesn't try hard to go straight. In his past three or four pictures, he played more or less 'legitimate' roles . . . [but] *Larceny, Inc.* finds him on the shady side of the street. And, considering the traffic is very hectic and amusing over there, it is a passing pleasure to see him back with the mob. As 'Pressure' Maxwell, [he] is a neat hand at blowing safes and such. But when dressed up as J. Chambers Maxwell, he is definitely in the gilt-edge, blue-chip class . . . Mr. Robinson, as usual, is a beautifully hard-boiled yegg. The principal joy is to watch him. His 'Pressure' cooks with gas."—Bosley Crowther, *The New York Times*

"[It] has all sorts of pretentious trimmings. It has the ebullient Edward G. Robinson as star, a handsome production and a notable supporting cast . . . [but] it has lost much of the Perelman nonsense humor that gave a certain zest to the play . . . Broderick Crawford plays a dumb safecracker with considerable comic effort. Jack Carson and Edward Brophy go all the way in mugging, and so does Mr. Robinson on more than one occasion."—Howard Barnes, *New York Herald-Tribune*

125

TALES OF MANHATTAN: With James Gleason and Mae Marsh

TALES OF MANHATTAN: With George Sanders

TALES OF MANHATTAN: With Don Douglas and James Rennie

TALES OF MANHATTAN

1942   20th Century-Fox

Producers, Boris Morros and S. P. Eagle; Director, Julien Duvivier; Screenplay and original stories by Ben Hecht, Ferenc Molnar, Donald Ogden Stewart, Samuel Hoffenstein, Alan Campbell, Ladislas Fodor, Laslo Vadnay, Laszlo Gorog, Lamar Trotti and Henry Blankfort; Photography, Joseph Walker; Art directors, Richard Day and Boris Leven; Set decorator, Thomas Little; Music, Sol Kaplan; Music director, Edward Paul; Songs by Saul Chaplin and Paul Francis Webster; Sound, W.D. Flick and Roger Heman; Editor, Robert Bischoff. 126 minutes (original running time); 118 minutes

Sequence A Orman (*Charles Boyer*), Ethel (*Rita Hayworth*), Halloway (*Thomas Mitchell*), Luther (*Eugene Pallette*), Actress (*Helene Reynolds*) **Sequence B** Diane (*Ginger Rogers*), George (*Henry Fonda*), Harry (*Cesar Romero*), Ellen (*Gail Patrick*), Edgar, The Butler (*Roland Young*) **Sequence C** Charles Smith (*Charles Laughton*), Mrs. Smith (*Elsa Lanchester*), Arturo Bellini (*Victor Francen*), Wilson (*Christian Rub*), Grandmother (*Adeline DeWalt Reynolds*), Piccolo Player (*Sig Arno*), Skeptic (*Will Wright*), Proprietor (*Dewey Robinson*), Latecomer (*Tom O'Grady*), Dignified Man (*Forbes Murray*) **Sequence D** Browne (*Edward G. Robinson*), William (*George Sanders*), Father Joe (*James Gleason*), Prof. Lyons (*Harry Davenport*), Hank Bronson (*James Rennie*), Davis (*Harry Hayden*), Judge (*Morris Ankrum*), Henderson (*Don Douglas*), Molly (*Mae Marsh*), Mary (*Barbara Lynn*), Spud (*Paul Renay*), Whistler (*Don Brodie*), Woman (*Esther Howard*) **Sequence E** Luke (*Paul Robeson*), Esther (*Ethel Waters*), Lazarus (*Rochester (Eddie Anderson)*), Costello (*J. Carrol Naish*), Hall Johnson Choir (*Themselves (40 voices)*), Grandpa (*Clarence Muse*), Christopher (*George Reed*), Nicodemus (*Cordell Hickman*), Monk (*John Kelly*)

The all-star, multi-episode *Tales of Manhattan*, using the services of ten writers, was Edward G. Robinson's first post-Warners movie. Initially producer Boris Morros tried to interest his partner on the film, S. P. Eagle (later to be known as Sam Spiegel), to use six different directors, a la Paramount's *If I Had a Million* a decade earlier. When Charles Boyer, however, became interested in the project, he urged them to use just one, Julien Duvivier, his friend from French films living in the U.S. for the duration. Boyer, Robinson and Duvivier subsequently were reunited on another multi-episode film, *Flesh and Fantasy*. A dress tailcoat was the prop which tied together the various episodes of *Tales of*

Manhattan. Initially there were six, one with W. C. Fields, but his was dropped after several previews indicated that it broke the general tone of the movie. (It has rarely been seen since, and remains effectively a lost Fields short.)

The sequence with Robinson, the fourth of the remaining five and thought by critics to be the best, has him playing an attorney who'd fallen on hard times, and when an invitation to his twenty-fifth college reunion turns up, he acquires the now pretty much threadbare tailcoat from a pawn shop so he can go "in style." At the function, he is wrongly accused by a pompous former classmate (played by George Sanders) of picking another man's pocket. Ashamedly, he confesses his state of poverty and leaves the banquet hall, but three other classmates intercept him and offer him a new career opportunity.

Despite its stellar cast, a Radio City Music Hall engagement, and generally favorable reviews, *Tales of Manhattan* was not the success the studio had hoped, and it failed to encourage other producers to mount similar projects.

CRITICAL VIEWS

"*Tales of Manhattan* is one of those rare films . . . Neither profound nor very searching, it nevertheless manages to convey a gentle, detached comprehension of the irony and pity of life . . . Edward G. Robinson gives a masterful performance as the bum who has seen better days . . . altogether, Julien Duvivier has directed the film with surprising evenness and has matched the moods and tempos of the various episodes with delicacy."—Bosley Crowther, *The New York Times*

"An impressive line-up of stars is to be found in *Tales of Manhattan.* High-ranking scenarists have spun the plot. The distinguished French director Julien Duvivier has staged the show. If it is big names you want, [it] is a prodigal offering. Obviously they lend an aura of glamor and fascination to the proceedings. What they fail to do is make *Tales of Manhattan* more than a disjointed and pretentious picture."—Howard Barnes, *New York Herald-Tribune*

DESTROYER

1943   Columbia Pictures

Producer, Louis F. Edelman; Director, William A. Seiter; Screenplay, Frank Wead, Lewis Meltzer and Borden Chase; Based on a story by Frank Wead; Photography, Franz F. Planer; Art director, Lionel Banks; Music, Anthony Collins, Editor, Gene Havlick. 99 minutes

DESTROYER: With Marguerite Chapman and Regis Toomey

Steve (Boley) Boleslavski (*Edward G. Robinson*), Mickey Donohue (*Glenn Ford*), Mary Boleslavski (*Marguerite Chapman*), Kansas Jackson (*Edgar Buchanan*), Sarecky (*Leo Gorcey*), Lt. Comm. Clark (*Regis Toomey*), Casey (*Ed Brophy*), Lt. Morton (*Warren Ashe*), Bigbee (*Craig Woods*), Yasha (*Curt Bois*), Admiral (*Pierre Watkin*), Knife Eating Sailor (*Al Hill*), Sobbing Sailor (*Bobby Jordan*), Chief Engineer (*Roger Clark*), Fireman Moore (*Dean Benton*), Fireman Thomas (*David Alison*), Doctor (*Paul Parry*), Chief Quartermaster (*John Merton*), Helmsman (*Don Peters*), Spinster (*Virginia Sale*), Sarecky's Girl (*Eleanor Counts*), Sailor (*Dale Van Sickel*), Gerguson (*Addison Richards*), 1st Ship Fitter (*Lester Dorr*), 2nd Ship Fitter (*Bud Geary*), Survivor (*Eddie Dew*), Doctor No. 1 (*Tristram Coffin*), Ensign Johnson (*Larry Parks*), Chief Gunner's Mate (*Eddy Chandler*), 2nd Fireman (*Lloyd Bridges*), Communications Officer (*Dennis Moore*), 1st Workman (*Edmund Cobb*), Riveter (*Eddy Waller*), Asst. Chief Engineer (*Charles McGraw*), Postman (*Pat O'Malley*), Bigbee's Girl (*Shirley Patterson*), Bucker (*Billy Bletcher*), Captain Thompson (*Kenneth MacDonald*)

One of Robinson's two wartime movies that had him in uniform (at age 49), *Destroyer* was a propaganda film that flag-waved for our side and cast him rather improbably as a petty officer—though not as improbably as a private in his subsequent *Mr. Winkle Goes to War*! A tenuous combination of comedy and melodrama, it has him playing Steve Boleslavski, known as "Boley," a ship's welder who regales his co-workers, often to the point of making a nuisance of himself. He tells them of his previous Navy experience, as mentor to the commander of the ship on which he was serving. With the launching of the new destroyer on which he has been working, Boley goes back into the Navy and gets himself stationed on it as Chief Bo'sun's Mate, deplacing a resentful Mickey Donohue who tries to get along with Boley. The latter, as usual, seeks absolute perfection and nags the crew mercilessly. Lt. Commander Clark, Boley's old friend, is urged by his superiors to replace him but refuses.

A violent sea battle between the destroyer and the Japanese brings Boley into his own and a hero among his mates. Feeling his mission complete, he then steps aside in favor of Mickey, who also wins the hand of Boley's daughter whom he had met on shore leave. Boley meanwhile watches with paternal pride as "his" destroyer steams out to rejoin the Pacific fleet.

CRITICAL VIEWS

"The film catches the spirit of naval camaraderie in one scene in which Mr. Robinson relates the story of the

DESTROYER: With Glenn Ford

DESTROYER: With Leo Gorcey, Glenn Ford and Edgar Buchanan

Bon-homme Richard's last fight, but on the whole, the film contains none of the incisive character lines and sharp technique that made such a stirring film out of *In Which We Serve*."—Otis Guernsey, Jr., *New York Herald-Tribune*

"Another ripe old-timer in the Hollywood actor ranks has been mustered into service for the movies' own particular brand of war. This time it is Edward G. Robinson, complete with haunch, paunch and scowl, who has been given a petty officer's rating in Columbia's *Destroyer* and may now be seen heaving Navy spirit onto the screen . . . The grey-beard fits into this story as sensibly as he fits into his World War I uniform. As the indestructible hero, Mr. Robinson utilizes the same tough snarl, the same withering looks and mute sarcasm that made him the scourage of muggs in days gone by. He also possesses a humility and a rare streak of tenderness which may not be wholly consistent but which set well in such a role as this . . . The best way to take *Destroyer* is with a sizable sprinkling of salt. It is a leaky and top-heavy vessel on which Mr. Robinson serves."—Bosley Crowther, *The New York Times*

"Edward G. Robinson plays Boley with a skillful mixture of comedy and sentiment. This is the kind of role that might have had Wallace Beery afloat with tears. Mr. Robinson keeps Boley within the bounds of reason, a likeable and believable fellow."—Eileen Creelman, *New York Sun*

DESTROYER: With Glenn Ford

FLESH AND FANTASY

1943   *Universal Pictures*

Producers, Charles Boyer and Julien Duvivier; Director, Julien Duvivier; Screenplay, Ernest Pascal, Samuel Hoffenstein and Ellis St. Joseph; Based on Oscar Wilde's *Lord Arthur Saville's Crime* and stories by Laslo Vadnay and Ellis St. Joseph; Photography, Paul Ivano and Stanley Cortez; Art directors, John B. Goodman, Richard Riedel and Robert Boyce; Set decorators, R. A. Gausman and E. R. Robinson; Costumes, Edith Head and Vera West; Music, Alexander Tansman; Music director, Charles Previn; Editor, Arthur Hilton. 93 minutes

Marshall Tyler (*Edward G. Robinson*), Paul Gaspar (*Charles Boyer*), Joan Stanley (*Barbara Stanwyck*), Henrietta (*Betty Field*), Michael (*Robert Cummings*), Septimus Podgers (*Thomas Mitchell*), King Lamarr (*Charles Winninger*), Rowena (*Anna Lee*), Lady Pamela Hardwick (*Dame May Whitty*), Dean of Chichester (*C. Aubrey Smith*), Doakes (*Robert Benchley*), Stranger (*Edgar Barrier*), Davis (*David Hoffman*), Lady Thomas (*Mary Forbes*), Librarian (*Ian Wolfe*), Mrs. Caxton (*Doris Lloyd*), Angel (*June Lang*), Equestrienne (*Grace McDonald*), Acrobat (*Joseph Crehan*), Detectives (*Arthur Loft, Lee Phelps*), Radio Announcer (*James Craven*), Justine (*Marjorie Lord*), Policeman (*Eddie Acuff*), Pierrot (*Peter Lawford*), Satan (*Lane Chandler*), Death (*Gil Patrick*), Harlequins (*Paul Bryar, George Lewis*), Old Negro (*Clinton Rosemond*), Old Man Prospector (*Charles Halton*), Angel (*Jacqueline Dalya*)

Somewhat in the style of *Tales of Manhattan* of the year before in which Edward G. Robinson also was involved with Charles Boyer and director Julien Duvivier, *Flesh and Fantasy* brought together a stellar cast in several disparate episodes tied together by a gimmick—here, the meaning of dreams, predictions and the supernatu-

FLESH AND FANTASY

ral as discussed by two members of a private club (played by Robert Benchley and David Hoffman). And like *Tales of Manhattan*, there was yet another episode filmed and later dropped. In this case, economy-minded Universal got its money's worth by releasing the deleted segment as *Destiny*, a "B" movie (with extra footage to expand it to an acceptable 65 minutes).

Robinson stars in the second of the three episodes (the one based on Oscar Wilde) as Marshall Tyler, an eminent American attorney who meets a theatrical palmist, Septimus Podgers, performing at a social gathering in London. He scoffs at Podgers's predictions but nonetheless submits to a reading and becomes intrigued when he is told that he will commit murder. The prediction preys on his mind and he finally embarks on a plan to commit the predestined crime. After making unsuccessful attempts on two victims, Tyler tries to remove the hex by strangling Podgers. In attempting to elude the police, he then runs through a circus and dies as the result of an accident.

CRITICAL VIEWS

"Seldom has murder been contemplated on the screen with more diabolical delight (for the audience) than

FLESH AND FANTASY: With Thomas Mitchell

130

FLESH AND FANTASY: With Dame May Whitty and Anna Lee

FLESH AND FANTASY

when Mr. Robinson of the flesh argues with Mr. Robinson on the fantasy, or the failure, about who the victim should be or how the crime would be committed . . . Julien Duvivier, the director, has underscored the sequence with mounting suspense, but unfortunately brings it to a disappointing climax by permitting Mr. Robinson to fulfill his destiny in a very routine manner. Yet this is still the best part of the picture."—Thomas M. Pryor, *The New York Times*

"*Flesh and Fantasy* is an example of one-act play techniques adapted for motion picture . . . The second [act] is a melodrama with Edward G. Robinson playing a rich lawyer who has been told by a fortune teller, Thomas Mitchell, that he will commit a murder. Things pick up in this sequence as the fantasy becomes mixed with excitement and good performances by the two above-mentioned actors. But here again, the one-act form is marred by repetition of the same effect and long conversational pauses."—Otis Guernsey, Jr., *New York Herald-Tribune*

TAMPICO: With Mona Maris, Victor McLaglen and Lynn Bari

TAMPICO: With Lynn Bari

TAMPICO

1944   20th Century-Fox

Producer, Robert Bassler; Director, Lothar Mendes; Screenplay, Kenneth Gamet, Fred Niblo, Jr., and Richard Macaulay; Story, Ladislas Fodor; Photography, Charles Clarke; Art directors, James Basevi and Albert Hogsett; Set decorator, Thomas Little; Music, David Raksin; Music director, Emil Newman; Choreography, Geneva Sawyer; Special effects, Fred Sersen; Sound, W. D. Flick; Editor, Robert Fritch. 75 minutes

Capt. Bart Manson (*Edward G. Robinson*), Kathie Ball (*Lynn Bari*), Fred Adamson (*Victor McLaglen*), Watson (*Robert Bailey*), Valdez (*Marc Lawrence*), Silhouette Man (*E. J. Ballantine*), Dolores (*Mona Maris*), Kruger (*Tonio Selwart*), Mueller (*Carl Ekberg*), Crawford (*Roy Roberts*), Stranger (*George Sorel*), Gun Crew Naval Officer (*Charles Lang*), Quartermaster O'Brien (*Ralph Byrd*), Immigration Inspector (*Daniel Ocko*), Naval Commander (*Nestor Paiva*), Messenger Boy (*David Cota*), Rodriguez (*Muni Seroff*), Photographer (*Juan Varro*), Justice of Peace (*Antonio Moreno*), Dr. Brown (*Ben Erway*), Mrs. Kelly (*Helen Brown*), Serra (*Martin Garralaga*), Steward (*Martin Black*), Waiter (*Chris-Pin Martin*), Proprietor (*Margaret Martin*), Waiter (*Trevor Bardette*), Seaman (*Virgil Johansen*), Navigator (*Arno Frey*), Pilot (*Jean Del Val*), Bit (*Karen Palmer*)

In this routine tale of wartime espionage—essentially a variation on the two-middle-age-buddies-whose-heads-are-turned-by-a-seductive-young-thing theme (like *Tiger Shark, Manpower*, et al.)—Edward G. Robinson is a tanker captain and Victor McLaglen his first mate, battling not only the elements and the Nazis but also each other over Lynn Bari, playing a mysterious vixen whom they have rescued from a ship torpedoed by a U-boat.

Kathie Ball (Bari) is not recognized by any of the sinking ship's other survivors, and she has no identification papers. Manson (Robinson) gets her released to his custody after port authorities in Tampico decide to hold her for investigation, and eventually, despite the objections of Adamson (McLaglen), he marries her. Ordered back to sea, Manson refuses to tell Kathie the date, but she finds out and goes aboard his ship to say goodbye. At sea, Manson's ship is halted by a German submarine. Adamson urges him to surrender the ship to the Nazis but Manson decides to fight, and it is sunk with Adamson aboard. En route back to port, Manson broods: only Kathie knew his ship's course. Can she be mixed up in a Nazi spy ring? Manson cannot bring himself to turn her in.

Appearing embittered, Manson begins making the rounds of Tampico's bars. Actually he is setting a trap. He casually leaves his papers on a bar and follows a mysterious man who picks them up, leading Manson straight to the ring preying on tankers. In a climactic battle, Manson captures the plotters—including his pal Adamson, who was working for the Nazis. Then he sets out to find Kathie and go on with his life.

CRITICAL VIEWS

"Mr. Robinson's role as a love-chastened ship's captain is carried off in his usual businesslike manner, although his admirers will likely feel that the chastening isn't particularly advantageous to his traditional characterization."—Paul P. Kennedy, *The New York Times*

"If the film has any virtue at all, it is that of underplaying, but while this has proved to be the outstanding feature of many of our most exciting pictures, this quality in itself is not sufficient . . . Wearing the four stripes of the merchant marine, Edward G. Robinson comes off with most of the acting honors."—Bert McCord, *New York Herald-Tribune*

". . . at the very best, trivial. Yet deep in my heart, I was grateful that anybody could find a role for a fifty-one-year-old man."—Edward G. Robinson

TAMPICO: With Lynn Bari

TAMPICO: With Mona Maris and Victor McLaglen

MR. WINKLE GOES TO WAR

1944   Columbia Pictures

Producer, Jack Moss; Associate producer, Norman Deming; Director, Alfred E. Green; Screenplay, Waldo Salt, George Corey and Louis Solomon; Based on the novel by Theodore Pratt; Photography, Joseph Walker; Art directors, Lionel Banks and Rudolph Sternad; Music, Carmen Dragon; Music director, Paul Sawtell; Sound, Lambert Day; Assistant director, Earl Bellamy; Editor, Richard Fantl. 80 minutes

Wilbert Winkle (*Edward G. Robinson*), Amy Winkle (*Ruth Warrick*), Barry (*Ted Donaldson*), Jack Pettigrew (*Bob Haymes*), Sergeant "Alphabet" (*Richard Lane*), Joe Tinker (*Robert Armstrong*), Ralph Wescott (*Richard Gaines*), Plummer (*Walter Baldwin*), McDavid (*Art Smith*), Martha Pettigrew (*Ann Shoemaker*), A. B. Simkins (*Paul Stanton*), Johnson (*Buddy Yarus, [George Tyne]*), Company Commander (*William Forrest*), Gladys (*Bernardene Hayes*), Hostess #1 (*Jeff Donnell*), Mayor Williams (*Howard Freeman*), M.P. (*Larry Thompson*), Captain (*Warren Ashe*), Sergeant #1 (*James Flavin*), Corporal (*Bob Mitchum*), Doctor (*Herbert Heyes*), Sergeant #2 (*Fred Kohler Jr.*), Draftee #1 (*Fred Lord*), Draftee #2 (*Cecil Ballerino*), Draftee #3 (*Ted Holley*), Doctor (*Ben Taggart*), Doctor (*Sam Flint*), Dentist (*Nelson Leigh*), Doctor (*Forbes Murray*), Doctor (*Ernest Hilliard*), Draftee (*Les Sketchley*), Draftee (*Ed Jenkins*), Draftee (*Paul Stupin*), M.P. (*Terry Frost*), Range Officer (*Hugh Beaumont*), Sergeant (*Dennis Moore*), Barber (Reporter) (*Emmett Vogan*), 4th Kid (*Tommy Cook*), Girl Bit (*Nancy Evans*), Girl Bit (*Ann Loos*), Girl Bit (*Early Cantrell*)

As an over-age inductee who overcomes his meekness to become a war hero, Robinson had yet another role not worthy of his talents. Three writers toiled over Theodore Pratt's lighthearted novel to hammer out a limp script which Robinson, doing yeoman work, made not much more than mildly amusing. Wilbert George Winkle, you see, had been a bank clerk for fourteen years and was pretty sick of the routine, quitting, finally, to devote full time to the fix-it business he has been running in a little shop he built next to his home, much to his wife Amy's consternation. Suddenly a draft notice turns up in his mail. Winkle at 44 does not believe he will pass the physical but he goes to the induction center with Jack Pettigrew, his neighbor's son. Both are inducted and are sent to the Ordnance Corps. Basic training almost kills Winkle, but he perseveres and then

MR. WINKLE GOES TO WAR

refuses to leave the Army when the draft age is lowered to 38.

He eventually finds himself in the South Pacific and, with Pettigrew and other members of the squad, pinned down during a mission against the Japanese. Winkle, who had been tinkering with a bulldozer when the attack came, heads it for the foxhole in which the enemy is hiding and plows them under, saving his men while being wounded himself. Army red-tape is ultimately cut through, and because of his age, he is honorably discharged and sent home—to return to his quiet, unassuming life in his fix-it shop where Amy welcomes him home and forgives his past eccentricities.

CRITICAL VIEWS

"Columbia has made the grave error of casting Edward G. Robinson in the Mr. Winkle part. He never succeeds in being either meekly amusing or properly courageous. Since the script has him involved with a small boy who is never completely identified, and a mean wife whose ultimate understanding of his true worth is quite incredible, it is not altogether Robinson's fault. The truth remains that he merely walks through his role in *Mr. Winkle Goes to War*, leaving a trail of tiny, tiresome situations behind him . . . [He] swaggers through most

MR. WINKLE GOES TO WAR: With Richard Gaines and Ruth Warrick

135

of the sequences, not quite sure whether he is Little Caesar or a timid bookkeeper."—Howard Barnes, *New York Herald-Tribune*

"If you can take Edward G. Robinson as a very mouse of a man, henpecked beyond endurance and virtually subsisting on a diet of pills, then you may find modest entertainment in [this picture] . . . True, the erstwhile Little Caesar does everything within his power to give a comic situation of a Casper Milquetoast turned G.I. And some of his flashes of bewilderment are briefly amusing, too. But somehow, his granite chiseled visage and his plainly hardboiled voice betray a contradiction which insistently muddles his act. It is hard to believe that Mr. Robinson would take what he does lying down."—Bosley Crowther, *The New York Times*

DOUBLE INDEMNITY

1944   Paramount Pictures

Producer, Joseph Sistrom; Director, Billy Wilder; Screenplay, Billy Wilder and Raymond Chandler; Based on a short story by James M. Cain in his book *Three of a Kind*; Photography, John Seitz; Art directors, Hans Dreier and Hal Pereira; Set decorator, Bertram Granger; Costumes, Edith Head; Music, Miklos Rozsa; Sound, Stanley Cooley and Walter Oberst; Editor, Doane Harrison. 107 minutes

Walter Neff (*Fred MacMurray*), Phyllis Dietrichson (*Barbara Stanwyck*), Barton Keyes (*Edward G. Robinson*), Jackson (*Porter Hall*), Lola Dietrichson (*Jean Heather*), Mr. Dietrichson (*Tom Powers*), Nino Zachette (*Byron Barr*), Mr. Norton (*Richard Gaines*), Sam Gorlopis (*Fortunio Bonanova*), Joe Pete (*John Philliber*), Norton's Secretary (*Bess Flowers*), Conductor (*Kernan Cripps*), Redcap (*Harold Garrison*), Pullman Porter (*Oscar Smith*), Nettie (Maid) (*Betty Farrington*), Woman (*Constance Purdy*), Pullman Conductor (*Dick Rush*), Pullman Porter (*Frank Billy Mitchell*), Train Conductor (*Edmund Cobb*), Pullman Porter (*Floyd Shackelford*), Pullman Porter (*James Adamson*), Garage Attendant (*Sam R. McDaniel*), Colored Man (*Clarence Muse*), Pacific All-Risk Telegraph Operator (*Judith Gibson*), Keyes' Secretary (*Miriam Franklin*), Bit (*George Magrill*)

After a number of less-than-worthy parts, Edward G. Robinson was back in full stride in this memorable drama which Billy Wilder and Raymond Chandler adapted from the James M. Cain story that Cain had crafted from the real-life 1927 slaying of New Yorker

Albert Snyder by his wife Ruth and her lover Judd Gray for Snyder's insurance. Taking less than top billing for the first time in many years (other than the alphabetical billing in *Tales of Manhattan*), Robinson in top form skillfully portrayed insurance claims manager Barton Keyes whose suspicions about a particularly puzzling death lead him to the complicity of the company's ace salesman he had come to think of as a son, Walter Neff (Fred MacMurray took this role after George Raft turned it down and after Billy Wilder convinced him he could do more than just light comedy).

As the sizzler opens, Neff, seriously wounded with a bullet in his shoulder, is reciting into a dictaphone a memo to Keyes, recounting the events leading up to his shooting. Some months earlier, Neff had met Phyllis Dietrichson when he stopped by her house to check her oilman husband's automobile policy. Although she expressed more than casual interest in accident insurance, Neff passed off the matter, but later became suspicious, especially when she pursued it with particular stress on the double indemnity clause. Gullible Neff and nefarious Phyllis not long afterwards become lovers, and she begins talking seriously about getting rid of her husband. They hatch the perfect crime and pull it off by faking the husband's fatal fall from the back of a train after he, in fact, had been killed by Neff sometime earlier and his body placed on the tracks. Sharp-nosed Keyes then enters the picture and immediately looks askance at Dietrichson's death.

Returning to the Dietrichson house with Phyllis, Neff discovers that she not only had been two-timing her husband but was doublecrossing Neff as well. She doesn't want him, just the $100,000 from her husband's double indemnity policy. A violent argument ensues and they grapple over a gun. It goes off, wounding him and killing her. While Neff is recounting the story, Keyes happens in on him and overhears the confession. He decides he must turn Neff over to the police for murder.

The film ends at this point. A concluding sequence in which Fred MacMurray is placed in the gas chamber while Edward G. Robinson sadly looks on with other prison officials was cut before the film's release. *Double Indemnity* remains far superior to author James M. Cain's somewhat similar *The Postman Always Rings Twice*, to say nothing of the much later copycat movie *Body Heat*, thanks primarily to director Wilder and Chandler's incisive script and the high-powered cast. It was Oscar-nominated as Best Picture of the Year (losing to *Going My Way*). Barbara Stanwyck also was nominated (Bergman won the award for *Gaslight*), as were Billy Wilder as Best Director, Wilder and Chandler for their screenplay adaptation, cinematographer John Seitz, and Miklos Rozsa for his score.

DOUBLE INDEMNITY: With Fred MacMurray

DOUBLE INDEMNITY: With Fred MacMurray

DOUBLE INDEMNITY: With Barbara Stanwyck and Fred MacMurray

137

DOUBLE INDEMNITY: With Fred MacMurray (in scene cut from film)

In 1973, an almost scene-for-scene remake was done for television with Richard Crenna, Samantha Eggar and Lee J. Cobb in the MacMurray-Stanwyck-Robinson parts. (There also was an abbreviated version on TV's Lux Video Theatre in 1954 starring Laraine Day and Frank Lovejoy—without a part comparable to Robinson's!)

CRITICAL VIEWS

"With perfectly coordinated acting by Fred MacMurray, Barbara Stanwyck and Edward G. Robinson and the lesser players, it hits clean and hard right between the eyes . . . Robinson plays an insurance company sleuth with splendid authority."—Howard Barnes, *New York Herald-Tribune*

"The performance of Mr. Robinson [as] a smart adjustor of insurance claims is a fine bit of characterization within its allotment of space. With a bitter brand of humor and irritability, he creates a formidable guy. As a matter of fact, [he] is the only one you care two hoots for in the film. The rest are just neatly carved pieces in a variably intriguing crime game."—Bosley Crowther, *The New York Times*

"It was, in fact, the third lead. I debated accepting it. Emanuel Goldenberg told me that at my age it was time to begin thinking of character roles, to slide into middle and old age with the same grace as that marvelous actor, Lewis Stone . . . The decision made itself . . . It remains one of my favorites."—Edward G. Robinson

THE WOMAN IN THE WINDOW

1944   RKO Radio Pictures

Producer, Nunnally Johnson; Director, Fritz Lang; Screenplay, Nunnally Johnson; Based on the novel *Once Off Guard* by J. H. Wallis; Photography, Milton Krasner; Art director, Duncan Cramer; Set decorator, Julia Heron; Special effects, Vernon Walker; Music, Arthur Lange; Music director, Hugo Friedhofer; Sound, Frank McWhorter; Editors, Gene Fowler, Jr. and Marjorie Johnson. 99 minutes

Prof. Richard Wanley (*Edward G. Robinson*), Frank Lalor
(*Raymond Massey*), Alice Reed (*Joan Bennett*), Dr. Barkstane
(*Edmond Breon*), Heidt (*Dan Duryea*), Mrs. Wanley (*Dorothy
Peterson*), Boy Scout (*Spanky McFarland*), Capt. Kennedy
(*Arthur Space*), Streetwalker (*Iris Adrian*), Claude Mazard
(*Arthur Loft*), Steward (Collins) (*Frank Dawson*), Elsie Wan-
ley (*Carol Cameron*), Inspector Jackson (*Thomas E. Jackson*),
Dickie Wanley (*Bobby Blake*), Garageman (*Alec Craig*), Traf-
fic Cop (*Ralph Dunn*), Toll Collector (*Joe Devlin*), Motorcycle
Cop (*Fred Graham*), Announcer (*Tom Hanlon*), Druggist
(*Harry Hayden*), Police Driver (*Eddy Chandler*), Magazine
Glamour Model (*Ruth Valmy*), Bar Extra (*Bess Flowers*)

An outstanding psychological thriller with a trick ending, *The Woman in the Window* has Edward G. Robinson
again enacting the milquetoast beset by circumstances
that bring him to a crisis. It is generally agreed to be one
of his finest mid-career performances. He is Richard
Wanley, a psychology professor who, with his family
out of town, innocently becomes embroiled with a
femme fatale (Joan Bennett played the part originally
intended for Merle Oberon) whose portrait he had
admired in the window of an art gallery. He is unaware
that she is the mistress of Claude Mazard, a famous financier, who arrives unexpectedly at her place when
Wanley happens to be there for a spot of tea and a bit of
conversation. In a burst of rage, Mazard, misunder-
standing the situation, makes a murderous assault on
Wanley. In self defense, the professor stabs Mazard

THE WOMAN IN THE WINDOW: With Joan Bennett (and Arthur
Loft in blanket)

139

with a pair of scissors handed him by the woman. To avoid disgrace and the ruin of his career, Wanley disposes of the body instead of calling the police.

Wanley is soon surprised to learn through his district attorney friend how much the police know about the killing and how close they are to the killer and his accomplice. He is forced further into a life of crime when Heidt, the dead man's bodyguard, begins blackmailing Wanley and the woman. Failing in his attempt to kill Heidt, Wanley decides on suicide. Ironically, at the fatal moment, the woman is phoning him with the information that the police have shot Heidt, convinced that he was Mazard's murderer.

At this point came the film's trick ending, which many critics of the time felt was a copout unfortunately tagged onto the story by the producer (who also happened to be the writer), a cheat, as one film historian put it, to rescue director Fritz Lang who had painted himself into a corner with the complex tale. *The Woman in the Window* won a sole Oscar nomination—for Best Scoring of a Dramatic Picture (by Arthur Lange and Hugo Friedhofer, but Miklos Rozsa's *Spellbound* got the Academy Award).

THE WOMAN IN THE WINDOW: With Joan Bennett

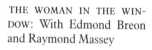

THE WOMAN IN THE WINDOW: With Edmond Breon and Raymond Massey

140

Robinson was to be reunited with Joan Bennett and Dan Duryea (the woman and the blackmailer) along with director Fritz Lang the following year in the not-too-dissimilar but more sensational *Scarlet Street*.

CRITICAL VIEWS

"Let it be noted that *The Woman in the Window* is a humdinger of a mystery melodrama . . . superlatively directed by Fritz Lang, and we couldn't imagine a better set of performers than the cast this picture boasts. Each player, from Edward G. Robinson and Joan Bennett as the unwitting principals in a celebrated murder to Thomas Jackson as the police homicide bureau chief, is almost letter perfect . . . Mr. Robinson, who was so good as the insurance investigator of *Double Indemnity*, gives a masterly performance as the professor."—Thomas M. Pryor, *The New York Times*

"Edward G. Robinson has seldom, if ever, been better than he is as the professor whose logical and ultimately desperate attempts to cover up his act are foiled at every turn."—Howard Barnes, *New York Herald-Tribune*

"Nunnally Johnson whips up a strong and decidedly suspenseful murder melodrama in *The Woman in the Window* . . . Robinson gives everything he has to the role as the reserved and reticent professor, scoring solidly."—*Variety*

OUR VINES HAVE TENDER GRAPES

1945   Metro-Goldwyn-Mayer

Producer, Robert Sisk; Director, Roy Rowland; Screenplay, Dalton Trumbo; Based on the novel *For Our Vines Have Tender Grapes* by George Victor Martin; Photography, Robert Surtees; Art director, Cedric Gibbons and Edward Carfagno; Set decorators, Edwin B. Willis and Hugh Hunt; Music, Bronislau Kaper; Sound, Douglas Shearer; Editor, Ralph E. Winters. 105 minutes

Martinius Jacobson (*Edward G. Robinson*), Selma Jacobson (*Margaret O'Brien*), Nels Halverson (*James Craig*), Bruna Jacobson (*Agnes Moorehead*), Arnold Hanson (*Jackie "Butch" Jenkins*), Bjorn Bjornson (*Morris Carnovsky*), Viola Johnson (*Frances Gifford*), Mrs. Bjornson (*Sara Haden*), Mr. Faraasen (*Louis Jean Heydt*), Minister (*Francis Pierlot*), Mrs. Faraasen (*Greta Granstedt*), Peter Hanson (*Arthur Space*), Kola Hanson

OUR VINES HAVE TENDER GRAPES: With Margaret O'Brien and Johnny Berkes

OUR VINES HAVE TENDER GRAPES: With Margaret O'Brien and Jackie "Butch" Jenkins

(*Elizabeth Russell*), Ingborg Jensen (*Dorothy Morris*), Kurt Jensen (*Charles Middleton*), Ivar Svenson (*Arthur Hohl*), Girl (*Abigail Adams*), Driver (*Johnny Berkes*), Marguerite Larsen (*Rhoda Williams*)

Set in a Norwegian farm community is southern Wisconsin, this excellent slice of Americana as viewed by a

141

OUR VINES HAVE TENDER GRAPES: With Margaret O'Brien Jackie "Butch" Jenkins and Agnes Moorehead

OUR VINES HAVE TENDER GRAPES: With Margaret O'Brien and Agnes Moorehead

seven-year-old girl has Edward G. Robinson—hiding behind a bushy mustache and a Scandinavian accent—being cast as the youngster's kind, understanding father (Wallace Beery had rejected the role), intimately concerned with not only his family but also the life of Benson Junction. There are, for instance, the arrival of the pretty new schoolteacher from Milwaukee; the growing friendship of the town newspaper's young editor with the newcomer; the events surrounding the young daughter and her cousin's adventures when the

circus comes to town; the near disaster when the two playmates go rowing in a metal bathtub; and the climactic fire that affects the neighbor whose farm was struck by lightning, leading the little girl to offer her prized calf to the farmer as a gift.

Robinson offered another top-notch performance, interacting wonderfully with co-star Margaret O'Brien, MGM's resident moppet, and freckle-faced Jackie "Butch" Jenkins (the fourth of his 11 movies), plus friends from the stage, Agnes Moorehead (as his wife) and Morris Carnovsky (as the neighbor). More importantly, as has been pointed out, it brought Robinson together with screenwriter Dalton Trumbo and a friendship that was to have career-shaking consequences when Hollywood came under investigation by the House Un-American Activities Committee. "I'd known Trumbo for a long while," Robinson recalled in his autobiography. "I knew he was hot-headed, wildly gifted, inordinately progressive, and it seemed to me, intensely logical. My relationship with him professionally and socially became, not very many years later, a subject for official concern of the Congress."

CRITICAL VIEWS

"Edward G. Robinson is solid and lovable as Martinius and in this role gives one of the finest performances in his long and varied career."—Thomas M. Pryor, *The New York Times*

"Edward G. Robinson [has] switched from tough roles

to that of a benevolent farmer who has a rather inordinate affection for his daughter. He plays the part for all it is worth, but it does not always make for entertainment."—Howard Barnes, *New York Herald-Tribune*

"Robinson gives a deft study of the farmer, an inarticulate, soil-bound man whose greatest dream is for a new barn. His groping for answers to his daughter's questions and drawing on parallels from farm life for explanations make empathetic points to the script's philosophy of simplicity."—*Variety*

JOURNEY TOGETHER

1945   RAF Film Unit/RKO British

Produced by the RAF Film Unit/Ministry of Information; Writer/Director, John Boulting; Story by Terence Rattigan; Photography, Harry Waxman and Gilbert Taylor; Production designer, John Howell; Music, Gordon Jacob; Special effects, Ray Morse; Editors,

Reginald Beck and Michael Del Campo. 95 minutes (cut to 80 minutes in the U.S. when released in 1946)

David Wilton (*Sgt. Richard Attenborough*), John Aynesworth (*Aircraftsman Jack Watling*), Smith (*Flying Officer David Tomlinson*), A Fitter (*Warrant Officer Sid Rider*), A Flight Sgt. Fitter (*Squadron Leader Stuart Latham*), An Acting Lt. (*Squadron Leader Hugh Wakefield*), A.C. 2 Jay (*Leading Aircraftsman Bromley Challenor*), An Anson Pilot (*Flying Officer Z. Peromowski*), Dean McWilliams (*Edward G. Robinson*), Flight Lt. Mander (*Patrick Waddington*), Squadron Leader Marshall (*Flight Lieutenant Sebastian Shaw*), The Commanding Officer (*Wing Commander Ronald Adam*), Mary McWilliams (*Bessie Love*), A Driver (*Sergeant Norvell Crutcher*), Guest Stars (*Rex Harrison, John Justin, George Cole, Miles Malleson, Ronald Squire, Fletcher Markle*), and Personnel of the Royal Air Force, Royal Canadian Air Force, United States Army

Robinson's participation in John Boulting's wartime flag-waver with an all-British cast of military personnel and actors then in uniform found him playing an American instructor who becomes the tough but understanding teacher of a squadron of RAF pilots training in the United States. The only other American in the cast was Bessie Love, playing Robinson's wife. At least one future "Sir"—a young actor named Richard Attenborough was in the film (as nominal star); another, the already established Rex Harrison, quite possibly was in the version that was initially shown in London, according to British writer Allen Eyles in his book on Harrison, but was not seen in the American print. Filmed during the summer of 1944 between Edward G. Robinson's assignments in *Double Indemnity* and *Our Vines Have Tender Grapes* (and not after *Scarlet Street*, as he erroneously recalls in his autobiography), *Journey Together* belatedy premiered in Great Britain in October

JOURNEY TOGETHER: With Jack Watling

JOURNEY TOGETHER: On the set with Lt. John Boulting, the director (left), and Maj. Roy Boulting (right)

1945 and was later shown in this country in a somewhat shortened version the following March. In the U.S., Robinson was given sole billing above the title whereas in the initial cast listing, he was rightly buried (because of the briefness of his role) 24th!

The well-written and superbly photographed film basically follows two young men, Dave Wilton, a Cockney lad, and John Aynesworth, a college graduate, who both enlist in the RAF about the same time, seeking to become pilots. Ultimately they come under the tutelage of Dean McWilliams when they go to flight school in Arizona, and he tries to impart some sense of teamwork to them without much success. Eventually the two find themselves on the same bomber, flying a mission over Berlin—each literally banking his life on the other.

CRITICAL VIEWS

"It is a dandy little picture about British airmen during the war, solidly authentic and full of character, action and suspense [that] neatly combines fact reporting on the steps in an airman's training course with a simple dramatic story of one trainee's experience . . . It is no reflection on Mr. Robinson or Miss Love (and their roles are naturally brief) to say that the actual airmen are much more credible in this film than they are."—Bosley Crowther, *The New York Times*

"Edward G. Robinson has been dragged into the picture as an American pilot-training officer. He does his bit in a fatherly way."—Joe Pihodna, *New York Herald-Tribune*

"The Royal Air Force Film Unit wanted me for a film written by Terence Rattigan and directed by Roy Boulting [ed.: actually it was his twin brother John]. The script was solidly authentic; it was about war; the role was wonderful—and I could get away [from Hollywood]."—Edward G. Robinson

JOURNEY TOGETHER: With Richard Attenborough and Jack Watling

SCARLET STREET

1946   Universal Pictures

A Diana Production; Executive producer, Walter Wanger; Producer/director, Fritz Lang; Screenplay, Dudley Nichols; Based on the novel and play *La Chienne* by Georges de la Fouchardiere and Mouezy-Eon; Photography, Milton Krasner; Art directors, Alexander Golitzen and John B. Goodman; Set decorators, Russell A. Gausman and Carl Lawrence; Music, H. J. Salter; Special effects, John P. Fulton; Editor, Arthur Hilton. 103 minutes

Christopher Cross (*Edward G. Robinson*), Kitty March (*Joan Bennett*), Johnny Prince (*Dan Duryea*), Janeway (*Jess Barker*), Millie (*Margaret Lindsay*), Adele Cross (*Rosalind Ivan*), Charles Pringle (*Samuel S. Hinds*), Dellarowe (*Arthur Loft*), Pop Lejon (*Vladimir Sokoloff*), Patcheye (*Charles Kemper*), Hogarth (*Russell Hicks*), Mrs. Michaels (*Anita Bolster*), Nick (*Cyrus W. Kendall*), Marchetti (*Fred Essler*), Policeman (*Edgar Dearing*), Policeman (*Tom Dillon*), Chauffeur (*Chuck Hamilton*), Employee (*Gus Glassmire*), Employee (*Ralph Littlefield*), Employee (*Sherry Hall*), Employee (*Howard Mitchell*), Employee (*Jack Statham*), Barney (*Rodney Bell*), Waiter (*Henri de Soto [Manuel Paris]*), Saunders (*Milton Kibbee*), Penny (*Tom Daly*), Holliday (*George Meader*), Tiny (*Lou Lubin*), Policeman (*Lee Phelps*), Policeman (*Matt Willis*), Ben (*Clarence Muse*), Hurdy Gurdy Man (*John Barton*), Prosecution Attorney (*Emmett Vogan*), Policeman (*Robert Malcolm*), Milkman (*Horace Murphy*), Loan Office Manager (*Will Wright*), Crocker (*Syd Saylor*), Derelict (*Dewey Robinson*), Evangelist (*Fritz Leiber*), Jones (*Byron Foulger*), 2nd Detective (*Dick Wessel*), 3rd Detective (*Dick Curtis*), Williams (*Joe Devlin*), Conway (*George Lloyd*)

SCARLET STREET: With Joan Bennett

Adapted from the French play *La Chienne*, which was filmed by Jean Renoir in 1931, sordid *Scarlet Street* is similar in plot (up to a point) to *The Woman in the Win-*

SCARLET STREET: With Rosalind Ivan

145

SCARLET STREET:
With Joan Bennett

SCARLET STREET: With Joan Bennett

dow, and has the same three stars and the same director. Edward G. Robinson this time is a henpecked clothing store clerk with a talent for painting, Joan Bennett the slinky femme fatale who takes him for a famous artist, and Dan Duryea a zoot-suited pimp with a sadistic streak. Robinson, as Christopher Cross (in no way to be confused with the pop singer of the early 1980s), rapidly falls under the spell of Kitty March, whom he had saved from a beating in the street one night. He is unaware of her attachment to an ungrateful punk, Johnny Prince. Kitty and Johnny decide to capitalize on Cross's supposed artistic genius, and it isn't long before she is accepting gifts from Cross—money stolen from his wife and embezzled from his employer—and allowing him to become her slave.

Ultimately he comes to recognize Kitty's relationship with Johnny, and in a blind rage after Johnny has left her one night, Cross stabs her to death with an ice pick and then arranges the evidence so that it points to Johnny as the killer. On the night of Johnny's execution, Cross climbs a pole nearby, hoping to hear the high voltage rushing through to the electric chair; then he descends to face his future. Now a derelict, he receives final retribution when he sees his portrait of Kitty sold for $10,000.

The picture was far too racy for the censors of the day, who demanded that the ice-picking of Joan Bennett be toned down (in the original, Robinson stabbed her six times; in the final print, only once) and a piece of dialogue be snipped. Director Lang, however, was able to have his film ultimately released, despite having the killer going free.

CRITICAL VIEWS

"Robinson, who is no mean art connoisseur, must have had a field day acting the part of the cashier who discovers that he has real talent in a thwarted love affair. He gives his all to the portrayal, sometimes a bit too much."
—Howard Barnes, *New York Herald-Tribune*

"In the role of the love-blighted cashier, Edward G. Robinson performs monotonously and with little illumination of an adventurous spirit seeking air."—Bosley Crowther, *The New York Times*

"Edward G. Robinson is the mild cashier and amateur painter whose love for Joan Bennett leads him to embezzlement, murder and disgrace. Two stars turn in top work to keep the interest high."—*Variety*

"I followed with *Scarlet Street* at Universal and hastened to finish it, so monotonous was the story and the character I played. So monotonous was I as an actor."
—Edward G. Robinson

THE STRANGER

1946   RKO International

Producer, S.P. Eagle; Director, Orson Welles; Screenplay, Anthony Veiller; Based on a story by Victor Trivas and Decla Dunning; Adaptation and dialogue, Anthony Veiller, John Huston and Orson Welles; Photography, Russell Metty; Art director, Perry Ferguson; Music, Bronislau Kaper; Editor, Ernest Nims. 94 minutes

Wilson (*Edward G. Robinson*), Mary Longstreet (*Loretta Young*), Prof. Charles Rankin (*Orson Welles*), Judge Longstreet (*Philip Merivale*), Noah Longstreet (*Richard Long*), Dr. Jeff Lawrence (*Byron Keith*), Potter (*Billy House*), Konrad Meinike (*Konstantin Shayne*), Sara (*Martha Wentworth*), Mrs. Lawrence (*Isabel O'Madigan*), Mr. Peabody (*Pietro Sosso*)

Edward G. Robinson (once again joining his leading lady from *The Hatchet Man* of 1932, Loretta Young) had top billing in Orson Welles' admirable *The Stranger*, playing a war crimes commissioner who has tracked a former Nazi to a small Connecticut town. Welles signed on to play the Nazi and then convinced producer S.P. Eagle (later Sam Spiegel) into letting him direct the film in place of John Huston—busily engaged in rewriting Anthony Veiler's script with Welles and preparing for his own *The Treasure of the Sierra Madre*. It was to be Welles' third picture as a director—one he desperately had to do to reestablish himself in the Hollywood mainstream. He then urged that his old Mercury Theatre colleague Agnes Moorehead play the Federal Agent, but Eagle insisted on Robinson for the role.

The story was intriguing: A Nazi mass murderer who had slipped out of Germany after the war and had come to the U.S. by way of Argentina and Mexico, is hiding out in a small town where he has gained respectability, and has become a college professor. He has married a judge's daughter who adores him, only to be exposed by a dogged Federal Agent, who has ingratiated himself to his quarry by posing as an art collector. In the film's memorable climax, Orson Welles with Edward G. Robinson in pursuit, attempts to hide out in the clock tower in the town square, but falls to his death, impaled on the sword of a warrior, one of the hands on the huge clock.

The movie was shot in just 35 days. Charles Higham, in his biography of Orson Welles, notes: "Robinson was in a sour mood, only reluctantly taking on the part, and convinced from his first meetings with Welles that the director's genius was in abeyance." Indeed, in his autobiography, Robinson said: "Orson has genius, but in this film it seems to have run out. It was bloodless, and so was I." *The Stranger* garnered an Oscar nomination for Victor Trivas for Best Original Story, but he lost

THE STRANGER: With Richard Long

THE STRANGER: With Richard Long, Loretta Young, Isabel O'Madigan, Orson Welles, Philip Merivale, Martha Wentworth and Byron Keith

THE STRANGER: With Loretta Young and Orson Welles

to Britisher Clemence Dane for his *Vacation From Marriage*.

CRITICAL VIEWS

"It is true that Mr. Welles has directed his camera for some striking effects, with lighting and interesting angles much relied on his technique. The fellow knows how to make a camera dynamic in telling a tale. And it is true, too, that Edward G. Robinson is well restrained as the unrelenting sleuth . . . But the whole film comes off a bloodless, manufactured show."—Bosley Crowther, *The New York Times*

"Edward G. Robinson matches staccato line for staccato line with Welles as his nemesis, charged with bringing Nazi criminals to justice."—Howard Barnes, *New York Herald-Tribune*

THE RED HOUSE

1947   Film Guild Corporation/United Artists

Producer, Sol Lesser; Writer/Director, Delmer Daves; Based on the novel by George Agnew Chamberlain; Photography,

THE RED HOUSE: With Lon McCallister and Allene Roberts

Bert Glennon; Art director, McClure Capps; Set decorator, Dorcy Howard; Music, Miklos Rozsa; Editor, Merrill White. 100 minutes

Pete Morgan (*Edward G. Robinson*), Nath Storm (*Lon McCallister*), Ellen Morgan (*Judith Anderson*), Meg Morgan (*Allene Roberts*), Tibby (*Julie London*), Teller (*Rory Calhoun*), Mrs. Storm (*Ona Munson*), Dr. Byrne (*Harry Shannon*), Officer (*Arthur Space*), Don Brent (*Walter Sande*), Cop (*Pat Flaherty*)

In this neat, widely admired little thriller adapted from George Agnew Chamberlain's novel, Edward G. Robinson, in his first and only excursion into the world of film producing, via the company he and Sol Lesser formed to make this movie, is farmer Pete Morgan, a moody cripple. He lives a life of rigid seclusion with his sister, Ellen (played by Judith Anderson), and his adopted daughter, Meg (newcomer Allene Roberts), whose parents mysteriously disappeared fifteen years before. To help on the farm, Morgan has hired a young neighbor, Nath Storm (Lon McCallister), but has warned Nath and all others away from Oxhead Woods—which borders on his farm—as well as "The Red House and the screams in the night." Nath, curious about Morgan's vague and erratic remarks about this Red House and its curse, arranges with Meg to spend Sunday searching for it.

Learning of the young folks' search, Morgan orders

THE RED HOUSE: With Allene Roberts

Teller, the caretaker he has hired, to use his gun on trespassers. Meg eventually locates the mysterious house, but breaks her leg as she flees from a fusillade of Teller's bullets. As the weeks pass, Ellen Morgan realizes that her brother's mental condition is deteriorating, and she

THE RED HOUSE: With Judith Anderson, Lon McCallister and Allene Roberts

THE RED HOUSE: With Allene Roberts

decides to burn the Red House that harbored his secrets in the hope that this act would aid him. She makes her way to the house but is shot by Teller. Before dying, she confides to Meg and Nath the secret she has kept for years: her brother, because of his unrequited love for Meg's mother, killed both of her parents in the Red House.

In the course of events, Morgan, now completely demented, lures Meg to the house, but Nath and the police have followed them and arrive in time to save her from a fate similar to her parents. Morgan, however, evades his pursuers and kills himself by driving his truck into the soggy mud near the house, where he had sunk the bodies of Meg's parents years earlier.

In addition to Lon McCallister, returning from the service and first-timer Allene Roberts (whose promise was never fulfilled), making their first important screen appearances were singer Julie London as a seductive local girl and Rory Calhoun as Teller, the caretaker.

CRITICAL VIEWS

"It's been a long time since the Hollywood artisans have turned out an adult horror number. *The Red House* is just such an edifying offering, which should supply horror-hungry audiences with the chills of the month . . . Edward G. Robinson is excellent as the crippled Peter, whose mind is cracking under the thrall of the horrible secret of *The Red House*, and Judith Anderson gives a taut performance as his sister who has silently shared his mental burden."—A. H. Weiler, *The New York Times*

"An ordinary mystery story has received a booster charge of good direction in *The Red House*, and the result is a moody hair-raiser of a melodrama . . . With veterans Edward G. Robinson and Judith Anderson pacing four talented newcomers to a round of convincing performances, this Sol Lesser production is a taut and steady item of menacing make-believe . . . Daves' direction has brought the scenery so much to life that it becomes the most important character of the piece, making the villainy of Edward G. Robinson as the farmer and Judith Anderson as his sister seem weak in comparison."—Otis Guernsey, *New York Herald-Tribune*

"It was a moody piece, got moody notices, but I think it made a few bucks."—Edward G. Robinson

ALL MY SONS: With Burt Lancaster and Mady Christians

ALL MY SONS

1948   Universal-International

Producer, Chester Erskine; Director, Irving Reis; Screenplay, Chester Erskine; Based on the play by Arthur Miller; Photography, Russell Metty; Art directors, Bernard Herzbrun and Hilyard Brown; Set decorators, Russell A. Gausman and Al Fields; Music, Leith Stevens; Sound, Leslie Carey and Corson Jowett; Editor, Ralph Dawson. 94 minutes

Joe Keller (*Edward G. Robinson*), Chris Keller (*Burt Lancaster*), Kate Keller (*Mady Christians*), Ann Deever (*Louisa Horton*), George Deever (*Howard Duff*), Herbert Deever (*Frank Conroy*), Jim Bayliss (*Lloyd Gough*), Sue Bayliss (*Arlene Francis*), Frank Lubey (*Henry (Harry) Morgan*), Lydia Lubey (*Elisabeth Fraser*), Charles (*Walter Soderling*), Minnie (*Therese Lyon*), Ellsworth (*Charles Meredith*), Attorney (*William Johnstone*), Wertheimer (*Herbert Vigran*), Judge (*Harry Harvey*), Bartender (*Pat Flaherty*), Headwaiter (*George Sorel*), Mrs. Hamilton (*Helen Brown*), McGraw (*Herbert Heywood*), Norton (*Joseph Kerr*), Halliday (*Jerry Hausner*), Foreman (*Frank Kreig*), Ed (*William Ruhl*), Tom (*Al Murphy*), Jorgenson (*Walter Bonn*), Bill (*Richard La Marr*), Workman (*Jack Gargan*), Attendants (*Victor Zimmerman, George Slocum*)

All My Sons was Arthur Miller's first major success on Broadway in 1947. (Earlier he had a now forgotten play called *The Man Who Had All the Luck*.) The hard-hit-

ALL MY SONS: With Louisa Horton and Mady Christians

ting screen version presented Edward G. Robinson—in the part played on Broadway by Ed Begley—with an especially powerful role as Joe Keller, a manufacturer

ALL MY SONS: With Burt Lancaster and Helen Brown

ALL MY SONS: With Mady Christians, Howard Duff, Burt Lancaster and Louisa Horton

Joe Keller's partner, Herbert Deever, is still in prison for the wartime crime (selling the parts), but Ann, his daughter, returns to the town where she grew up and goes to visit the Kellers, invited there by son Chris. She had been engaged to Chris's brother, whom Kate Keller still believes to be alive and because of that opposes the marriage of Chris and Ann. George Deever, Ann's brother, has been insisting that Joe also is guilty and urges her not to become part of the "blood-stained" Keller household. Although Chris worships his father, he is compelled by conscience to learn the truth and calls on Deever in prison, only to discover that Joe escaped conviction through a legal technicality.

Uncovering the whole story, Chris confronts his father with a letter Ann had sent to his brother, stating that the pilot intended to fly to his death in shame over the father's unpatriotic and criminal deed. A stunned and repentant Joe Keller is driven to suicide, as Ann and Chris leave together.

CRITICAL VIEWS

"Through a fine performance by Edward G. Robinson, it certainly reveals a character . . . [He] does a superior job of showing the shades of a personality in a little tough guy who has a softer side . . . Clearly he reveals the blank bewilderment of a man who can't conceive in the abstract the basic moral obligation of the individual to society."—Bosley Crowther, *The New York Times*

"While there are scenes of fine indignation in the motion picture, realized to the full by Edward G.

who supplied defective airplane parts to the military, resulting in the deaths of nearly two dozen WWII flyers, his own son included. This was Robinson's first film after becoming embroiled with the HUAC hearings in Washington, and was to test his standing in the Hollywood community (box office was not a consideration since the moviegoing public, it turns out, was unaware or simply did not care). Robinson was teamed with up-and-coming Burt Lancaster (doing Arthur Kennedy's Broadway part) as the younger son, stage star Mady Christians in an infrequent screen role as the wife, and newcomer Louisa Horton as the dead flyer's fiancée who switches her love to his brother.

Robinson, Burt Lancaster, Mady Christians and Frank Conroy, they do not off-set fabricated situations and blurred characterizations."—Howard Barnes, *New York Herald-Tribune*

"Edward G. Robinson gives an effective performance as the small town manufacturer who sends defective parts to the Army Air Force. It's a humanized study that rates among his best and lends the thought behind the film much strength."—*Variety*

". . . a picture of which I am inordinately proud . . . It was a part I played with such passion and intensity that the director, Irving Reis, told me constantly to take it easy. He also called me One-Take Eddie because rarely did I ever have to repeat a scene."—Edward G. Robinson

KEY LARGO

1948   Warner Bros.-First National

Producer, Jerry Wald; Director, John Huston; Screenplay, Richard Brooks and John Huston; Based on the play by Maxwell Anderson; Photography, Karl Freund; Art director, Leo K. Kuter; Set decorator, Fred M. MacLean; Music, Max Steiner; Sound, Dolph Thomas; Makeup, Perc Westmore; Special effects, William McGann and Robert Burks; Editor, Rudi Fehr. 101 minutes

Frank McCloud (*Humphrey Bogart*), Johnny Rocco (*Edward G. Robinson*), Nora Temple (*Lauren Bacall*), James Temple (*Lionel Barrymore*), Gaye Dawn (*Claire Trevor*), Curley Hoff (*Thomas Gomez*), Toots Bass (*Harry Lewis*), Deputy Clyde Sawyer (*John Rodney*), Ziggy (*Marc Lawrence*), Angel Garcia (*Dan Seymour*), Sheriff Ben Wade (*Monte Blue*), Ralph Feeney (*William Haade*), Tom Osceola (*Jay Silverheels*), John Osceola (*Rodric Redwing*), Bus Driver (*Joe P. Smith*), Skipper (*Alberto Morin*), Man (*Pat Flaherty*), Ziggy's Henchmen (*Jerry Jerome, John Phillips, Lute Crockett*), Old Indian Woman (*Felipa Gomez*)

In a return to his old studio, Edward G. Robinson was cast as Humphrey Bogart's antagonist for the fifth and final time—except that now Bogart was the leading star on the Warner lot, so Robinson had to be the bad guy—getting his when the two traded bullets at the climax. A high-powered cast created the electricity in this John Huston/Richard Brooks very loose adaptation of Maxwell Anderson's 1939 play which starred Paul Muni and Uta Hagen. Frederic Tozere had the role comparable to

Robinson's. (Also in the cast on stage were such young actors as Karl Malden, José Ferrer, James Gregory and Tom Ewell.)

In his first true gangster role since the early '40s, Robinson, in his sadistic Johnny Rocco that remains part of gangster movie folklore, gave one of the most memorable bad guy performances of his career, a virtuoso portrayal that begins from his first moment on the screen—luxuriating, cigar in mouth, in a bubble bath! Most of the action takes place in a small hotel in the Florida Keys run by James Temple and his daughter-in-law Nora. Frank McCloud, an ex-Army major, who had been a buddy of Nora's husband, killed in action, turns up for a visit and learns that the only other guests in the hotel are a mysterious "Mr. Brown" and his "entourage": an alcoholic floozy and four sinister-looking henchmen. When "Mr. Brown" at last puts in an appearance, McCloud recognizes him as Johnny Rocco, an infamous crime boss hiding out from the Feds until he can make his way to Cuba.

McCloud at first views Rocco with indifference, preferring to spend his energies on Nora Temple. When a fierce storm rakes the island, Rocco loses his cool and McCloud, who'd put up with his goading and sarcasm, comes to the aid of Rocco's moll, Gaye Dawn, and receives a beating for his efforts. Sheriff Ben Wade soon arrives in search of his deputy and finds him dead. Rocco thrusts the blame on a pair of local Indians. Convinced of Rocco's deviousness, McCloud agrees to pilot a boat for him to Cuba. With guns smuggled to him by Gaye, who is left behind with the Temples, McCloud plans to get rid of Rocco once out to sea, and one by one he picks off Rocco's henchmen. After a cat and mouse game on the small cruiser, McCloud lures Rocco, who has been cowering below in the cabin, into a final shootout, before heading back to Key Largo and Nora.

With the top-notch cast (Bogart and Bacall in the last of their four movies together, Robinson unsurpassed, Trevor earning an Oscar for her performance, Barrymore in the twilight of his career), *Key Largo* became even more of a hit for John Huston at the time than did *The Treasure of the Sierra Madre* which preceded it by less than six months. *Sierra Madre*, of course, became Warners' surprise hit in 1948 with Huston winning his Oscar for that one. *Key Largo* later was done on TV (Alcoa Theatre, 1956) with Alfred Drake, Anne Bancroft and J. Carrol Naish in the Bogart-Bacall-Robinson parts.

CRITICAL VIEWS

"Although not as honest and thoughtful a portrayal of human beings as its predecessor (*The Treasure of the Sierra Madre*), it is a bowstring-tight humdinger of

KEY LARGO: With Claire Trevor

KEY LARGO: With Humphrey Bogart

KEY LARGO

movie make-believe . . . Robinson is Little Caesar all over again, terrorizing both his henchmen and the bystanders trapped with him in a lonely seaside hotel. In a story of modern crime, his acting might seem extreme, but here its touch of the Twenties is exactly what is required of a brutish has-been who hopes that 'prohibition will come back in a couple of years.'"—Otis Guernsey, *New York Herald-Tribune*

"It is whimsical that Warners, who had a great deal to do with the rise of the gangster in the movies, should have been as persistent as they have in dispatching this legendary character to limbo over a period of years. Ever since *The Petrified Forest* . . . they have made several obvious occasions to kiss the boy goodbye. Now in their latest, *Key Largo*, they subject him to the final irony: they have him enacted again by no less than Edward G. Robinson and then let a reformed Humphrey Bogart bump him off . . . [Huston] got stinging performances out of most of his cast—notably out of Mr. Robinson, who plays the last of the red-hot gangsters in top-notch style. Indeed, Mr. Robinson's performance is an expertly timed and timbred scan of the vulgarity, corruption and egoism of a criminal mind."—Bosley Crowther, *The New York Times*

"Let me tell you something about Bogie. On the set *he* gave it all to me. Second billing or no, I got the star treatment because he insisted upon it—not in words but in action. When asked to come to the set, he would

KEY LARGO: With Humphrey Bogart, Lionel Barrymore and Lauren Bacall

ask: 'Is Mr. Robinson ready?' He'd come to my trailer dressing room to get me. Lionel Barrymore was in the picture, and we both gave *him* the deference he deserved."—Edward G. Robinson

NIGHT HAS A THOUSAND EYES

1948   Paramount Pictures

Producer, Endre Bohem; Director, John Farrow; Screenplay, Barré Lyndon and Jonathan Latimer; Based on the novel by Cornell Woolrich; Photography, John F. Seitz; Art directors, Hans Dreier and Franz Bachelin; Set decorators, Sam Comer and Ray Moyer; Costumes, Edith Head; Music, Victor Young; Sound, Hugo Grenzbach and Gene Garvin; Editor, Eda Warren. 80 minutes

NIGHT HAS A THOUSAND EYES: With Virginia Bruce

NIGHT HAS A THOUSAND EYES

John Triton (*Edward G. Robinson*), Jean Courtland (*Gail Russell*), Elliott Carson (*John Lund*), Jenny (*Virginia Bruce*), Lieut. Shawn (*William Demarest*), Peter Vinson (*Richard Webb*), Whitney Courtland (*Jerome Cowan*), Dr. Walters (*Onslow Stevens*), Mr. Gilman (*John Alexander*), Melville Weston (*Roman Bohnen*), Mr. Myers (*Luis Van Rooten*), Butler (*Henry Guttman*), Miss Hendricks (*Mary Adams*), Chauffeur (*Philip Van Zandt*), Dr. Ramsdell (*Douglas Spencer*), Edna (maid) (*Jean King*), 2nd Maid (*Dorothy Abbott*), Gowan (*Bob Stephenson*), Bertelli (*William Haade*), 3rd Scientist (*Stuart Holmes*), Young Chinese Woman (*Jean Wong*), Young Chinese Woman (*Anna Tom*), Young Chinese Man (*Weaver Levy*), Chinese Waiter (*Artarne Wong*), Newsstand Woman (*Jane Crowley*), Radio Announcer (*Joey Ray*), Scrubwoman (*Eleanore Vogel*), Bit Woman (Italian) (*Minerva Urecal*), 1st Secretary (*Renee Randall*), 2nd Secretary (*Marilyn Gray*), Mr. Byers (*Lester Dorr*), Husband of Frantic Mother (*Harland Tucker*), Deb's Mother (*Violet Goulet*), Bit Man (*Edward Earle*), 2nd Companion (*Julia Faye*), Agnes (*Margaret Field*), Deb's Father (*Major Sam Harris*), Elderly Doorman (*John Sheehan*), Secretary (*Betty Hannon*), Jailer (*James Davies*), Mrs. Byers (*Gladys Blake*), Frantic Mother (*Frances Morris*)

Robinson returned to Paramount to star in a mediocre melodrama based on the novel by Cornell Woolrich, playing a vaudeville mentalist, John Triton, who finds himself both blessed and cursed with the power of precognition. He can foretell tragic events but his inability to prevent their occurrence disturbs him, and he retires from the stage when he foresees the death of a friend in childbirth following her marriage to his partner, Whitney Courtland. Years later, he learns that Courtland, now a wealthy industrialist, is attempting to set a coast-to-coast speed record in his private plane and receives a premonition of Courtland's death. In an effort to save him, Triton pleads with Courtland's daughter, Jean, to stop the flight, but her fiancé, Elliott Carson, views Triton as a crackpot.

Courtland's plane crashes, and a distressed Triton becomes even more dejected when he foresees Jean's death in an accident. Jean agrees to let him help her avoid the accident, but Elliott becomes suspicious and calls the police. Having learned that Courtland's plane might have been tampered with, the police suspect that Triton was involved in what they consider murder and that he might really be trying to do away with Jean as well.

As the hour of Jean's impending death draws near, Triton, by correctly predicting the suicide of a convict, convinces the police of his strange powers. They release him and he rushes to Jean's home and bursts in as one of her father's former associates is preparing to kill her to

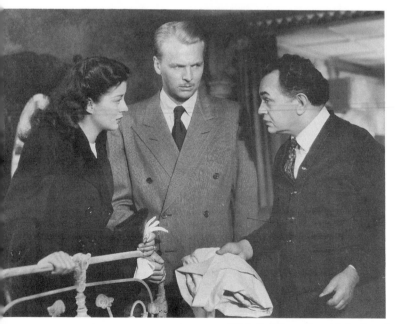

NIGHT HAS A THOUSAND EYES: With Gail Russell and John Lund

cover up a crooked stock deal. Triton rushes to her defense, but the police who have followed him mistake his motives and shoot him down. In his pocket, they find a note predicting his own death that night.

Not much has been seen of *Night Has a Thousand Eyes* in the years since it first saw light of day, but the title theme written by Buddy Mernier (words) and Jerry Brainin (music) has gone on to become a pop standard.

CRITICAL VIEWS

"[It] is such unadulterated hokum that it almost ingratiates itself . . . [except that] it tries to put over the pretense that it is serious stuff . . . From the very beginning to the very end of the film, we are asked to believe that a fellow really might have supernatural sight—that an ex-vaudevillian might forecast not only what horse will win but who will be killed in accidents and what attempts will be made on peoples' lives. Now, this sort of thing might be charming—or funny at least—if done in a spirit of thinly veiled fooling or out-and-out fantasy. But here it is done in sombre fashion with Edward G. Robinson playing the gent as a figure of tragic proportions."—Bosley Crowther, *The New York Times*

"Robinson labors diligently and sometimes effectively in the part of the crystal-ball gazer who is doomed to unhappiness and extinction by his supernatural powers."—Howard Barnes, *New York Herald-Tribune*

". . . unadulterated hokum that I did for the money."—Edward G. Robinson

HOUSE OF STRANGERS

1949   20th Century-Fox

Producer, Sol C. Siegel; Director, Joseph L. Mankiewicz; Screenplay, Philip Yordan; Based on the novel *I'll Never Go There Any More* by Jerome Weidman; Photography, Milton Krasner; Art directors, Lyle Wheeler and George W. Davis; Set decorators, Thomas Little and Walter M. Scott; Costumes, Charles Le Maire; Music, Daniele Amfitheatrof; Orchestrator, Maurice de Packh; Sound, W. D. Flick and Roger Heman; Editor, Harmon Jones. 101 minutes

Gino Monetti (*Edward G. Robinson*), Irene Bennett (*Susan Hayward*), Max Monetti (*Richard Conte*), Joe Monetti (*Luther Adler*), Pietro Monetti (*Paul Valentine*), Tony Monetti (*Efrem Zimbalist, Jr.*), Maria Domenico (*Debra Paget*), Hel-

NIGHT HAS A THOUSAND EYES: With Jerome Cowan and Virginia Bruce

HOUSE OF STRANGERS: With Tito Vuolo and Luther Adler

HOUSE OF STRANGERS: With Susan Hayward

HOUSE OF STRANGERS: With Richard Conte

HOUSE OF STRANGERS: With Richard Conte, Debra Paget, Esther Minciotti and Hope Emerson

ena Domenico (*Hope Emerson*), Theresa Monetti (*Esther Minciotti*), Elaine Monetti (*Diana Douglas*), Lucca (*Tito Vuolo*), Victoro (*Alberto Morin*), Waiter (*Sid Tomack*), Judge (*Thomas Browne Henry*), Prosecutor (*David Wolfe*), Danny (*John Kellogg*), Woman Juror (*Ann Morrison*), Night Club Singer (*Dolores Parker*), Bit Man (*Mario Siletti*), Pietro's Opponent (*Tommy Garland*), Guard (*Charles J. Flynn*), Bat Boy (*Joseph Mazzuca*), Cop (*John Pedrini*), 3rd Applicant (*Argentina Brunetti*), Bit Man (*Maurice Samuels*), Cop (*George Magrill*), Cop (*Mike Stark*), Neighbor (*Herbert Vigran*), Referee (*Mushy Callahan*), Preliminary Fighters (*Bob Castro*), (*Eddie Saenz*), Doorman (*George Spaulding*), Taxi Driver (*John "Red" Kullers*), Detectives (*Scott Landers, Fred Hillebrand*)

Robinson, with HUAC pressure increasing, found one of his last major roles in some time one of his best, and, other than his posthumous Oscar, it was to bring him his only major acting award: the Cannes Film Festival named him Best Actor for his portrayal of Gino Monetti, barber-turned-banker whose three sons turn out to be rotters and a fourth, Max, vindictive.

Gino Monetti moved from cutting hair during the Depression to loan-sharking as he began his banking empire. He was as ruthless in business as he was cruelly lording it over his family at home where his wife and four sons lived in increasing mistrust. Gino's banking methods eventually led to an indictment. But, as his three older boys, Joe, Tony and Pietro turned their backs on him, his youngest, Max, came to his defense—and even attempted to fix the jury. Tipped off by Joe, the police arrested Max and he was sent up the river. His brothers then moved in and ousted Gino—freed in a mistrial—from the family business. Tony married Max's fiancée and the brothers were living in luxury. Shortly before dying, Gino visited Max at Sing Sing and got a promise from him to exact revenge on his other sons.

Returning to New York's Little Italy after rotting in prison for seven years, Max goes straight to the trust company founded by his father to settle the old score with his brothers and leaves them in fear of his one-man vendetta. He then visits the apartment of Irene Bennett, a woman with whom he'd once had a torrid affair. She tries to get him to go away with her, but he refuses until he has avenged his father's betrayal by the other three. At the family mansion, the showdown is set. The brothers give Max a beating, but soon are fighting among themselves, leaving Max at last free, going off arm-in-arm with Irene.

House of Strangers was remade by Fox with a Western setting as *Broken Lance* (1954) with Spencer Tracy as the patriarch and with a circus setting as *The Big Show* (1961) with Nehemiah Persoff in a revised version of the Robinson role.

CRITICAL VIEWS

"As nasty a nest of vipers you're likely to see outside of a gangster picture or maybe a jungle film is assembled in *House of Strangers* . . . Indeed there's a very strong resemblance in this film to the gangster type, not only in the natures of the characters but in the pat manipulation of the plot . . . As a sizzling and picturesque exposure of a segment of nouveau-riche life within the Italian-American population, this film . . . has its decidedly entertaining points . . . Edward G. Robinson, as usual, does a brisk and colorful job of making 'Papa' Monetti a brassy despot with a Sicilian dialect."—Bosley Crowther, *The New York Times*

"It has solid characterizations by Edward G. Robinson, Richard Conte, Luther Adler, Susan Hayward and their assistants . . . Robinson gives [Monetti] ominous quality, but he lingers too fondly over reminiscences of his youth as a barber on Mulberry Street and makes far too much of an Italian accent."—Howard Barnes, *New York Herald-Tribune*

"Then there was a picture called *House of Strangers* for Fox, directed by Joe Mankiewicz. I loved it. Good thing I did, because suddenly the whole goddamn roof fell in again."—Edward G. Robinson

IT'S A GREAT FEELING: With Pat Flaherty, Jack Carson and Doris Day

Train Passenger (*Sandra Gould*), Jeffrey Bushdinkle (Groom) (*Errol Flynn*), Guest Stars (as Themselves) (*Gary Cooper, Joan Crawford, Sydney Greenstreet, Danny Kaye, Patricia Neal, Eleanor Parker, Ronald Reagan, Edward G. Robinson, Jane Wyman*), and directors (*David Butler, Michael Curtiz, King Vidor* and *Raoul Walsh*)

IT'S A GREAT FEELING

1949   Warner Bros.-First National

Producer, Alex Gottlieb; Director, David Butler; Screenplay, Jack Rose and Melville Shavelson; Story, I.A.L. Diamond; Photography, Wilfrid M. Cline; Art director, Stanley Fleischer; Set decorator, Lyle B. Reifsnider; Costumes, Milo Anderson; Music, Jule Styne; Music director, Ray Heindorf; Orchestrations, Sidney Cutner and Leo Shuken; Songs by Sammy Cahn and Jule Styne; Choreography, LeRoy Prinz; Sound, Dolph Thomas and David Forrest; Editor, Irene Morr. Technicolor. 85 minutes

Himself (*Dennis Morgan*), Judy Adams (*Doris Day*), Himself (*Jack Carson*), Arthur Trent (*Bill Goodwin*), Information Clerk (*Irving Bacon*), Grace (*Claire Carleton*), Publicity Man (*Harlan Warde*), Trent's Secretary (*Jacqueline deWit*), Mr. Adams (*Wilfred Lucas*), Gate Guard (*Pat Flaherty*), Manicurist (*Wendy Lee*), Models (*Nita Talbot, Eve Whitney, Carol Brewster, Sue Casey, Joan Vohs*), Saleslady (*Lois Austin*), Wrestling Fan in Bar (*Tom Dugan*), Soda Jerk (*James Holden*),

To celebrate its newest musical sensation, Doris Day (in her third picture), Warner Bros. created a lighthearted romp about a star-struck waitress in the studio's commissary hoping to break into films. It then rounded up a number of its current contract players, several of its directors, and Edward G. Robinson, not so long ago a member of the Warner family, and Danny Kaye, not yet one, to cavort with her. Robinson, in his first film in color, does a takeoff on the snarling gangster he virtually had patented. Dennis Morgan and Jack Carson costarred above the title with Doris Day. They played themselves. *It's a Great Feeling* was to be Robinson's last Hollywood movie for several years.

CRITICAL VIEWS

"Credit the Warner Brothers with being able to take a joke . . . lightly lampooning its stars, directors, producers and publicity men and having a genuinely nice time doing it. And what is more important, it is a gay and impudent lark which transmits its broad humor to the viewer with a helping of surprises . . . In fact the company's varsity has been trotted out for this Techni-colored frolic . . . Edward G. Robinson contributes a travesty on his hard-boiled gangster characterization . . ."—A. H. Weiler, *The New York Times*

"A broad takeoff on Broadway and picture making. It has a gay light air, color and lineup of surprise guest stars that greatly enhance word-of-mouth values . . . Edward G. Robinson gives a swell takeoff on his stock hard-boiled gangster character in a sequence played for loud chuckles."—*Variety*

". . . an all-star piece of baloney called *It's a Great Feeling*, starring Doris Day and Dennis Morgan and with a whole bunch of stars playing themselves: Gary Cooper, Joan Crawford, Danny Kaye, and Ronnie Reagan. Imagine, Ronnie Reagan! (Of course, at the time, I think he was still a Democrat.)"—Edward G. Robinson

MY DAUGHTER JOY

(U. S. title: OPERATION X)

1950   Columbia Pictures

Producer and director, Gregory Ratoff; Associate producer, Phil Brandon; Screenplay, Robert Thoeren and William Rose; Based on the novel *David Goldner* by Irene Nemirowsky; Photography, Georges Perinal and Andre Beck; Art director, Andre Andrejew; Music, R. Gallois-Montbrun; Music director, Dr. Hubert Clifford; Sound, Jack Drake; Editor, Raymond Poulton. 79 minutes

George Constantin (*Edward G. Robinson*), Ava Constantin (*Nora Swinburne*), Georgette (Joy) Constantin (*Peggy Cummins*), Larry Boyd (*Richard Greene*), Sir Thomas MacTavish (*Finlay Currie*), Marcos (*Gregory Ratoff*), Colonel Fogarty (*Ronald Adam*), Andreas (*Walter Rilla*), Professor Karol (*James Robertson Justice*), Ennix (*David Hutcheson*), Polato (*Dod Nehan*), Sultan (*Peter Illing*), Dr. Schindler (*Ronald Ward*), Prince Alzar (*Roberto Villa*), Barboza (*Harry Lane*)

In Great Britain, Edward G. Robinson took the role of a ruthless businessman named George Constantin in a so-so adaptation of the not-too-well known novel, *David Goldner*. Made in 1949, it did not arrive on these shores until around Christmas time of 1950—and then only briefly.

Constantin is brilliant, and he's not one to let anyone forget it. His days as a youngster in Constantinople, where he earned pennies as a bootblack, have long been

MY DAUGHTER JOY: With Peggy Cummins

MY DAUGHTER JOY: With Gregory Ratoff, Ronald Adam and Nora Swinburne

seared in his mind, and created a consuming passion to one day rule the world. Next to this driving force, he has room for only one other thing in his life, his beloved daughter, Georgette. Constantin supposedly has found

MY DAUGHTER JOY: With Peggy Cummins, Richard Greene and Nora Swinburne

the key to supreme power, a project he calls Operation X, but one ingredient is missing: a vital material controlled by a mideastern sultan. To obtain it, Constantin plans to give his daughter in marriage to the potentate's son.

Georgette, meanwhile, has become engaged to Larry Boyd, a resourceful young journalist, who has been doing a bit of investigation and has stumbled upon Operation X. Enraged, Constantin orders Boyd out of his house. Constantin's wife intercedes, pleading with her husband to give Georgette the happiness he has been promising her for so long. When he refuses, she confesses that Georgette is not his daughter. The shock of the news dooms both Operation X and its scheming backer, who almost ruled the world.

CRITICAL VIEWS

"Edward G. Robinson gives the film's solitary rounded performance. He is a restrained schemer whose dreams of 'mastery of the world' seem ominously real." —A. H. Weiler, *The New York Times*

"Edward G. Robinson strides through the leading role in a suitable imitation of megalomania . . . [His] version of a power-hungry millionaire is who strides into a room, confronts three resentful graybeards, and announces, 'Gentlemen, whether you like it or not, you are going to loan me two million dollars!'"—Otis Guernsey, *New York Herald-Tribune*

"Late in 1949 I went to London to make a picture in England. There it was called *My Daughter Joy*. In this country it was called *Operation X*. In either country it should have been called unspeakable."—Edward G. Robinson

ACTORS AND SIN

1952   United Artists

A Sid Kuller production; Produced, directed and written by Ben Hecht; Co-director and photography, Lee Garmes; Set decorator, Howard Bristol; Music, George Antheil; Editor, Otto Ludwig. 85 minutes

Actor's Blood: Maurice Tillayou (*Edward G. Robinson*), Marcia Tillayou (*Marsha Hunt*), Alfred O'Shea (*Dan O'Herlihy*), Otto Lachsley (*Rudolph Anders*), Tommy (*Alice Key*), Clyde Veering (*Rick Roman*). **Woman of Sin:** Orlando Higgens (*Eddie Albert*), J.B. Cobb (*Alan Reed*), Miss Flannigan (*Tracey Roberts*), Mr. Blue (*Paul Guilfoyle*), Mr. Devlin (*Doug Evans*), Daisy Marcher (*Jenny Hecht*), Mrs. Egelhofer (*Jody Gilbert*), Movie Hero (*John Crawford*)

161

ACTORS AND SIN: With Dan O'Herlihy and Marsha Hunt

With film offers not forthcoming on a regular basis, "the drought," as he called it, Robinson returned to the stage in the national company of Sidney Kingsley's *Darkness at Noon* (in the role Claude Rains was doing on Broadway). Following that, he joined writer Ben Hecht in a middling two-part movie which Hecht was producing independently and himself directing. Robinson starred in the first segment, *Actor's Blood*, playing fading Shakespearean actor Maurice Tillayou who devotes himself to his actress daughter who has let success go to her head. She has alienated her friends, driven her husband away, and found her own career on the skids. When she poisons herself, Tillayou, rather than admitting her failure to the world, decides to make her suicide look like murder. At a party of those suspected by the police of committing the crime, the lights suddenly go out and Tillayou is found dying from a dagger wound, unable to put his hand on the man he thinks is the murderer. His ruse is discovered: he stabbed himself, and the assembled guests salute his melodramatic flair.

CRITICAL VIEWS

"'Actor's Blood' is a stiff, glum and narcissistic tale of a retired actor's devotion to his daughter, a neurotic, dim-ming Broadway star who commits suicide . . . Edward G. Robinson and Marsha Hunt, the leads, bleakly intone some of Mr. Hecht's most sonorous dialogue."—Howard Thompson, *The New York Times*

"The characters are pretty familiar, including the star's doting father, played by Edward G. Robinson in a combination of pride and anxiety."—Otis Guernsey, *New York Herald-Tribune*

"And so I entered the 'B' picture phase of my career as a movie star—or former movie star, if that's a better way of putting it, or has-been, if that's still a better way." —Edward G. Robinson

ACTORS AND SIN: With Marsha Hunt

B. Willis; Music director, Alberto Colombo; Sound, Douglas Shearer; Editor, Ben Lewis. 73 minutes

John B. "Hans" Lobert (*Edward G. Robinson*), Christy (*Vera-Ellen*), Adam Polachuk (*Jeff Richards*), Bobby Bronson (*Richard Jaeckel*), Julie Davis (*William Campbell*), Carl Hubbell (*Himself*), Brian McLennan (*Paul Langton*), Chuy Aguilar (*Lalo Rios*), Tippy Mitchell (*Bill Crandall*), Wally Mitchell (*Frank Ferguson*), Dale Alexander (*John McKee*), Mr. Polachuk (*Mario Siletti*), Pomfret (*Robert Caldwell*), Little Joe (*Donald "Chippie" Hastings*), Themselves (*Al Campanis, Bob Trocolor, Tony Ravish*)

BIG LEAGUER

1953   Metro-Goldwyn-Mayer

Producer, Matthew Rapf; Director, Robert Aldrich; Screenplay, Herbert Baker; Based on a story by John McNulty and Louis Morheim; Photography, William Mellor; Art directors, Cedric Gibbons and Eddie Imazu; Set decorator, Edwin

Rather unusual, and little appreciated on its initial release (MGM threw it away on the bottom half of double bills and didn't even give it a Manhattan opening), this fictionalized story of New York Giants manager John "Hans" Lobert gave Edward G. Robinson the starring role. It also was Robert Aldrich's first film as a director, had Lobert himself as "technical consultant," and offered the studio's resident dance star Vera-Ellen a straight dramatic role.

The film begins with veteran third baseman Hans Lobert finding himself in charge of the Florida training camp of the New York Giants. Among the rookie players he must whip into shape are Adam Polachuk, the son of a poor immigrant who'd wanted him to study law; Tippy Mitchell, a famed fast-baller's shy son

BIG LEAGUER: With Jeff Richards

BIG LEAGUER: With Vera-Ellen

BIG LEAGUER: With Jeff Richards

who'd rather be an architect than a first baseman; Julie Davis, a brash know-it-all from Hell's Kitchen; and Bobby Bronson, a showoff pitcher from Ohio. Lobert's niece (and assistant) Christy warns him that the Giants might shut the camp if he doesn't show better results this year, but he seems unconcerned. The four roommates survive the first "cut" but egos and personal problems begin sidetracking them, despite Lobert's fatherly gruffness. Ultimately, he turns one into a star, convinces another he simply doesn't have what it takes, loses one for whom he'd lost hope to the Dodgers. Christy falls for Adam, whose dad arrives to see him play in an exhibition game and goes away filled with pride. And Lobert prepares for another season and another batch of rookie hopefuls.

CRITICAL VIEWS

"A human interest story on the training of baseball-minded youth, [and] the presence of Edward G. Robinson helps bolster the presentation . . . [He] is good as the camp founder and believable in the hokum that has been mixed in with fact."—*Variety*

"The surprise of *Big Leaguer*, Aldrich's first film as director, is that such routine studio material should be so confidently and cleverly wrought. On the other hand, given the way Aldrich has consistently tackled the subject head on, it should not be so surprising that he has both respected his material and brought out rather than imposed its interesting formal and thematic elements."—*Monthly Film Bulletin* (1988)

VICE SQUAD

1953   United Artists

Producers, Jules Levy and Arthur Gardner; Director, Arnold Laven; Screenplay, Lawrence Roman; Based on the novel *Harness Bull* by Leslie T. White; Photography, Joseph C. Biroc; Art director, Carroll Clark; Music, Herschel Burke Gilbert; Editor, Arthur H. Nadel. 88 minutes

Captain Barnaby (*Edward G. Robinson*), Mona Ross (*Paulette Goddard*), Ginny (*K. T. Stevens*), Jack Hartrampf (*Porter Hall*), Marty Kusalich (*Adam Williams*), Al Barkis (*Edward Binns*), Pete Monte (*Lee Van Cleef*), Frankie Pierce (*Jay Adler*), Vickie Webb (*Joan Vohs*), Lt. Bob Imlay (*Dan Riss*), Carol Lawson (*Mary Ellen Kay*), Dwight Foreman (*Barry Kelley*), Detective Lacy (*Harlan Warde*), Policeman (*Murray*

VICE SQUAD:
With Porter Hall

Alper), Reporter (*Russ Conway*), Lou (*Robert Karnes*), Dutch (*Charles Tannen*), Detective at Lineup (*Edgar Dearing*), Lt. Ed Chisholm (*Lewis Martin*), Landlord (*Lee Phelps*), Mr. Jurner (*Percy Helton*), Mr. Lawson (*George Eldredge*), Fred (Desk Sergeant) (*Lennie Bremen*), Detective (*Paul Bryar*)

As a no-nonsense Captain of Detectives named Barnaby, Edward G. Robinson gives authority to this rather routine "just another day at the station house" drama, thwarting a swindling attempt of a not-too-wise middle-aged woman, attending early morning lineups for petty thieves and other suspects, setting up the machinery to stop a bank heist on a stoolie's tip, taking personal charge of the investigation involving a cop shooting by a pair of hoods. Also sashaying into the proceedings is one-time Paramount queen Paulette Goddard—having a tougher time than Robinson getting a good role in the early Fifties (and finally chucking it all to marry Erich Maria Remarque and live in luxury on a Swiss mountaintop)—as Mona, an escort bureau proprietress with wide underworld connections. It is through Mona and one of her girls that Barnaby gets the

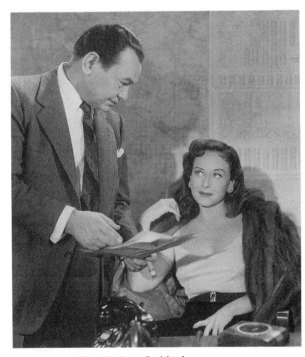

VICE SQUAD: With Paulette Goddard

VICE SQUAD: With Harlan Warde (left), Paul Bryar (right foreground) and players

165

THE GLASS WEB: With Kathleen Hughes

THE GLASS WEB

time as a captain of detectives plagued by a variety of cons, stoolies, gunmen and molls, and the problem of running down a cop-killing gang of bank robbers . . . Mr. Robinson's hands, to put it bluntly, are full, but he is always the typically grim, tolerant and terribly efficient officer."—A. H. Weiler, *The New York Times*

"Edward G. Robinson plays the tired captain with conviction and sour patience."—Paul V. Beckley, *New York Herald-Tribune*

THE GLASS WEB

1953   Universal-International

Producer, Albert J. Cohen; Director, Jack Arnold; Screenplay, Robert Blees and Leonard Lee; Based on the novel by Max S. Ehrlich; Photography, Maury Gertsman; Art directors, Bernard Herzbrun and Eric Orbom; Set decorators, Russell A. Gausman and Ruby A. Levitt; Gowns, B. V. Thomas; Music director, Joseph Gershenson; Sound, Leslie I. Carey and Robert Pritchard; Editor, Ted J. Kent. Filmed in 3-D. 81 minutes

Henry Hayes (*Edward G. Robinson*), Don Newell (*John Forsythe*), Louise Newell (*Marcia Henderson*), Paula Ranier (*Kathleen Hughes*), Dave Markson (*Richard Denning*), Lt. Stevens (*Hugh Sanders*), Sonia (*Jean Willes*), Jake (*Harry O. Tyler*), Bob Warren (*Clark Howat*), Other Man (*Paul Dubov*), Announcer (*John Hiestand*), Plainclothesman (*Bob Nelson*), Everett (*Dick Stewart*), Barbara Newell (*Jeri Lou James*), Jimmy Newell (*Duncan Richardson*), First Engineer (*Jack Kelly*), Waitress (*Alice Kelley*), Ad Lib (*Lance Fuller*), Lew (*Brett Halsey*), Mrs. O'Halloran (*Kathleen Freeman*), Viv (*Eve McVeagh*), Sally (*Beverly Garland*), Cliffie (*Jack Lomas*), Mrs. Doyle (*Helen Wallace*), Weaver (*Howard Wright*), Gilbert (Lawyer) (*Herbert C. Lytton*), Mr. Weatherby (*James Stone*), Fred Abbott (*John Verros*), Tramp Comic (*Benny Rubin*), Tourist (*Eddie Parker*), District Attorney (*Tom Greenway*), Paper Man (*Donald Kerr*)

The television game was the background for this convoluted noirish drama in which Edward G. Robinson, as Henry Hayes, a lonely, officious researcher and would-be writer for a weekly series that reenacts famous crimes, gets involved with and taken by a smart cookie—an ambitious, small-time actress clawing her way to the top—and knows too much about a fact-based murder. Filmed in 3-D for no particular reason, except

lead in his homicide investigation. That takes him to Marty Kusalich, whose two gunsels, Pete and Al, killed the cop while trying to steal a car for Kusalich's planned bank robbery. Barnaby and his vice squad round up the perpetrators and his day comes to a close—not much different, he decides, from other "ordinary" ones.

CRITICAL VIEWS

"Edward G. Robinson, who hasn't been around lately to glower at movie audiences, is back in harness, this to make it "in" during the era, *The Glass Web* was directed by Jack Arnold, one of Universal's house directors whose reputation has grown over the years through his 3-D sci-fi horror work on *It Came From Outer Space* (made just before this one) and *Creature From the Black Lagoon* (made just after it) as well as his later *The Incredible Shrinking Man*.

Hayes has been contributing to the luxury of femme fatale Paula Ranier, thinking he has a spot in her heart, only to discover that Don Newell, the head writer for the show, also is seeing her and is being blackmailed by her—the two had previously had a summer fling which he wishes to keep from his wife. Learning that he had been played for a patsy, Hayes, who secretly wants Newell's job, kills Paula in a fit of rage just before Newell shows up at her place. The cops' prime suspect is her estranged husband, with whom she had recently quarreled, but he comes up with an alibi, and the police are stymied.

Seeing a way to pin the rap on Newell, Hayes then sells the show's producer, Dave Markson, on the idea of using the murder case for reenactment on their weekly program case, and reluctantly Newell scripts it. Hayes also puts together a meticulously detailed script and gives it to Markson. However, in his plan to prove Newell's guilt, Hayes gives himself away by one mistake. Realizing that Newell knows that he is the murderer, Hayes traps him in an empty studio, but the police arrive and shoot him before he can kill Newell.

CRITICAL VIEWS

"The rats and the hoods and the killers came back to the Palace screen yesterday . . . The reintroduction of the traffic was provided with Universal's *The Glass Web*, a minor criminal excursion with Edward G. Robinson and John Forsythe as its stars . . . [Robinson] plays the

THE GLASS WEB: With John Forsythe and Richard Denning

THE GLASS WEB: With John Forsythe

BLACK TUESDAY

research expert for a TV crime show who murders a beautiful blonde number for giving him the air."—Bosley Crowther, *The New York Times*

"Edward G. Robinson meanders through the part of a studio technician who is in love with Kathleen Hughes, the TV actress out to get all she can."—Joe Pihodna, *New York Herald-Tribune*

"An inside look at the workings of a television studio gives an interesting background to *The Glass Web* . . . Robinson gives an excellent account of the frustrated researcher who feels his true worth isn't appreciated."—*Variety*

BLACK TUESDAY

1954   United Artists

A Leonard Goldstein Production; Producers, Leonard and Robert Goldstein; Director, Hugo Fregonese; Story and screenplay, Sydney Boehm; Photography, Stanley Cortez; Art director, Hilyard Brown; Set decorator, Al Spencer; Music, Paul Dunlap; Sound, Tom Lambert; Editor, Robert Golden. 80 minutes

Vincent Canelli (*Edward G. Robinson*), Peter Manning (*Peter Graves*), Hatti Combest (*Jean Parker*), Father Slocum (*Milburn Stone*), Joey Stewart (*Warren Stevens*), Frank Carson (*Jack Kelly*), Ellen Norris (*Sylvia Findley*), John Norris (*James Bell*), Dr. Hart (*Victor Perrin*), Lou Mehrtens (*Hal Baylor*), Boland (*Harry Bartell*), Parker (*Simon Scott*), Howard Sloane (*Russell Johnson*), Fiaschetti (*Philip Pine*), Donaldson (*Paul Maxey*), Collins (*William Schallert*), Selwyn (*Don Blackman*), Benny (*Dick Rich*)

Robinson was on back on the wrong side of the law in this prison picture throwback to the old Warner Bros. days. Working with Hugo Fregonese, the Argentine-born director making the last of 11 US movies during the 1950-54 period, he took sole above-the-title billing in this threadbare prison melodrama that at another time would have emerged as an acceptable made-for-

BLACK TUESDAY: With Peter Graves

BLACK TUESDAY:
With Jean Parker

television movie. He headed a cast that included future
TV names like Peter Graves (*Mission: Impossible*),
Milburn Stone (*Gunsmoke*) and Jack Kelly (*Maverick*)
as well as fading "B" movie queen Jean Parker—the gal
who perennially kept the likes of Richard Arlen and
Chester Morris apart.

Robinson stars as Vincent Canelli, a vicious death-
row resident whose days are numbered. Displaying his
usual arrogance, Canelli spends his time formulating a
daring scheme to beat Black Tuesday (the official execution day in New Jersey). Next Tuesday, he is scheduled
for the chair along with Peter Manning, another killer,
who hid his swag from a big bank robbery before being
captured. The night before his execution, Canelli has
his moll Hatti contact a death house guard with the
news that the latter's daughter Ellen has been kidnapped, and that the price of the ransom is his help in
springing Canelli.

Along with the reporters gathered for the execution is
Joey Stewart, one of Canelli's henchmen. In the ensuing breakout attempt, Joey kills the guard as Canelli
makes a bloody escape and goes to a deserted warehouse where Ellen and four others are being held,
among them a doctor who is forced to patch up Manning, wounded while fleeing. Next day, Manning
retrieves the stolen money from a safe-deposit box, but
the trail he leaves from the blood dripping from his
wounds leads the cops to the warehouse. Canelli threatens to kill his five hostages unless he and Manning are
given safe passage out. The cops refuse, and Canelli
sends out the first dead hostage. When Canelli, however, threatens the life of another, a priest, Manning
draws the line, gets into a fight with Canelli and kills
him. Then he heads downstairs, knowing he will probably be shot by the police.

CRITICAL VIEWS

"Edward G. Robinson plays his old, snarling, savage
self . . . In contrast to [his] wholesale sputtering, the
supporting cast of comparatively unfamiliar faces are
brought, one by one, into personal but perceptive focus
. . . It's a pleasure to see Mr. Robinson shedding his
good citizenship in such a colorful, lively show. But the
picture needs a good stool pigeon to tell us what makes
Eddie run."—Howard Thompson, *The New York Times*

"Mr. Robinson is still the old pro in this kind of thing
and at no point in this film imitates his own past portrayals but gives a fresh and convincing portrait of an
egomaniacal killer."—Paul V. Beckley, *New York Herald-Tribune*

"Edward G. Robinson makes a return to gang czar roles
in this story and has lost none of his menacing qualities."—*Variety*

"The players are handled with tact, and even the powerful histrionics of Edward G. Robinson are kept in
proper perspective. His performance is remarkable: in

THE VIOLENT MEN: With Barbara Stanwyck

THE VIOLENT MEN

1955   Columbia Pictures

Producer, Lewis J. Rachmil; Director, Rudolph Mate; Screenplay, Harry Kleiner; Based on the novel *Rough Company* by Donald Hamilton; Photography, Burnett Guffey and W. Howard Greene; Art directors, Ross Bellah and Carl Anderson; Set decorator, Louis Diage; Costumes, Jean Louis; Music, Max Steiner; Music director, Morris Stoloff; Editor, Jerome Thoms. CinemaScope and Technicolor. 96 minutes

John Parrish (*Glenn Ford*), Martha Wilkison (*Barbara Stanwyck*), Lew Wilkison (*Edward G. Robinson*), Judith Wilkison (*Dianne Foster*), Cole Wilkison (*Brian Keith*), Caroline Vail (*May Wynn*), Jim McCloud (*Warner Anderson*), Tex Hinkleman (*Basil Ruysdael*), Elena (*Lita Milan*), Wade Matlock (*Richard Jaeckel*), Magruder (*James Westerfield*), Derosa (*Jack Kelly*), Sheriff Martin Kenner (*Willis Bouchey*), Purdue (*Harry Shannon*), George Menefee (*Peter Hanson*), Jackson (*Don C. Harvey*), Tony (*Robo Bechi*), Dryer (*Carl Andre*), Hank Purdue (*James Anderson*), Mrs. Vail (*Katharine Warren*), Mr. Vail (*Tom Browne Henry*), Bud Hinkleman (*Bill Phipps*), Anchor Rider (*Edmund Cobb*), Mahoney (*Frank Ferguson*), Dr. Henry Crowell (*Raymond Greenleaf*)

In his first Western, his second Technicolor movie, and his third picture with Barbara Stanwyck (although the other two might not qualify since the veteran stars shared no scenes in *Flesh and Fantasy* and were together for only about ten seconds in two scenes with no dialogue in *Double Indemnity*), Edward G. Robinson took third billing in the first substantial film he had been offered in years. He played the crippled cattle baron, Lew Wilkison, whose grasping wife Martha has been carrying on an affair with his younger brother Cole, much to the disgust of daughter Judith. Wilkison has been trying to build an empire by driving small ranchers and farmers from the valley, but his henchmen push too hard when John Parrish, a pacifist disillusioned by the war, comes on the scene. Soon he is forced to take on Wilkison's gunslingers after one of Parrish's ranch hands is gunned down. Before long, two big ranch fires, a horse stampede and an ambush see the violent ends of Martha—who, for good measure, robbed Lew of his crutches and left him to die in their

THE VIOLENT MEN: With Barbara Stanwyck

THE VIOLENT MEN: With
Dianne Foster and Glenn
Ford

flaming ranch house—and Cole Wilkison. Lew is left
sadder but wiser without Judith, who has run off with
Parrish, and his home, family and empire in ruins.

CRITICAL VIEWS

"Columbia has pulled out all the levers in making *The
Violent Men*, a broad-beamed and action-crammed
western . . . Robinson is a brooding and bitter cripple
as a consequence of his last big range war [and] is spared
destruction, possibly because his performance is the
best. His survival is the only surprise worth mentioning
in his pell-mell color film."—Bosley Crowther, *The
New York Times*

"Robinson plays Little Caesar in buckskin. He has
moved from urban vice dens to the wide open spaces,
but henchmen still jump to do his bidding. Where once
the command was 'Put the body in cement and drop it
in the East River!,' now it's 'Clean out the valley! I don't
care if you have to burn every ranch and string up all the
ranchers!'"—William Zinsser, *New York Herald-Tribune*

THE VIOLENT MEN: With Barbara Stanwyck, Brian Keith and Glenn
Ford

171

TIGHT SPOT

1955   Columbia Pictures

Producer, Lewis J. Rachmil; Director, Phil Karlson; Screenplay, William Bowers; Based on the play *Dead Pigeon* by Lenard Kantor; Photography, Burnett Guffey; Art directors, Ross Bellah and Carl Anderson; Set decorator, Louis Diage; Costumes, Jean Louis; Music director, Morris Stoloff; Sound, John Livadary; Editor, Viola Lawrence. 97 minutes

Sherry Conley (*Ginger Rogers*), Lloyd Hallett (*Edward G. Robinson*), Vince Striker (*Brian Keith*), Prison Girl (*Lucy Marlow*), Benjamin Costain (*Lorne Greene*), Mrs. Willoughby (*Katherine Anderson*), Marvin Rickles (*Allen Nourse*), Fred Packer (*Peter Leeds*), Mississippi Mac (*Doye O'Dell*), Clara Moran (*Eve McVeagh*), Warden (*Helen Wallace*), Jim Hornsby (*Frank Gerstle*), Miss Masters (*Gloria Ann Simpson*), Carlyle (*Robert Shield*), Arny (*Norman Keats*), Harris (*Ed "Skipper" McNally*), Detective (*John Marshall*), Plainclothesman (*Will J. White*), Doctor (*Tom de Graffenried*), Judge (*Joseph Hamilton*), Bailiff (*Alan Reynolds*), Tonelli (*Alfred Linder*), 1st Detective (*John Larch*), 2nd Detective (*Ed Hinton*), TV Salesman (*Bob Hopkins*), Bit Girl Honeymooner (*Kathryn Grant*), Bit Man (*Erik Paige*), Bit Man (*Kevin Enright*), Bit Man (*Tom Greenway*), Bit Boy Honeymooner (*Robert Nichols*)

Edward G. Robinson, as tough U. S. Attorney Lloyd Hallett, took second billing to Ginger Rogers, as hardened gangland moll Sherry Conley, in this gangster flick adaptation of Lenard Kantor's short-lived 1953 Broadway play *Dead Pigeon*. The equally stage-bound film had much of the same crew (other than director and writer) who had previously worked on Robinson's *The Violent Men*. Sherry has been released from prison into Hallett's custody as a reluctant material witness in the pending trial of big-time gangster Benjamin Costain. Since there are no living witnesses to testify in court to Costain's criminal activities, Hallett hopes to break down Sherry's resistance in a plusher hotel setting.

Hallett, however, finds Sherry staunchly uncooperative until the police matron on duty at the hotel is killed while protecting her from the sniper shot of Costain's henchman. It also turns out that Vince Striker, the police detective assigned to guard her, and with whom she has a tentative romance, is in Costain's pay. At the last minute, he tries to save her from Costain's thugs but is killed for his troubles. At last Sherry tells Hallett she's ready to testify. When he asks her on the stand what her profession is, she replies, "gang buster."

CRITICAL VIEWS

"*Tight Spot* is a pretty good little melodrama, the kind

TIGHT SPOT: With Ginger Rogers

TIGHT SPOT: With Brian Keith

you keep rooting for as generally happened when Lenard Kantor's *Dead Pigeon* appeared on Broadway a while back . . . Miss Rogers' self-sufficiency throughout hardly suggests anybody's former scapegoat [but] Mr. Keith and Mr. Robinson are altogether excellent. . . . If Academy Awards aren't in order, neither are apologies."—Howard Thompson, *The New York Times*

"Eddie Robinson, in the relatively quiet part of the dis-

TIGHT SPOT: With Brian Keith and Ginger Rogers

trict attorney, once more proves what a really expert trouper he is. He has a wonderful authority in the scenes requiring it, but it's even more exciting to watch the skill with which he supports and builds the effects of the actors he is working with. His listening helps the audience to listen and the subtle methods by which he directs spectator attention make him the all-important underscoring factor in many of Ginger's big scenes."— Jack Moffitt, *The Hollywood Reporter*

"Robinson is very good as the Fed down to his last witness."—*Variety*

A BULLET FOR JOEY

1955   United Artists

Producers, Samuel Bischoff and David Diamond; Director, Lewis Allen; Screenplay, Geoffrey Homes and A. I. Bezzerides; Story, James Benson Nablo; Photography, Harry Neumann; Art director, Jack Okey; Music, Harry Sukman; Editor, Leon Barsha. 85 minutes

Inspector Raoul Leduc (*Edward G. Robinson*), Joe Victor (*George Raft*), Joyce Geary (*Audrey Totter*), Carl Macklin (*George Dolenz*), Fred (*Peter Hanson*), Eric Hartman (*Peter Van Eyck*), Mrs. Hartman (*Karen Verne*), Paola (*Ralph Smiley*), Dubois (*Henri Letondal*), Morrie (*John Cliff*), Nick (*Joseph Vitale*), Jack Allen (*Bill Bryant*), Paul (*Stan Malotte*),

TIGHT SPOT: With Lorne Greene, Ginger Rogers, Eve McVeagh, Allen Nourse

Yvonne Temblay (*Toni Gerry*), Marie (*Sally Blane*), Garcia (*Steven Geray*), Percy (*John Alvin*), Artist (*Bill Henry*), Bartender (*Frank Hagney*)

"Edward G. Robinson celebrates his 32nd year of stardom on the screen with *A Bullet for Joey*," the copy for this rather mundane thriller's promotion campaign touted. Teamed once again with a rather mellowed

A BULLET FOR JOEY: With George Raft

George Raft after 15 years, one-time tough guy Robinson is a police inspector with the Royal Canadian Mounted Police, out to get his man—exiled gangster Joe Victor, played by one-time tough guy Raft. Set against the backdrop of Montreal, this modestly budgeted feature has Inspector Raoul Leduc trying to tie together three murders, all seemingly connected with Carl Macklin, an atomic scientist targeted by the Commies for kidnapping and a journey behind the Iron Curtain. Joe Victor has been tapped by Eric Hartman, head of a spy ring, to be smuggled in from Lisbon to carry out the snatch with the help of his girlfriend, Joyce Geary, and some of his old mob. Victor's scheme is for Joyce to seduce Macklin and for Jack Allen, one of his gunsels, to make a play for Macklin's secretary, Yvonne Temblay. When Yvonne becomes too serious, however, Jack bumps her off. Meanwhile, Joyce has fallen for Macklin, complicating matters.

During this time, while tracing Yvonne's killer, Leduc trails Hartman and cronies to a ship ready to sail. Macklin already is on board, a drugged prisoner. Leduc and Victor shoot it out in a gun battle and the latter is killed. Quashing the caper, Leduc and his men round up the remaining members of the spy ring.

CRITICAL VIEWS

"Age cannot wither nor custom stale the infinite uniformity of Edward G. Robinson and George Raft . . . We only need scan the details of Mr. Raft's laying out

A BULLET FOR JOEY: With George Dolenz and Audrey Totter

the job and Mr. Robinson's patient checking on him every step of the way. These are the things Mr. Raft and Mr. Robinson can do with their eyes shut—and sometimes do."—Bosley Crowther, *The New York Times*

"The veterans of make-believe, mayhem, murder and other sordid crimes are Edward G. Robinson—in this case, a right guy—and George Raft, a fugitive called in to pull the big job."—Joe Pihodna, *New York Herald Tribune*

ILLEGAL

1955   Warner Bros.

ILLEGAL: With Jayne Mansfield, Ellen Corby and Nina Foch

Producer, Frank P. Rosenberg; Director, Lewis Allen; Screenplay, W. R. Burnett and James R. Webb; Based on the play *The Mouthpiece* by Frank J. Collins; Photography, J. Peverell Marley; Art director, Stanley Fleischer; Wardrobe, Moss Mabry; Music, Max Steiner; Sound, Stanley Jones; Editor, Thomas Reilly. 88 minutes

Victor Scott (*Edward G. Robinson*), Ellen Miles (*Nina Foch*), Ray Borden (*Hugh Marlowe*), Joe Knight (*Robert Ellenstein*), Edward Clary (*DeForest Kelley*), Joseph Carter (*Jay Adler*), Allen Parker (*James McCallion*), Ralph Ford (*Edward Platt*), Frank Garland (*Albert Dekker*), Andy Garth (*Jan Merlin*), Miss Henkel (*Ellen Corby*), Angel O'Hara (*Jayne Mansfield*), George Graves (*Clark Howat*), Taylor (*Henry Kulky*), Steve Harper (*Addison Richards*), E. A. Smith (*Howard St. John*), Al Carol (*Lawrence Dobkin*), Policeman (*George Ross*), Detectives (*John McKee, Larry Hudson*), Blonde Girl (*Kathy Marlowe*), Bailiff (*Ted Stanhope*), Judge (*Charles Evans*), Doctor (*Jonathan Hale*), Night Orderly (*Marjorie Stapp*), Third Guard (*Fred Coby*), Bartender (*Max Wagner*), Barfly (*John Cliff*), Jailer (*Henry Rowland*), Miss Worth (*Julie Bennett*), Woman (*Pauline Drake*), Miss Hathaway (*Roxanne Arlen*), Mr. Manning (*Archie Twitchell*), Phillips (*Stewart Nedd*), First Policeman (*Herb Vigran*), Second Policeman (*Chris Alcaide*)

Frank Collins' 1929 play *The Mouthpiece* had been filmed by Warners in 1931 with Warren William in the starring role and again nine years later (as *The Man Who*

ILLEGAL: With Charles Evans and Nina Foch

ILLEGAL: With Albert Dekker

Talked Too Much) with George Brent in the lead. Edward G. Robinson, in this third version, put his stamp on the role of the conscience-stricken district attorney who learned he sent an innocent man to the chair, took to drink, and then went into private practice as a defense attorney.

A star vehicle for Robinson, it also had such seasoned actors as Nina Foch, Hugh Marlowe, Albert Dekker, Ellen Corby and Jay Adler, as well as a pre-*Star Trek* DeForest Kelley and an on-the-verge-of-stardom Jayne Mansfield as a mobster's tootsie. Robinson plays Victor Scott, who, at the urging of his assistant, Ellen Miles, and his former investigator, Ray Borden, whom she has married, goes on the wagon and puts his legalistic knowledge to work as a tough defense lawyer. Racketeer Frank Garland is one of his first clients and he rapidly finds that he's become a mouthpiece for the mob. Garland, it seems, has had free reign for some time through inside help at the DA's office when Scott had the job. The finger, it turns out, points to Borden, who is on the take. Ellen discovers this and is forced to shoot her husband in self-defense when he makes an attempt on her life.

The new DA, believing Ellen to be an informer, puts her on trial for murder, and Scott antagonizes Garland by insisting on undertaking her defense. Garland orders a hit on Scott, but though wounded, he enters the courtroom with his star witness, Angel O'Hara, Garland's ex-mistress. Her testimony clears Ellen and incriminates Garland.

"We'd be willing to bet a nickel that the people who wrote and made Warner Bros.' *Illegal* had *The Asphalt Jungle* in mind and were doing their best to imitate it, difficult though that would be . . . [It] invades the higher echelons of crime, with a fast-thinking, double-dealing lawyer as the principal character . . . The fact that this hard-bitten lawyer is played by Edward G. Robinson in his old vein of stinging sarcasm is a clue to what you might expect."—Bosley Crowther, *The New York Times*

"Edward G. Robinson plays the swivel-hipped lawyer, who swings from the right side to the wrong side of the law and then reverses the field again to the right side."—Joe Pihodna, *New York Herald-Tribune*

ILLEGAL

HELL ON FRISCO BAY

1956   Warner Bros.

A Jaguar Production. Associate producer, George C. Bertholon; Director, Frank Tuttle; Screenplay, Sydney Boehm and Martin Rackin; Based on a *Collier's* story "The Darkest Hour" by William P. McGivern; Photography, John Seitz; Art director, John Beckman; Music, Max Steiner; Sound, Charles B. Lang; Editor, Folmar Blangsted. CinemaScope and WarnerColor. 98 minutes

Steve Rollins (*Alan Ladd*), Victor Amato (*Edward G. Robinson*), Marcia Rollins (*Joanne Dru*), Dan Bianco (*William Demarest*), Joe Lye (*Paul Stewart*), Kay Stanley (*Fay Wray*), Mario Amato (*Perry Lopez*), Anna Amato (*Renata Vanni*), Lou Fiaschetti (*Nestor Paiva*), Hammy (*Stanley Adams*), Lt. Neville (*Willis Bouchey*), Detective Connors (*Peter Hanson*), Bessie (*Tina Carver*), Brody Evans (*Rodney (Rod) Taylor*), Sebastion Pasmonick (*Anthony Caruso*), George Pasmonick (*Peter Votrian*), Father Larocca (*George J. Lewis*), Blonde (*Jayne Mansfield*), Landlady (*Mae Marsh*)

The only screen teaming of Edward G. Robinson and Alan Ladd was in this crime drama which Ladd chose for the second movie of his newly formed Jaguar Productions, working with Frank Tuttle (the director of his *This Gun for Hire* and *Lucky Jordan* back in 1942). Robinson is ruthless crime czar Victor Amato, who owns the San Francisco docks; Ladd is Steve Rollins, an embittered ex-cop who was framed for manslaughter

HELL ON FRISCO BAY: With Alan Ladd

and served five years for it. Rollins, now out, begins hunting for the man who put him behind bars and learns from an old waterfront boss, Lou Fiaschetti, that the frame was made by Amato. Rollins soon gets an offer to join Amato's gang, but goes with cop pal Dan Bianco to personally turn down the offer. Amato is not used to being rejected and orders his boys to ambush

HELL ON FRISCO BAY: With Nestor Paiva and Stanley Adams

HELL ON FRISCO BAY: With Paul Stewart and Fay Wray

HELL ON FRISCO BAY: With Joanne Dru

the pair as they leave. The henchman, however, ends up dead and Rollins collars Amato's cocky nephew, Mario, and works him over until he fingers the man who bumped off the material witness in the killing that sent Rollins to prison.

Learning that Mario has talked, Amato has his lieutenant, Joe Lye, take care of Mario, and then plans to take care of Lye himself. Kay Stanley, Lye's girlfriend,

NIGHTMARE: With Kevin McCarthy and Virginia Christine

finds Rollins and tells him she overheard Amato order Mario's death. She also admits to Rollins knowing enough about the earlier murders to clear him. Rollins goes after Amato, who is about to make his getaway in a speedboat, and while a wild battle is going on aboard in an exciting climactic chase, the boat crashes into a bridge piling. The police arrive to pull Rollins and Amato from the water. Amato is captured; Rollins is cleared.

In the cast were Paul Stewart, an old Robinson pal from the stage, as his trusted right hand; veteran star Fay Wray in an infrequent latter-day performance as an aging moll; and, in a tiny role, Jayne Mansfield once again.

CRITICAL VIEWS

"Thanks to Edward G. Robinson, who wears his role snugly as he wears his shoes, and to some sardonic dialogue written for him by Martin Rackin and Sydney Boehm, Warner Brothers' latest crime drama, *Hell on Frisco Bay*, is two or three cuts above the quality of the run of pictures in this hackneyed genre."—Bosley Crowther, *The New York Times*

"[In it] it is Robinson who reigns supreme. Even after all these years he is a fascinating boss, in his pearl gray homburg and gray silk vest, glaring out of settled eyes at a man he is soon to kill, flicking the ashes of an expensive cigar nonchalantly on the rug. His commands are edged with a sardonic wit, and he is quick to give a girl the back of his hand if she spurns his advance. This is the old meanie at the top of his form, relishing every black minute of his role."—William K. Zinsser, *New York Herald-Tribune*

"The resident devil is Edward G. Robinson, a sort of menace emeritus who is invited by Alan Ladd, a cop he once framed, to retire from the daily grind to a peaceful chair at San Quentin. Eddie replies at some length: 'Oh y-a-a-a-a-a-a?' . . . Cut to Mr. Robinson (in his role as Mr. Big), the ruthless killer of the San Francisco wharfs, and slowly this routine, senseless fable takes on a little flash and style . . . Every time Mr. Robinson slouches upon the scene, gnawing cigars and slobbering cynicisms, it is amusing, interesting—and good."—*Time*

NIGHTMARE

1956   United Artists

A Pine-Thomas Production. Producers, William Thomas and William Pine; Writer/Director, Maxwell Shane; Based on the short story by Cornell Woolrich; Photography, Joseph Biroc; Art director, Frank Sylos; Music, Herschel Burke Gilbert; Sound, Jack Solomon and Paul Wolff; Editor, George Gittens. 89 minutes

Rene Bressard (*Edward G. Robinson*), Stan Grayson (*Kevin*

NIGHTMARE: With Kevin McCarthy

McCarthy), Gina (*Connie Russell*), Sue Bressard (*Virginia Christine*), Torrence (*Rhys Williams*), Belnap (*Gage Clarke*), Warner (*Barry Atwater*), Madge (*Marian Carr*), Louie Simes (*Billy May*)

In this interesting but routinely presented new version of the Cornell Woolrich story (filmed by the same director in 1947 as *Fear in the Night*), Edward G. Robinson is cast as the detective brother-in-law of an increasingly terrified New Orleans jazz musician who discovers that his recurring dream of committing a bizarre murder isn't a dream at all.

Stan, the musician, finds himself unable to account for his strange feeling of having killed somebody, and a mysterious key and button in his hotel room add to his worry and confusion. He seeks help from Rene, the detective, to unravel the truth. Rene feels Stan's mood is based on his nervous condition, and not on fact, and to cheer him up, plans a picnic with Stan's girlfriend Gina (played by '50s pop singer Connie Russell) and Sue, Stan's sister and Rene's wife. Caught in a rainstorm the four take refuge in what seems to be a vacant house, but Rene's suspicions are aroused when Stan seems to know the place and takes Rene to the room in which a murder has been committed. This convinces

NIGHTMARE: With Kevin McCarthy

Rene that his brother-in-law is guilty and he urges Stan to flee. Stan tries suicide and Rene saves him, determining to prove his innocence.

Matching clues and information, Rene discovers that Stan's next door neighbor, Belnap, hypnotized him and used him to kill selected victims. To get Belnap to repeat the events, Rene and Stan stage a scene in the murder house and Belnap finally confesses. In the process, though, he again hypnotizes Stan and almost succeeds in drowning him. Saved at the last minute by Rene, Stan is ultimately cleared of all charges thanks to his brother-in-law the detective and his clever ruse in unmasking the real killer.

CRITICAL VIEWS

"Nightmares are sometimes induced by (a) mistakes in diet, (b) nervous disorders, (c) imperfect ventilation, or (d) cramped sleeping positions. But that's not the simple case with jazz musician Stan Grayson's *Nightmare* . . . And what a nightmare it was! It was enough to mix up even a Freud . . . This Pine-Thomas-Shane production is a modest melodrama with some crooked but neat performances by Messrs. Robinson and McCarthy, Connie Russell and Virginia Christine."—Milton Esterow, *The New York Times*

"Mr. Robinson does the best he can, as usual, with his lean material, but the fact is good acting does little more than remind one of the waste."—Paul V. Beckley, *New York Herald-Tribune*

NIGHTMARE: With Kevin McCarthy

THE TEN COMMANDMENTS

1956   Paramount Pictures

Producer and director, Cecil B. DeMille; Associate producer, Henry Wilcoxon; Screenplay, Aeneas MacKenzie, Jesse L. Lasky, Jr., Jack Gariss and Fredric M. Frank; Based on the novels *Prince of Egypt* by Dorothy Clarke Wilson, *Pillar of Fire* by Rev. J. H. Ingraham, and *On Eagle's Wings* by Rev. G. E. Southon, in accordance with The Holy Scriptures and the ancient texts of Josephus, Eusebius, Philo, The Midrash; Photography, Loyal Griggs; Additional photography, J. Peverell Marley, John Warren and Wallace Kelley; Art directors, Hal Pereira, Walter Tyler and Albert Nozaki; Costumes, Edith Head; Music, Elmer Bernstein; Choreography, LeRoy Prinz; Editor, Anne Bauchens. VistaVision and Technicolor. 221 minutes

Moses (*Charlton Heston*), Rameses (*Yul Brynner*), Nefretiri

THE TEN COMMANDMENTS: With Yul Brynner

THE TEN COMMANDMENTS:
With Debra Paget

THE TEN COMMANDMENTS

(*Anne Baxter*), Dathan (*Edward G. Robinson*), Sephora (*Yvonne De Carlo*), Lilia (*Debra Paget*), Joshua (*John Derek*), Sethi (*Sir Cedric Hardwicke*), Bithiah (*Nina Foch*), Yochabel (*Martha Scott*), Memnet (*Judith Anderson*), Baka (*Vincent Price*), Aaron (*John Carradine*), Jethro (*Eduard Franz*), Miriam (*Olive Deering*), Mered (*Donald Curtis*), Jannes (*Douglass Dumbrille*), Hur Ben Caleb (*Lawrence Dobkin*), Abiram (*Frank DeKova*), Korah (*Ramsay Hill*), Amminadab (*H. B. Warner*), Pentaur (*Henry Wilcoxon*), Elisheba (*Julia Faye*), Jethro's Daughter (*Lisa Mitchell*), Korah's Wife (*Joan Woodbury*), Simon (*Francis J. McDonald*), The Blind One (*John Miljan*), Rameses I (*Ian Keith*), King of Ethiopia (*Woodrow (Woody) Strode*), Slave Woman (*Dorothy Adams*), Commander of the Hosts (*Henry Brandon*), Amalekite Herder (*Touch (Michael) Connors*), Pretty Slave Girl (*Gail Kobe*), Foreman (*Fred Kohler Jr.*), Slave (*Kenneth MacDonald*), Fanbearer (*Addison Richards*), Lugal (*Onslow Stevens*), Sardinian Captain (*Clint Walker*), Wazir (*Frank Wilcox*), Old Hebrew—Moses' House (*Luis Alberni*), First Taskmaster (*Michael Ansara*), Hebrew at Golden Calf (*Zeev Bufman*), Slave (*Frankie Darro*), High Official (*Franklin Farnum*), Child Slave (*Kathy Garver*), Herald (*Walter Woolf King*), Old Man Praying (*Frank Lackteen*), Slave (*Carl Switzer*), Hebrew at Golden Calf (*Robert Vaughn*), Cretan Ambassador (*John Hart*)

The movie that brought Edward G. Robinson back to "A" films couldn't have been bigger. And it was all thanks to Cecil B. DeMille. "No more conservative or patriarchal figure existed in Hollywood, no one more opposed to Communism or any permutation or combinations thereof. And no fairer one, no man with a greater sense of decency and justice," Robinson wrote in his autobiography. "Cecil B. DeMille returned me to films. Cecil B. DeMille restored my self-respect." In preparing for his biggest production, *The Ten Commandments*, DeMille overruled his associates that Robinson was, under the circumstances, unacceptable, and ordered them to offer him the part of Dathan, the traitorous Hebrew overseer who betrayed Moses, who is then exiled into the desert with his people by Rameses. It is also Dathan who, during the forty-day absence of Moses and Joshua as they ascend the mountain to receive the Ten Commandments, plots a return to Egypt and whips the multitude into a frenzy of fear, forcing Moses' brother Aaron to make them a Golden Calf to worship.

The Ten Commandments, which DeMille had produced once before in 1923, would be the highlight of his career and the last movie he directed. (Unable because of health problems to move forward with his next production, his remake of *The Buccaneer*, he turned the directorial reigns over to his son-in-law, Anthony Quinn.) The film won Academy Award nominations as Best Picture, for Color Cinematography, Film Editing, Color Art Direction, Color Costume Design and Sound Recording. It lost to *Around the World in 80 Days* in the first three categories and to *The King and I* in the last three.

THE TEN COMMANDMENTS: On the set

THE TEN COMMANDMENTS: With Charlton Heston and Israelites

183

"Mr. DeMille has worked photographic wonders. And his large cast of characters is very good, from Sir Cedric Hardwicke as a droll and urbane Pharaoh to Edward G. Robinson as a treacherous overlord."—Bosley Crowther, *The New York Times*

"This new version of DeMille's silent saga, *The Ten Commandments*, overwhelms its audience, it's that big. Pictorially it is greatly impressive, dwarfing all cinematic things that have gone before it . . . Competent work is done by Edward G. Robinson as the evil Hebrew."—*Variety*

A HOLE IN THE HEAD

1959   United Artists

A Sincap Production; Producer and director, Frank Capra; Co-producer, Frank Sinatra; Screenplay, Arnold Shulman; Based on his play; Photography, William H. Daniels; Art director, Edward Imazu; Set decorator, Fred MacLean; Costumes, Edith Head; Music, Nelson Riddle; Songs, "High Hopes" and "All My Tomorrows" by Sammy Cahn and James Van Heusen; Sound, Fred Lau; Editor, William Hornbeck. CinemaScope and DeLuxe Color. 120 minutes

Tony Manetta (*Frank Sinatra*), Mario Manetta (*Edward G. Robinson*), Ally Manetta (*Eddie Hodges*), Mrs. Rogers (*Eleanor Parker*), Shirl (*Carolyn Jones*), Sophie Manetta (*Thelma Ritter*), Jerry Marks (*Keenan Wynn*), Dorine (*Joi Lansing*), Mendy (*George DeWitt*), Julius Manetta (*Jimmy Komack*), Fred (*Dub Taylor*), Miss Wexler (*Connie Sawyer*), Mr. Diamond (*Benny Rubin*), Sally (*Ruby Dandridge*), Hood (*B. S. Pully*), Alice (*Joyce Nizzari*), Master of Ceremonies (*Pupi Campo*)

After having been off the screen for two years while starring on Broadway in *Middle of the Night*, Robinson came back to take second billing to ring-a-ding-ding era Frank Sinatra (and playing Frank's sensible but dull older brother!) in Frank Capra's production of Arnold Shulman's stage comedy, *A Hole in the Head*. The Jewish family of the original play (Paul Douglas and David Burns had roles taken on the film by Sinatra and Robinson) became the Italian Manettas because, presumably it was more convenient to make Robinson Italian than Sinatra Jewish—and besides, it was Sinatra's movie.

Edward G. Robinson is Mario Manetta, a New York clothing manufacturer, who is called upon by his improvident, devil-may-care younger brother Tony, a 40-year-old widower who lives with a young son, Ally, in a run-down Miami Beach hotel he owns. Tony is asking for help to bail him out when the place is threatened with foreclosure. Leaving his business in the hands of his own inept son, Julius, Mario flies South with his wife, Sophie, learns the truth about Tony's wheeling and dealing and scheming to become a big promoter, and turns down his requests for money. However, Mario does offer to assist him, if Tony will give up the hotel, start a practical business in the Bronx, and consider marrying Mrs. Rogers, a very attractive widow who'd always had a thing for Tony.

Although interested in Mrs. Rogers, Tony refuses Mario's offer. Instead, he contacts his old crony Jerry Marks who has hit the big time, but gets another turn down. Ultimately, Tony decides to send Ally off with Mario and Sophie, telling the boy he no longer wants him. But then he has a change of heart. Ally comes back to his dad, who decides to marry Mrs. Rogers, leaving Mario and Sophie free to try to rescue their clothing business from their klutzy son.

A HOLE IN THE HEAD: With Thelma Ritter

A HOLE IN THE HEAD: With Frank Sinatra, Eleanor Parker and Thelma Ritter

A HOLE IN THE HEAD: With Thelma Ritter and Frank Sinatra

In his autobiography, *The Name Above the Title*, Frank Capra observed: "Sinatra plays his best scenes *without* rehearsing, and Robinson plays his best scenes after an hour of rehearsing. If I rehearse them together they'll wreck each other. So I rehearse Robinson with someone else playing Sinatra's lines. Robinson says 'No!' Sinatra *must* rehearse with him. I say, I'll tell Sinatra what to do, not Robinson. So Eddie ups and runs and says he'll quit. If he does, he's a damn fool. He's great in the picture." Capra eventually struck a compromise. "It was a happy picture from then on, so happy that I think neither Sinatra nor Robinson—nor Thelma Ritter for that matter—ever gave a warmer or better performance."

A Hole in the Head had a convoluted history. Written in 1950, it had a tryout at the Westport Country Playhouse in Connecticut under the title *My Fiddle Has Three Strings*. Maureen Stapleton and J. Edward Bromberg starred and Lee Strasberg directed. It was rewritten for television in 1956 as *The Heart's a Forgotten Hotel* with Edmond O'Brien and Sylvia Sidney, with Arthur Penn directing. It ultimately opened on Broadway in 1957 and had a middling run as *A Hole in the Head* and later became a summer stock item. The Sinatra-Robinson movie followed. In 1968, it was resurrected as the Broadway musical *Golden Rainbow* with Steve Lawrence and Eydie Gorme. The film version, Capra's penultimate movie, remains best known not for

the performances but for the Oscar-winning song "High Hopes."

CRITICAL VIEWS

"[It] does have two yeasty performances by Thelma Ritter and Edward G. Robinson as the brother and sis-

185

A HOLE IN THE HEAD: With Jimmy Komack and Thelma Ritter

SEVEN THIEVES: With Joan Collins

ter-in-law who bail Frank Sinatra out of his financial difficulties in Florida . . . As entertainment, it owes most of its success to Miss Ritter and Robinson, whose sense of timing in dialogue is fascinating to watch."—Paul V. Beckley, *New York Herald Tribune*

"As the brother, a narrow-minded dullard, Edward G. Robinson is superb; funny while being most officious and withering while saying the drollest things."—Bosley Crowther, *The New York Times*

SEVEN THIEVES

1960   20th Century-Fox

Producer, Sydney Boehm; Director, Henry Hathaway; Screenplay, Sydney Boehm; Based on the novel *Lions at the Kill* by Max Catto; Photography, Sam Leavitt; Art directors, Lyle Wheeler and John DeCuir; Set decorators, Walter M. Scott and Stuart A. Reiss; Costumes, Bill Thomas; Music, Dominic Frontiere; Sound, Charles Peck and Harry M. Leonard; Editor, Dorothy Spencer. CinemaScope. 102 minutes.

Paul Mason (*Rod Steiger*), Theo Wilkins (*Edward G. Robin-*

son), Melanie (*Joan Collins*), Poncho (*Eli Wallach*), Louis (*Michael Dante*), Raymond Le May (*Alexander Scourby*), Hugo Baumer (*Berry Kroeger*), Director of Casino (*Sebastian Cabot*), Duc Di Salins (*Marcel Hillaire*), Chief of Detectives (*John Berardino*), Governor (*Alphonse Martell*), Seymour (*Jonathan Kidd*), Governor's Wife (*Marga Ann Deighton*)

Robinson, back in harness as a star and getting second billing, was the mastermind of an elaborate casino heist in this underrated thriller, his lone film with director Henry Hathaway. He's aging American gangster Theo Wilkins, hoping to pull off one last grand coup before he dies, and putting together a sensational plot to rob the casino at Monte Carlo of $4-million, enlisting the aid of six others.

Accordingly, Melanie, a stripper, inveigles the casino director's secretary, Raymond Le May, into arranging for the others' admittance on the night of the Governor's Ball. While Paul Mason, Theo's right arm, and Louis, a safecracker, break into the vaults, Theo himself poses as the personal physician of an eccentric wheelchair-bound millionaire, The Baron, impersonated by Melanie's partner, Poncho. The Baron has a "heart attack" at the tables, is pronounced dead by his doctor, and is taken to the director's office where Paul and Louis are waiting with the stolen money. The loot is then stuffed into the "corpse's" wheelchair, and despite

SEVEN THIEVES: With Rod Steiger, Joan Collins and Eli Wallach

several setbacks, the thieves make a successful getaway in an ambulance driven by their cohort Hugo Baumer.

On the way Poncho "revives," only to discover that

SEVEN THIEVES: With Joan Collins and Rod Steiger

Theo, for whom the excitement has proven too much, has suffered a fatal heart attack. Melanie, who has fallen in love with Paul, suddenly realizes that he is Theo's son. Paul discovers that the stolen money is in large, new, serialized bills, and useless to them, and he forces the others, already fighting among themselves, to return the boodle to the casino. After leaving the valise with the money in the checkroom, Paul and Melanie stop briefly at the roulette table, make a small bet and win big.

CRITICAL VIEWS

"Simply as entertainment, it is altogether good—well-conceived for suspense and excitement, well directed by Henry Hathaway, and well-played . . . Edward G. Robinson and Rod Steiger do have the most elaborate roles, but Mr. Wallach, Miss Collins and Mr. Scourby support them manfully and womanly."—Bosley Crowther, *The New York Times*

"[It] does not come up to the expectations one would reasonably have of a crime suspense movie aided by Edward G. Robinson, Rod Steiger and Eli Wallach."—Paul V. Beckley, *New York Herald-Tribune*

PEPE

1960   Columbia Pictures

Producer and director, George Sidney; Associate producer, Jacques Gelman; Screenplay, Dorothy Kingsley and Claude Binyon; Story, Leonard Spigelgass and Sonya Levien; Based on the play *Broadway Magic* by Ladislas Bus-Fekete; Photography, Joe MacDonald; Art director, Ted Haworth; Set decorator, William Kiernan; Costumes, Edith Head; Music supervisor, Johnny Green; Special musical material, Sammy Cahn and Roger Edens; Songs, Andre Previn and Dory Langdon; Choreography, Eugene Loring and Alex Romero; Editors, Viola Lawrence and Al Clark. Technicolor. 195 minutes

Pepe (*Cantinflas*), Ted Holt (*Dan Dailey*), Suzie Murphy (*Shirley Jones*), Rodruguez (*Carlos Montalban*), Lupita (*Vicki Trickett*), Dancer (*Matt Mattox*), Manager (*Hank Henry*), Carmen (*Suzanne Lloyd*), Jewelry Salesman (*Stephen Bekassy*), Waitress (*Carol Douglas*), Priest (*Francisco Reguerra*), Charro (*Joe Hyams*), Immigration Inspector

PEPE: With Greer Garson

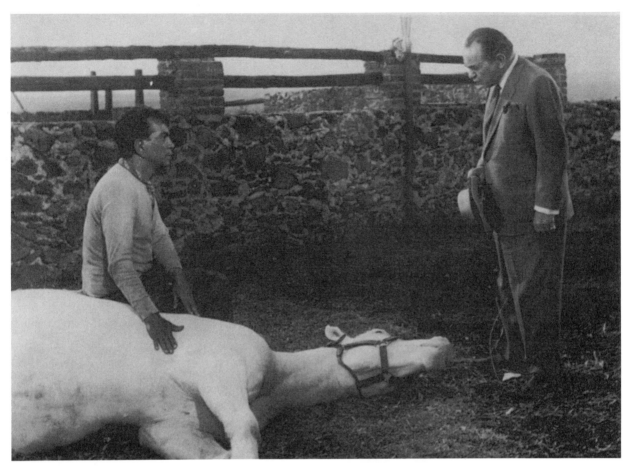

PEPE: With Cantinflas

(*Ernie Kovacs*), Studio Gateman (*William Demarest*), And (as themselves): (*Maurice Chevalier, Bing Crosby, Michael Callan, Tony Curtis, Richard Conte, Bobby Darin, Sammy Davis, Jr., Jimmy Durante, Zsa Zsa Gabor, voice of Judy Garland, Greer Garson, Hedda Hopper, Joey Bishop, Peter Lawford, Janet Leigh, Jack Lemmon, Dean Martin, Jay North, Kim Novak, Andre Previn, Donna Reed, Debbie Reynolds, Edward G. Robinson, Cesar Romero, Frank Sinatra, Billie Burke, Ann B. "Schultzy" Davis, Jack Entratter, Col. E. E. Fogelson, Jane Robinson, Bunny Waters, Charles Coburn*).

Joining 32 other "guest stars" in this Cantinflas comedy adventure (his only American movie other than the similarly stellar *Around the World in 80 Days*), Edward G. Robinson has several scenes. He is a movie producer who buys, from film director Ted Holt (Dan Dailey), the beloved stallion that is the object of an odyssey by Pepe, a Mexican ranchhand, that takes him to Las Vegas and Hollywood. Holt has sold the horse to Robinson to finance a film project, but at film's end, refuses to sell control of his movie back to Robinson unless Robinson returns the horse to Pepe. Wandering in and out of this bare bones "plot" in this overblown three hour and fifteen minute movie are the other entertainment business names who cross paths with Pepe.

CRITICAL VIEWS

"The rare and wonderful talents of Mexican comedian Cantinflas . . . are pitifully spent and dissipated amid a great mass of Hollywooden dross in the over-sized, over-peopled *Pepe* . . . What we mean, simply, is you won't 'find' the spirited comedian in these scenes. You will merely see a patient shadow of the real Cantinflas. Nor will you see him in the lengthy stretches of 'plot,' wherein Dan Dailey as the booze-bogged film director spars with Edward G. Robinson, as a producer, and jousts with a Hollywood hopeful, Shirley Jones."—Bosley Crowther, *The New York Times*

"When Robinson sees the completed film (within a film), he assures Dailey: 'Nothing to worry about. Pure entertainment.' Which may hint at the credos of screenwriters Dorothy Kingsley and Claude Binyon and of producer-director George Sidney."—Paul V. Beckley, *New York Herald-Tribune*

MY GEISHA: With Shirley MacLaine

MY GEISHA

1961   Paramount Pictures

A Sachiko Production; Producer, Steve Parker; Director, Jack Cardiff; Screenplay, Norman Krasna; Photography, Shunichiro Nakao; Art directors, Hal Pereira, Arthur Lonergan and Makoto Kikuchi; Costumes, Edith Head; Music, Franz Waxman; Song "You Are Sympathy to Me" by Franz Waxman and Hal David; Sound, Harold Lewis and Charles Grenzbach; Editor, Archie Marshek. Technirama and Technicolor. 120 minutes

Lucy Dell (alias Yoko Mori) (*Shirley MacLaine*), Paul Robaix (*Yves Montand*), Sam Lewis (*Edward G. Robinson*), Bob Moore (*Bob Cummings*), Kazumi Ito (*Yoko Tani*), Kenichi Takata (*Tatsuo Saito*), Amatsu Hisako (*Tamae Kiyokawa*), Kaida (*Ichi Hayakawa*), Leonard Lewis (*Alex Gerry*), Shiga (*Tsugundo Maki*), Maid (*Satoko Kuni*), Geisha (*Kazue Kaneko*), Geisha (*Junko Aoki*), Head Waitress (*Nariko Muramatsu*), Geisha (*Akemi Shimomura*), Geisha (*Mayumi Momose*), Geisha (*Kyoko Takeuchi*), Head Waitress (*Akiko Tsuda*), Bob's Girlfriend (*Marion Furness*), Butler (George) (*George Furness*)

This amiable romantic comedy provided Edward G. Robinson with a rather thankless role, once again as a movie producer, in a star vehicle assembled around Shirley MacLaine by her then-husband Steve Parker, whose base of operations in the entertainment business was in the Far East. The film, if nothing else, provided Robinson with a showcase for his deft scene-stealing of which he took full advantage, as well as a free trip to Japan.

Playing Sam Lewis, father confessor and good friend of film star Lucy Dell, he accompanies her to Tokyo as she attempts to win back her husband, Paul Robaix, a movie director fed up with being known as "Mr. Dell" and anxious to make a "new wave" film of *Madama Butterfly* starring an unknown geisha. Lucy decides to disguise herself under a black wig, don a kimono, and audition for the part—which she gets at the expense of a long line of Japanese actresses. Sam Lewis' (and Edward G. Robinson's) role then merely becomes that of a sounding board for Lucy; a chaperone to make certain her wolf of a leading man, Bob Moore, keeps his hands off of her; a matchmaker to bring Lucy and Paul together again; and in effect simply to add an extra dollop of class to a perfectly harmless, moderately amusing but visually stunning movie.

MY GEISHA: With Bob Cummings, Yves Montand and Shirley MacLaine

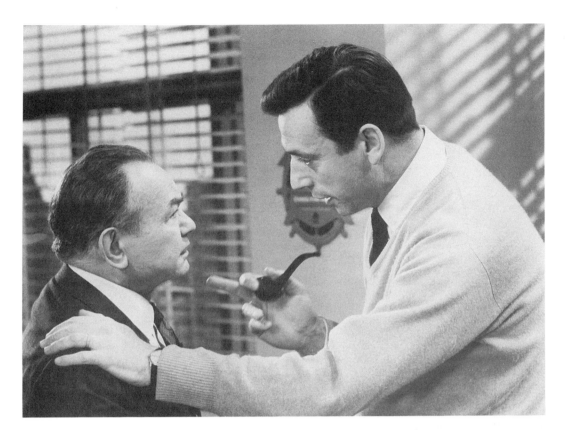

MY GEISHA:
With Yves Montand

My Geisha, filmed on location in and around Tokyo in late 1960 and early 1961, premiered in the Far East and played elsewhere in the world toward the end of that year but did not make it to the U.S. until mid-1962. It was, for a number of years, the last of Yves Montand's four Hollywood films—despite being made in the Orient—and the first in many years for veteran actor Robert Cummings (now calling himself Bob) after a lengthy stint or two in television. For costumer Edith Head, there was an Oscar nomination. For Robinson, it was a diverting stage wait.

CRITICAL VIEWS

"[It is] a visually beautiful if only temporarily convincing romantic comedy drama . . . amiable and easy on the eyes and ears, but unfortunately it does not have too much to say that hasn't been said before this troupe made its trek to Japan . . . Edward G. Robinson takes the role of [MacLaine's] understanding producer-mentor in casual but effective stride."—A. H. Weiler, *The New York Times*

"Much of it reminds you of television situation comedy, which is endurable only to those fascinated by the personalities of the players."—Paul V. Beckley, *New York Herald-Tribune*

"It is perhaps a tribute to the cast that the film often

MY GEISHA: With Shirley MacLaine

191

TWO WEEKS IN ANOTHER TOWN: With Claire Trevor

appears less crass and vulgar than it might have been: Edward G. Robinson gives his customary relaxed and beautifully timed performance."—*Monthly Film Bulletin*

TWO WEEKS IN ANOTHER TOWN

1962   Metro-Goldwyn-Mayer

Producer, John Houseman; Associate producer, Ethel Winant; Director, Vincente Minnelli; Screenplay, Charles Schnee; Based on the novel by Irwin Shaw; Photography, Milton Krasner; Art directors, George W. Davis and Urie McCleary; Set decorators, Keogh Gleason and Henry Grace; Wardrobe, Walter Plunkett; Music, David Raksin; Special visual effects, Robert R. Hoag; Sound, Franklin Milton; Editors, Adrienne Fazan and Robert J. Kern, Jr. CinemaScope and Metrocolor. 107 minutes

Jack Andrus (*Kirk Douglas*), Maurice Kruger (*Edward G. Robinson*), Carlotta (*Cyd Charisse*), Davie Drew (*George Hamilton*), Veronica (*Dahlia Lavi*), Clara Kruger (*Claire Trevor*), Brad Byrd (*James Gregory*), Barzelli (*Rosanna Schiaffino*), Janet Bark (*Joanna Roos*), Lew Jordan (*George Macready*), Tucino (*Mino Doro*), Zeno (*Stefan Schnabel*), Assistant Director (*Vito Scotti*), Dr. Cold Eyes (*Tom Palmer*),

TWO WEEKS IN ANOTHER TOWN: With Claire Trevor

192

Ravinski (*Erich Von Stroheim, Jr.*), Chanteuse (*Leslie Uggams*), Noel O'Neill (*Janet Lake*), Signora Tucino (*Joan Courtenay*), Liz (*Margie Liszt*), 1st Henchman (*Franco Corsaro*), 2nd Henchman (*Edward Colmans*), German Tourist (*Edit Angold*), Soundman (*Don Orlando*), George Jarrett (*Red Perkins*), Electrician (*Albert Carrier*), Sound Engineer (*James Garde*), Cameraman (*Alberto Morin*), Chinese Sister (*Beulah Quo*), Lady Godiva (*Cilly Feindt*), 1st Bar Girl (*Lilyan Chauvin*), 2nd Bar Girl (*Ann Molinari*), Bouncers (*Charles Horvath, John Indrisano*), Ad Libs in Lounge (*Benito Prezia, Tony Randall, Joe Dante*)

Two Weeks in Another Town, a companion piece of sort to—and sadly, several pegs below—the 1952 *The Bad and the Beautiful* (same producer, director, star, writer and composer), brought Edward G. Robinson to MGM once again with an exceptionally strong role in a series

TWO WEEKS IN ANOTHER TOWN: With Rosanna Schiaffino

of major parts over the next few years. Taking second billing to Kirk Douglas, Robinson was reunited with Claire Trevor (they had co-starred in the 1930s in *The Amazing Dr. Clitterhouse*, in the 1940s in *Key Largo*, and she was the first Lorelei Kilbourne to his Steve Wilson on radio's "Big Town"). They played a fading film director and his possessive wife, Maurice and Clara Kruger. Maurice has been given a film to shoot in Rome but things on the set are getting out of control, between his egotistical, demanding leading man, Davie Drew, who thinks his director to be an old fool who doesn't have it anymore, and his tempestuous leading lady, Barzelli, whose command of the English language is wanting. The film is running far behind schedule and over budget and the producer is on Kruger's back. In desperation, he turns to old protegé Jack Andrus, a washed-up, alcoholic actor just out of a stay in a New England sanitarium, and offers him the job of dubbing the film.

Andrus comes on board bringing with him all the old megalomania and braggadocio that had made him a major but obnoxious star earlier. And then his ex-wife Carlotta turns up in Rome to prove that she can still dominate him. Their tenuous relationship gives Kruger added pause. Throwing an anniversary party for his shrewish wife Clara, Kruger is accused by her of having an affair with Barzelli, and a few hours afterward, the harried director has a heart attack. Andrus is again prevailed upon, this time to finish directing Kruger's movie, and he rises to the challenge. Although he salvages the film, he incurs the wrath of his mentor, Kruger, who is bitterly aware of his own failure. Andrus, however, survives the professional and emotional attack, and now free of Kruger, he sets off for Hollywood and a new career in directing.

Among the actors, Robinson received the best reviews—at this point, almost by tradition. It was his only movie with Vincente Minnelli, himself coming to the end of his illustrious MGM career (he'd make only two more films for the studio, and three elsewhere), and also his only teaming with Kirk Douglas, from the next generation of movie tough guys.

CRITICAL VIEWS

"The 'other town' is Rome, where an Italo-American co-production is under way—a penny-pinching, coldly calculated affair that is being ineptly directed by a frightened has-been . . . tellingly played by Edward G. Robinson [who] grinds out footage to the best of his dwindling ability [and] knows that his work can be taken away from him at any time and completed by other, unsympathetic hands."—Hollis Alpert, *Saturday Review*

TWO WEEKS IN ANOTHER TOWN: With Kirk Douglas and Claire Trevor

"*Two Weeks in Another Town* [is] a drippy drama on a theme of degradation . . . As the expatriate American director, [Edward G.] Robinson snarls and gives but the barest impression of a human being in genuine distress."—Bosley Crowther, *The New York Times*

"Only remotely life-like characters in the story are Robinson and Claire Trevor as an ambiguous married couple whose personalities transform under the secretive cover of night. But the characters are as despicable as they are complex, and the film is desperately in need of simpler, nicer people. Robinson and Miss Trevor, two reliable performers, do all they can with the roles."—*Variety*

"*Two Weeks in Another Town* is filled with fascinating incident and sharply sophisticated relationships. Minnelli's flair for melodrama and heightened characterization has never been more apparent: Robinson and Trevor squabbling with each other, acidly cutting at every opportunity; and then, in bed at night, he starts to weep self-pityingly and she mothers him like a small child—it is a devastating scene."—Peter Bogdanovich, *Film Culture*

SAMMY GOING SOUTH

SAMMY GOING SOUTH

(*in the U.S.*, A BOY TEN FEET TALL)

1963   British Lion/Bryanston-Seven Arts

A Michael Balcon Production; Producer, Hal Mason; Director, Alexander Mackendrick; Screenplay, Denis Cannan; Based on the novel by W. H. Canaway; Photography, Erwin Hillier; Art director, Edward Tester; Music, Tristram Carey; Second-unit photography, Norman Warwick; Sound, H. L. Bird; Editor, Jack Harris. Cinema Scope and Eastman Color. 128 minutes. (U.S. running time: 88 minutes)

Cocky Wainwright (*Edward G. Robinson*), Sammy Hartland (*Fergus McClelland*), Gloria von Imhoff (*Constance Cummings*), Lem (*Harry H. Corbett*), Spyros Dracondopolous (*Paul Stassino*), The Syrian (*Zia Mohyeddin*), Abu Lubaba (*Orlando Martins*), Heneker (*John Turner*), Aunt Jane (*Zena Walker*), District Commissioner (*Jack Gwillim*), Cathie (*Patricia Donahue*), Bob (*Jared Allen*), Doctor (*Guy Deghy*), Hassan (*Marne Maitland*), Egyptian Policeman (*Steven Scott*), Head Porter (*Frederick Schiller*)

In Great Britain for this colorful, delightful film version of W. H. Canaway's adventure tale of a young boy who is orphaned and off on an odyssey to find his aunt in

SAMMY GOING SOUTH: With Fergus McClelland

195

SAMMY GOING SOUTH: With Zena Walker

South Africa, Edward G. Robinson was given top billing for star power, but it was Fergus McClelland—an unknown then and since—who had the title role and the lion's share of the movie. Robinson began the movie in Nairobi, but a serious heart attack forced the producers to close it down, with the promise to wait for him. Doctors insisted that the rest of his scenes be done in Britain as the 9,000-foot altitude in Africa would be too much for him. It was to be nearly two years before the movie got to the United States, released by Paramount Pictures as *A Boy Ten Feet Tall*, and shorn of nearly 40 minutes of footage (since restored for television showings).

Robinson turns up mid-journey as grizzled Cocky Wainright, an old-time hunter and diamond smuggler, who comes upon adventuresome ten-year-old Sammy Hartland—orphaned during the Suez War and making his way to Durban to find his Aunt Jane. The two get along famously, with Sammy telling Cocky about his journey thus far—there were a sinister Syrian peddler with whom he trekked to Luxor and who was shackled to the boy after being blinded; a rich American lady tourist who proposed to take him north by train while he insisted on going south; her Greek guide who tried to waylay the lad and then demand a ransom from his patron; and now Cocky, his pal from the Bush. And there's Cocky, regaling the boy about his golden past.

The police, however, close in on Cocky and the boy and Cocky's pilot associate Lem, who has flown in to pick up another batch of stolen diamonds. Lem flies off, Cocky is nabbed and Sammy escapes into the jungle.

At police headquarters, Cocky wills his fortune to young Sammy, and then gets the assurance of Aunt Jane, who has come for the boy, that she will allow Sammy to finish his journey on his own. Back in Durban, she is there to meet the boy/man after his arduous trek.

Other than Edward G. Robinson, the sole American in the cast is expatriate veteran Constance Cummings, as the rich lady who takes a shine to young Sammy.

CRITICAL VIEWS

"It's been a long time since Alexander Mackendrick directed a film and even longer since he and Sir Michael Balcon worked together. Watching *Sammy Going South*, however, one gets the feeling that time has stood still . . . [but] it is left to Edward G. Robinson, with a Hemingway fringe of whiskers, to bring a welcome injection of personality, robust and professional."—*Monthly Film Bulletin* (1963)

"With the exception of Robinson, looking like a slightly junior Ernest Hemingway, and Paul Stassino, as a glib

196

SAMMY GOING SOUTH

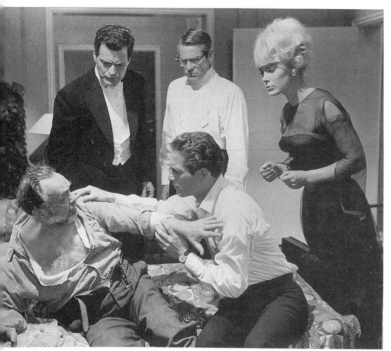

THE PRIZE: With Sergio Fantoni, Kevin McCarthy, Paul Newman and Elke Sommer

THE PRIZE: With Paul Newman

crook of a guide, the others are cardboard."—*Variety* (1963)

"Most fortunately, indeed, at about mid-point, that wonderful old actor, Edward G. Robinson saunters into view as a grizzled, warm-hearted diamond smuggler, and gives the picture its real substance."—Howard Thompson, *The New York Times* (1965)

THE PRIZE

1963   Metro-Goldwyn-Mayer

A Roxbury Production; Producer, Pandro S. Berman; Associate producer, Kathryn Hereford; Director, Mark Robson; Screenplay, Ernest Lehman; Based on the novel by Irving Wallace; Photography, William H. Daniels; Art directors, George W. Davis and Urie McCleary; Set decorators, Henry Grace and Dick Pefferle; Wardrobe, Bill Thomas; Makeup, William Tuttle; Music, Jerry Goldsmith; Special visual effects, J. McMillan Johnson, A. Arnold Gillespie and Robert R. Hoag; Editor, Adrienne Fazan. Panavision and Metrocolor. 135 minutes

Andrew Craig (*Paul Newman*), Dr. Max Stratman (*Edward G. Robinson*), Inger Lisa Andersen (*Elke Sommer*), Emily Stratman (*Diane Baker*), Dr. Denise Marceau (*Micheline Presle*), Dr. Claude Marceau (*Gerard Oury*), Dr. Carlo Farelli (*Sergio Fantoni*), Dr. John Garrett (*Kevin McCarthy*), Count Bertil Jacobsson (*Leo G. Carroll*), Daranyi (*Sacha Pitoeff*), Monique Souvir (*Jacqueline Beer*), Hans Eckart (*John Wengraf*), Ivar Cramer (*Don Dubbins*), Mrs. Bergh (*Virginia Christine*), Mr. Bergh (*Rudolph Anders*), Saralee Garrett (*Martine Bartlett*), Hilding (*Karl Swenson*), Oscar (*John Qualen*), Clark Wilson (*Ned Wever*), Steen Ekberg (*Martin Brandt*), Hotel Porter (*Ivan Triesault*), Mrs. Farelli (*Grazia Narciso*), Davis Garrett (*Larry Adare*), Amy Garrett (*Robin Adare*), BBC News Correspondent (*Lester Mathews*), German Correspondent (*John Banner*), Tokyo Correspondent (*Teru Shimada*), American TV News Correspondent (*Jerry Dunphy*), French Correspondent (*Michael Panaieff*), Mrs. Ahlquist (*Edith Evanson*), Miss Fawley (*Queenie Leonard*), British Reporter (*Ben Wright*), Photographer (*Erik Holland*), Swedish Woman (*Alice Frost*), Burly Swedes (*Carl Rydin, Ronald Nyman*), Swedish Bellboy (*Sven Peterson*), Officer (*Peter Coe*), American Reporter (*Anna Lee*)

The Grade A filming of Irving Wallace's somewhat untidy melodrama of mistaken identity and chase intrigue gave Edward G. Robinson—special billing at the end of the cast on the ads; second on the screen—a dual role (for the first time since *The Whole Town's Talk-*

ing): that of a bewhiskered physicist kidnapped by the Russians and spirited onto a Soviet ship in Stockholm harbor just before he can accept his Nobel Prize, and his evil twin brother who had defected behind the Iron Curtain some years earlier. Top-billed Paul Newman, in the first of his two pictures with Robinson, is Andrew Craig, a Nobel laureate who is sucked into the shenanigans surrounding the strange behavior of Dr. Max Stratman, unaware that this isn't the real Dr. Max, but the imposter whom the Reds, with the help of Dr. Max's niece, Emily, are using to offer an anti-American diatribe for his acceptance speech at the ceremony. When he comes to discover more than he should know about the Stratman kidnapping plot, Craig finds himself at the center of the intrigue, involved in murder and, in escaping his pursuers after being unable to convince the Swedish police that "Stratman" is an imposter, at a nudist camp.

With the aid of a comely member of the Swedish Foreign Office, Inger Andersen, Craig manages to track the real Stratman to the ship where he is being held, and smuggles him back to his hotel. There Stratman, exhausted, suffers a heart seizure but recovers in time to join the other prize winners at the ceremony. The other "Stratman," seeing him there, flees, but is shot down by a Russian agent to conceal the aborted plan. As he lays dying, he pulls off a mask to reveal he is actually an

THE PRIZE: With Paul Newman, Diane Baker, Elke Sommer, Virginia Christine and Leo G. Carroll

actor impersonating Stratman's brother who had died in Russia years before.

The Swedish government reportedly took a dim view of this film, which they felt denigrated the dignity of the Nobel Prize, vulgarizing it by putting it at the center of a pretentious and somewhat silly spy story with lively dialogue by Ernest Lehman, a suspense melodrama played, intentionally or not, for laughs—mainly at the nudist colony, where Newman is urged to stand up and give a speech after being recognized. This film also was billed as Elke Summer's American debut (although she was seen earlier in *The Victors*).

CRITICAL VIEWS

"This florid farrago of fiction . . . plays fast and loose not only with the prestige of the Nobel affair but also with simple conventions of melodrama and with the intelligence of the customers . . . It gathers together as recipients of Nobel awards about as lurid a lot of performers as might walk up to receive Oscars at one of those Academy Nights in Hollywood . . . Well, at least it's a fast-paced movie picture [and] Mr. Robinson in both of his roles is good."—Bosley Crowther, *The New York Times*

"[The film] stands barefaced amid the pomp of Panavision, Metrocolor and Elke Sommer's physique . . . You and I already know this: good old Edward G. Robinson, playing an umlaut-accented physicist, has had a meeting with a queer Iron Curtain type ('So we meet again, Ekhart!') and has been kidnapped after he refuses to defect to the East—and good old Edward G. Robinson, with a slightly lighter umlaut accent, is busy impersonating himself in order to make un-American remarks at the Nobel ceremonies while the real Edward G. Robinson is being shanghaied to Leningrad aboard a freighter."—Judith Crist, *New York Herald-Tribune*

"The able old pro, Edward G. Robinson, seen briefly as Dr. Max Stratman, gives a performance of strength and dignity, the best in the film."—Wanda Hale, *New York Daily News*

GOOD NEIGHBOR SAM

1964 Columbia Pictures

A David Swift Production; Produced and directed by David Swift; Associate producer, Marvin Miller; Screenplay, James Fritzell, Everett Greenbaum and David Swift; Based on the novel by Jack Finney; Photography, Burnett Guffey; Production designer, Dale Hennesy; Set decorator, Ray Moyer; Music, Frank DeVol; Sound, James Z. Flaster; Editor, Charles Nelson. In Eastman Color by Pathe. 130 minutes

Sam Bissel (*Jack Lemmon*), Janet Lagerloi (*Romy Schneider*), Minerva Bissel (*Dorothy Provine*), Simon Nurdlinger (*Edward G. Robinson*), Howard Ebbets (*Michael Connors*), Mr. Burke (*Edward Andrews*), Reinhold Shiffner (*Louis Nye*), Earl (*Robert Q. Lewis*), Girl (*Joyce Jameson*), Irene (*Anne Seymour*), Jack Bailey (*Charles Lane*), Edna (*Linda Watkins*), Phil Reisner (*Peter Hobbs*), Sonny Blatchford (*Tris Coffin*), Larry Boling (*Neil Hamilton*), Miss Halverson (*Riza Royce*), Millard Mellner (*William Forrest*), The Hi-Los (*Themselves*), Taragon (*Bernie Kopell*), Wyeth (*Patrick Waltz*), Hausner (*William Bryant*), Jenna (*Vickie Cos*), Ardis (*Kym Karath*), Marsha (*Quinn O'Hara*), McVale (*Hal Taggart*), Gloria (*Jan Brooks*), French Waiter (*Peter Camlin*), Assistant Director (*Tom Anthony*), Mrs. Burke (*Bess Flowers*), Hertz Commercial Man (*Dave Ketchum*), Director (*David Swift*), Truck Driver (*George Savalas*), Mrs. Nurdlinger (*Elsie Baker*)

In the David Swift comedy showcasing Jack Lemmon, *Good Neighbor Sam*, Edward G. Robinson was given "Guest Star" billing playing Simon Nurdlinger, a puritanical head of a dairy produce company for whose ad agency Lemmon—as Sam Bissel—works. Nurdlinger, it turns out, wants his advertising campaign to be as pure as his products and insists that anyone remotely connected with his company to have an irreproachable private life, and happily-married Sam Bissel fits the bill nicely.

Sam innocently takes on a good neighbor role and agrees to pose as the "husband" of his wife's sexy friend so she can inherit $15 million, if she's still living with her real hubby from whom she's actually separated. She then joins Sam at a party tossed by Nurdlinger, who hires the "perfect couple" to endorse his dairy products on billboards all over town. Sam really gets into hot water—or milk. Before Nurdlinger can decide that his ace adman is engaged in hanky-panky, Sam and his good neighbor have to race the night away painting over all the billboards that show them lovey-dovey. They then get the real Mrs. Bissel into Nurdlinger's benevolent presence with Sam. The next day, the neighbor and her husband are back together again and fighting, and Sam and mate are wealthier by one of the inherited millions gifted them by their neighbor. And Nurdlinger is none the wiser.

CRITICAL VIEWS

"*Good Neighbor Sam*, who is none other than Jack Lemmon, the screen's perennially confused and harried young-man-about-town, is hardly a changed citizen in

GOOD NEIGHBOR SAM: With Edward Andrews

GOOD NEIGHBOR SAM: With Romy Schneider

GOOD NEIGHBOR SAM: With Edward Andrews, Romy Schneider, Jack Lemmon (right) and players

ROBIN AND THE SEVEN HOODS: With Dean Martin

ROBIN AND THE SEVEN HOODS

this swiftly-paced, pleasantly wacky but loosely assembled farce . . . Aiding in these manufactured frolics [is] Edward G. Robinson, as the rich, Bible-spouting client."—A. H. Weiler, *The New York Times*

"This unremarkable comedy scrapes through on the professionalism of its stars. Romy Schneider and Dorothy Provine are pleasantly relaxed in their lushly colorful suburban setting, and Jack Lemmon as amusing as ever in his accustomed, clean-living role, although his talent is rather wasted on slapstick scenes . . . In general the humor is much too naïve to provide a suitable niche for Edward G. Robinson."—*Monthly Film Bulletin*

ROBIN AND THE 7 HOODS

1964   Warner Bros.

A P-C Production; Executive producer, Howard W. Koch; Producer, Frank Sinatra; Associate producer, William H. Daniels; Director, Gordon Douglas; Screenplay, David R. Schwartz; Photography, William H. Daniels; Art director, LeRoy Deane; Set decorator, Raphael Bretton; Costumes, Donfeld; Music, Nelson Riddle; Songs, Sammy Cahn and James Van Heusen; Sound, Everett Hughes and Vinton Vernon; Editor, Sam O'Steen. Panavision and Technicolor. 123 minutes

Robbo (*Frank Sinatra*), John (*Dean Martin*), Will (*Sammy Davis, Jr.*), Allen A. Dale (*Bing Crosby*), Guy Gisborne (*Peter Falk*), Marian (*Barbara Rush*), Sheriff Potts (*Victor Buono*), Six Seconds (*Hank Henry*), Blue Jaw (*Robert Carricart*), Vermin (*Allen Jenkins*), Tomatoes (*Jack LaRue*), Robbo's Hoods (*Sonny King, Phil Crosby, Richard Bakalyan*), Sheriff Glick (*Robert Foulk*), Gimp (*Phil Arnold*), Soup Meat (*Harry Swoger*), Tick (*Joseph Ruskin*), Liver Jackson (*Bernard Fein*), Gisborne's Hoods (*Harry Wilson, Joe Brooks, Richard Sinatra, Roger Creed*), Cocktail Waitress (*Caryl Lee Hill*), House Girl (*Carolyn Morin*), Guard (*Al Silvani*), Hoods (*Joe Gray, John Delgado, Boyd "Red" Morgan, John Pedrini, Al Wyatt, Tony Randall*), Prosecuting Attorney (*Bill Zuckert*), Judge (*Milton Rudin*), Lawyers (*Ed Ness, Frank Scannell*), Mr. Ricks (*Hans Conried*), Butler (*Thom Conroy*), 2nd Butler (*Joey Jackson*), Woman Derelict (*Linda Brent*), Boys (*Jerry Davis, Manuel Padilla, Mark Sherwood*), Hammacher (*Sig Ruman*), Big Jim (*Edward G. Robinson*)

In this musical Robin Hood-themed gangster spoof back at his long-ago home studio, Edward G. Robinson does an unbilled gag bit at the opening, playing the No.

ROBIN AND THE 7 HOODS: With Joseph Ruskin, Harry Wilson, Robert Carricart, Frank Sinatra, Peter Falk, Robert Foulk and Allen Jenkins

1 mobster in Prohibition Era Chicago, who is being honored at a lavish birthday party by the crooked local sheriff, his equally crooked deputy and an assortment of gangland's finest and meanest. He is bumped off after being serenaded with a sentimental rendition of "For He's a Jolly Good Fellow." A crook named Guy Gisborne declares himself the new top gunsel and an all-out gang war starts with the dead mobster's turf being claimed by a hood named Robbo and his merry little band. Robinson's presence is not snuffed out by a few bullets however. A painted likeness of him looms above the mantel of the paneled conference room of gang headquarters throughout the film as if to remind the actors one and all, and the audience as well, who the No. 1 gangster was and always will be.

Concocted as a Runyeonesque romp for Sinatra and his pared-down Rat Pack plus Bing Crosby, turning up as a pious Allen A. Dale, secretary of an orphanage who would be delighted to get his hands on the mob's money, this "home movie," as most critics called the Sinatra & Co. films of the time, misfired. It did, however, serve as a showcase for some terrific Cahn and Van Heusen songs such as "My Kind of Town" (Oscar-nom-inated but a loser to "Chim Chim Cher-ee"), "Style," "Don't Be a Do-Badder," etc., and Nelson Riddle's scoring, which also was nominated for an Oscar.

CRITICAL VIEWS

"[It] is almost as strained and archaic in the fable it has to tell of Prohibition-era gangsters in Chicago as the fable of Robin Hood it travesties . . . For all those magnificent talents, it is an artless and obvious film. The brightest thing about it is its color photography."—Bosley Crowther, *The New York Times*

"It's shades of *Little Caesar* and *Guys and Dolls* and every orphanage musical Crosby ever enhanced—but how wrong can it go when you start out with Edward G. Robinson as the top hood of 'em all?"—Judith Crist, *New York Herald-Tribune*

"The spirit of a hit is apparent and [the] picture stacks up nicely as mass entertainment . . . [It] opens in 1928 with the gangster kingpin of the day—Edward G. Robinson doing a cameo bit here—as the guest of honor at a lush birthday party."—*Variety*

THE OUTRAGE: With William Shatner and Howard Da Silva

THE OUTRAGE: With William Shatner and Howard Da Silva

THE OUTRAGE

1964   Metro-Goldwyn-Mayer

A Martin Ritt Production; Producer, A. Ronald Lubin; Associate producer, Michael Kanin; Director, Martin Ritt; Screenplay, Michael Kanin; Based on the film *Rashomon* by Akira Kurosawa, from stories by Ryunosuke Akutagawa, and the play *Rashomon* by Fay and Michael Kanin; Photography, James Wong Howe; Art directors, George W. Davis and Tambi Larsen; Set decorators, Henry Grace and Robert R. Benton; Costumes, Donfeld; Music, Alex North; Special visual effects, J. McMillan Johnson and Robert R. Hoag; Second-unit director, Lesley Selander; Editor, Frank Santillo. Panavision. 97 minutes

Juan Carrasco (*Paul Newman*), Husband (*Laurence Harvey*), Wife (*Claire Bloom*), Con Man (*Edward G. Robinson*), Preacher (*William Shatner*), Prospector (*Howard Da Silva*), Sheriff (*Albert Salmi*), Judge (*Thomas Chalmers*), Indian (*Paul Fix*)

The landmark 1951 Japanese movie, *Rashomon*, that put Akira Kurosawa on the cinematic map, and the hugely successful 1959 stage adaptation of it by Fay and Michael Kanin were the inspiration for Martin Ritt's moderately successful *The Outrage*—reset from feudal Japan to 19th century Arizona. Edward G. Robinson has the role of an Old West con man, who meets up with a preacher and a prospector at a remote depot waiting for a train. The other two had been at the trial of a notorious Mexican bandit (played by Paul Newman), who was convicted and hanged for a particularly violent "outrage" against a Southern colonel and his wife. At the trial, the two tell the con man, they were puzzled by three varying stories of the incident. The bandit confessed that he had tied up the Colonel and raped his wife, then stabbed him in a duel of honor. The wife claimed that after attacking her, the bandit fled, and her husband, believing that she had encouraged the bandit, looked at her with such loathing that she killed him. Another witness, an Indian medicine man who said he happened onto the scene, told the husband's story, that the Colonel killed himself in shame at his wife's dishonor.

The prospector then confesses that he saw the whole incident but failed to come forward at the trial. His version is that the wife actually relished the attention of the bandit and goaded him and her husband to fight for her, and after their duel, the Colonel was accidentally killed

when he tripped on his own dagger, which was never found. The con man and the preacher realize that the prospector must have stolen the jewel-encrusted dagger.

As the tale ends, the three come upon an abandoned baby at the depot, and the prospector's willingness to adopt it restores the preacher's faith in humanity, shaken by the trial. The con man, however, merely ponders, bemused. In the stage version, Rod Steiger starred as the bandit, Claire Bloom as the wife (repeating her role in the screen version) and Noel Willman was the husband. The roles of the con man, preacher and prospector were created as a device for storytelling on the screen and to account for the flashbacks.

CRITICAL VIEWS

"Edward G. Robinson's portrayal of the bearded, seedy, cocky con artist is earthy and direct. 'You tell people what they want to hear,' he says scornfully after a session of truthseeking. In focusing cynically on 'truths' that remain a mystery at the film's end, Martin

THE OUTRAGE

Ritt and his willing company have done nobly by the original in their provocative and engrossing drama."—A. H. Weiler, *The New York Times*

"Edward G. Robinson is delightful as the cruddy old con man, a cynic who hears the various versions of the crimes and believes none."—Wanda Hale, New York *Daily News*

"Edward G. Robinson shows up as a Little Caesar-ized hobo-con man."—Judith Crist, *New York Herald-Tribune*

"The script is absolutely faithful to the plot line of *Rashomon*, but divorced from the exotic background of medieval Japan and rather uneasily accommodated to the American West, it is seen to be a fairly shabby bag of tricks . . . Edward G. Robinson provides some enjoyably cynical comments as the con man."—*Monthly Film Bulletin*

CHEYENNE AUTUMN

1964   Warner Bros.

Producer, Bernard Smith; Director, John Ford; Screenplay, James R. Webb; Suggested by the novel by Mari Sandoz; Associate director, Ray Kellogg; Photography, William Clothier; Art director, Richard Day; Set decorator, Darrell Silvera; Music, Alex North; Sound, Francis E. Stahl, Jack Solomon; Editor, Otho Lovering. Super-Panavision 70 and Technicolor. 159 minutes (cut to 145 minutes)

Captain Thomas Archer (*Richard Widmark*), Deborah Wright (*Carroll Baker*), Captain Oscar Wessels (*Karl Malden*), Wyatt Earp (*James Stewart*), Carl Schurz (*Edward G. Robinson*), Red Shirt (*Sal Mineo*), Spanish Woman (*Dolores Del Rio*), Little Wolf (*Ricardo Montalban*), Dull Knife (*Gilbert Roland*), Doc Holliday (*Arthur Kennedy*), Second Lieutenant Scott (*Patrick Wayne*), Miss Guinevere Plantagenet (*Elizabeth Allen*), Major Jeff Blair (*John Carradine*), Tall Tree (*Victor Jory*), Major Dog Kelly (*Judson Pratt*), First Sergeant Stanislaus Wichowsky (*Mike Mazurki*), Homer (*Ken Curtis*), Major Braden (*George O'Brien*), Trail Boss (*Shug Fisher*), Pawnee Woman (*Carmen D'Antonio*), Deborah's Uncle (*Walter Baldwin*), Little Bird (*Nancy Hseuh*), Trail Hand (*Chuck Roberson*), Running Deer (*Moonbeam*), Medicine Man (*Many Muleson*), Svenson (*John Qualen*), Dr. O'Carberry (*Sean McClory*), Lieutenant Peterson (*Walter Reed*), Sergeant Of The Guard (*James Flavin*), Entertainers (*Stephanie Epper, Mary Statler, Jean Epper, Donna Hall*), Trooper Plumtree (*Ben Johnson*), Trooper Smith (*Harry Carey, Jr.*), Telegrapher (*Bing Russell*), Townsman (*Major Sam Harris*), Senator

Henry (*Denver Pyle*), Secretary To Schurz (*Carleton Young*), Infantry Captain (*William Henry*), Woman (*Louise Montana*), Colonel (*Zon Murray*), Officer (*Chuck Hamilton*)

John Ford's stellar Western epic about the Cheyenne Nation's trek back to their homeland in Wyoming from the Oklahoma reservation forced on them by the United States government—some called this film Ford's apology to the Indians who, in his many earlier Westerns, he had presented so one-dimensionally—found Edward G. Robinson forceful, as usual, in the relatively small role as Carl Schurz, Secretary of the Interior in the late 1870s. The Schurz role had been scheduled for Spencer Tracy, but his illness forced a change in casting and it fell to Robinson.

When the Cheyenne begin their long march under Chief Dull Knife, Chief Little Wolf and elder Chief Tall Tree (accompanied by Deborah Wright, a Quaker school teacher), Captain Thomas Archer and his regiment are ordered to pursue them and return them to Oklahoma. However the outfit is mauled in battle by Little Wolf. Obtaining reinforcements, Archer tries to arrange a capture without bloodshed, but one of his aides instigates another battle, bringing on a second military defeat. Ultimately, he finally negotiates a truce. But, when he learns that the government is planning to renege on it, he seeks the help of Carl Schurz in Washington, just as the Army is preparing to move in on the survivors of the march, who are temporarily interned at Fort Robinson.

Schurz suggests a truce that will allow the Cheyenne to return to their homeland and, in the spring of 1879, after a 1,500-mile trek, they are back in Yellowstone country. Dull Knife, one of the renegades of the tribe (in one of the many subplots), goes into exile, and Archer, who has come to be fascinated by Deborah Wright, decides to remain with the Indians.

This marked Robinson's reunion with Ford after nearly thirty years, and it was Ford's final Western, as sprawling as they make them, and had a number of rambling interludes into which he could bring some of his favorite actors for whom he couldn't find a spot in the story's main action. One humorous sequence has James Stewart turning up as Wyatt Earp and Arthur Kennedy as Doc Holliday in a rambunctious but extraneous poker game with John Carradine and Judson Pratt. It was cut after the film's premier engagements but since has been restored in home video prints.

CRITICAL VIEWS

"In *Cheyenne Autumn*, John Ford, that old master of the Western, has come up with an epic frontier film . . .

[But] the climax with Carl Schurz [Robinson] interceding on behalf of the Indians after a hurried trip to Washington is neither effective and convincing drama nor is it faithful to the novel of Mari Sandoz on which the script is based."—Bosley Crowther, *The New York Times*

"The secretary [of the Interior] herein is Carl Schurz, as park-loving New Yorkers may guess, and it's Edward G. Robinson in cameo."—Judith Crist, *New York Herald-Tribune*

CHEYENNE AUTUMN

CHEYENNE AUTUMN: With Richard Widmark

CHEYENNE AUTUMN: With Chuck Hamilton (foreground), Zon Murray and players

"Edward G. Robinson, playing Carl Schurz, Secretary of the Interior, seems extremely earnest, too earnest to shave all the time."—Archer Winsten, *New York Post*

"Edward G. Robinson plays Carl Schurz . . . who complains of his lumbago and eventually solves the problems of the Cheyenne in a confrontation scene that is just as hilarious [as the James Stewart-Arthur Kennedy interlude] but unintentially."—*Life*

THE CINCINNATI KID

1965   Metro-Goldwyn-Mayer

A Filmways-Solar Picture; A Martin Ransohoff Production. Producer, Martin Ransohoff; Associate producer, John Calley; Director, Norman Jewison; Screenplay, Ring Lardner, Jr., and Terry Southern; Based on the novel by Richard Jessup; Photography, Philip H. Lathrop; Art directors, George

THE CINCINNATI KID: With Steve McQueen, Ann-Margret, Karl Malden, Joan Blondell and player

W. Davis and Edward Carfagno; Set decorators, Henry Grace and Hugh Hunt; Costumes, Donfeld; Music, Lalo Schifrin; Title song by Lalo Schifrin and Dorcas Cochran; Sung by Ray Charles; Sound, Franklin Milton; Editor, Hal Ashby. Metrocolor. 113 minutes

The Cincinnati Kid (*Steve McQueen*), Lancey Howard (*Edward G. Robinson*), Melba (*Ann-Margret*), Shooter (*Karl Malden*), Christian (*Tuesday Weld*), Lady Fingers (*Joan Blondell*), Slade (*Rip Torn*), Pig (*Jack Weston*), Yeller (*Cab Calloway*), Hoban (*Jeff Corey*), Felix (*Theo Marcuse*), Sokal (*Milton Selzer*), Mr. Rudd (*Karl Swenson*), Cajun (*Emile Genest*), Danny (*Ron Soble*), Mrs. Rudd (*Irene Tedrow*), Mrs. Slade (*Midge Ware*), Dealer (*Dub Taylor*), Hoban's Wife (*Joyce Perry*), Gambler (*Claude Hall*), Desk Clerk (*Olan Soule*), Eddie (*Barry O'Hara*), 1st Player (*Pat McCaffrie*), Poker Player (*Bill Zuckert*), 2nd Player (*John Hart*), 3rd Player (Charlie) (*Howard Wendell*), Referee (*Andy Albin*), Bettor (*Hal Taggart*), Philly (*Robert Do Qui*), Poker Player (*Sandy Kevin*)

THE CINCINNATI KID

pah was fired over "artistic differences" with both Steve McQueen and producer Martin Ransohoff. Jewison, a Canadian director best known for the light Doris Day-type comedies he had been turning out at Universal, was to prove his mettle with heavier material here and go on to a distinguished career in a variety of genres (*The Russian Are Coming, The Russians Are Coming, In the Heat of the Night, Fiddler on the Roof, Moonstruck*). He brought with him his favorite editor, Hal Ashby, who also was to have an important career later as a director.

With Robinson in the role of Lancey Howard, opposite McQueen as the kid who would take away his title, he was reunited with Joan Blondell as an ace card dealer/gambler named Lady Fingers. Robinson and Blondell had costarred in *Bullets or Ballots* nearly thirty years earlier. In the star-laden film, set in the late Thirties, The Kid, weary of hustling for nickle and dime stakes, decides to challenge the reigning stud poker king for the title of "The Man." The Man currently is and for the last three decades has been Lancey. A game is set up with Slade, the wealthy owner of a New

THE CINCINNATI KID: With Steve McQueen

Edward G. Robinson had one of the last great roles of his career in the film version of Richard Jessup's novel about an epic poker game. *The Cincinnati Kid*, which was to poker what *The Hustler* was to pool-playing, had been on actor Steve McQueen's schedule for some time, and it went into production in January 1965 under Sam Peckinpah's direction from a script by the author of the source novel, Richard Jessup. Spencer Tracy had been signed to play the veteran poker king, Lancey Howard, but then bowed out. Peckinpah then changed the locale of the story from St. Louis of the novel to New Orleans, at which time Jessup took his typewriter and went home. In for Jessup, briefly, was Paddy Chayefsky, who was then replaced by Ring Lardner, Jr. His script was then worked over by Terry Southern and Charles Eastman, who came in with Norman Jewison after Peckin-

THE CINCINNATI KID: With Karl Malden, Joan Blondell and Cab Calloway (background)

Orleans gambling house; the dealer will be Shooter, widely respected in the gambling fraternity as fair and honest. Shooter is also The Kid's patron.

Meanwhile, Slade, who had been gutted by The Man, is bent on revenge. He reminds the Shooter of some unpaid debts and pressures him to fix the game by passing cards to The Kid. The big game finally begins and runs over a period of several days. The other players drop out one by one until only Lancey and The Kid remain. In the momentous final duel, in which Lady Fingers is relief dealer, The Kid, who has noticed that Shooter had been passing him cards, finds himself holding a full house. Lancey bluffs his all on a single card, and The Kid is beaten.

CRITICAL VIEWS

"The climax is [McQueen's] marathon duel with Edward G. Robinson who is one of the film's two genuine bright spots. The other is Joan Blondell, bless her . . . Appearing briefly, as a wily card king, Mr. Robinson is quiet, precise and deadly—all with his eyes. And fortunately, for spectators bored by cards, into that interminable climax, there breezes Joan Blondell, like a blowsy, good-natured gale."—Howard Thompson, *The New York Times*

"Mr. Robinson proves himself The Man both as an actor and as Lancey Howard, suave, weary and unyielding in his tenure as the shrewdest gentleman gambler of all . . . So skillfully is the contest dramatized that non-card players are swept into the suspenseful tale. Whether stud experts will agree with The Man's ultimate verdict that 'making the wrong move at the right time' is what the game and the gamble are all about is a matter for post-movie speculation."—Judith Crist, *New York Herald-Tribune*

"The elderly card shark [is] played consummately by Edward G. Robinson."—Hollis Alpert, *Saturday Review*

"Robinson is at his best in some years as the aging, ruthless Lancey Howard, champ of the poker table for more than thirty years and determined now to defend his title against a cocksure but dangerous opponent who believes he is ready for the big moment."—*Variety*

"Edward G. Robinson, dressed for the kill and packing his shaving kit before the big game to keep his beard in trim, dominates the film with his presence from the moment when the camera moves up from the steam issuing round the train's wheels to find him arriving in New Orleans."—*Monthly Film Bulletin*

LA BLONDE DE PEKIN
(THE BLONDE FROM PEKING)

1967   Paramount Pictures

A Co-production of Hans Eckelkamp Films (West Germany)/ Copernic Films (France)/Clesi Cinematografica (Italy); Producer, Raymond Danon; Director, Nicolas Gessner; Screenplay, Nicolas Gessner and Marc Behm; Adaptation, Jacques Vilfrid; Based on the novel *You Have Yourself a Deal* by James Hadley Chase; Photography, Claude Lecomte; Art director, Georges Petitot; Music, Francois de Roubaix; Editor, Jean-Michel Gautier. Franscope and Eastmancolor. 95 minutes (later cut to 80 minutes)

Christine (*Mireille Darc*), Gandler (*Claudio Brook*), Douglas (*Edward G. Robinson*), Secretary (*Pascale Roberts*), Erika Olsen (*Francoise Brion*), Doctor (*Jo Warfield*), Ginny (*Giorgia Moll*), Hardy (*Carl Studer*), Jackson (*Yves Elliot*), Olsen (*Jean-Jacques Delbo*), and: (*Valery Inkijinoff, Tiny Young, Aime de March*)

In this somewhat obscure spy programmer filmed on location in Hong Kong, Edward G. Robinson turns up as an aging CIA chief named Douglas, on the trail along with agents from various other countries of a blonde amnesiac named Christine. She may or may not be Erika Olsen, possibly the ex-mistress of a Chinese scientist, who unwittingly has obtained important nuclear secrets. Mark Gandler, an American actor, is hired by Douglas to pose as the woman's husband and lure her to a Swiss villa. There she reveals she is neither a spy nor Erika, but Erika's twin sister, Christine, and that Erika has the scientist's priceless Black Grape Pearl in her possession. Douglas wants the scientist's secrets and Gandler decides he wants the scientist's pearl. Gandler and Christine go to Hong Kong to find Erika and arrive in time to witness her murder by Chinese agents. Falling from Erika's neck, the Black Grape Pearl drops into the sea, leaving the Blonde from Peking and the erstwhile actor-turned-CIA agent to pursue other employments.

Alternately known as *Peking Blonde*, this film, the first of Robinson's that would be made for assorted European production companies, premiered in West Germany in October 1967 and opened in Paris several months later. It was virtually unseen theatrically in the United States.

THE BLONDE FROM PEKING: With Mireille Darc

THE BLONDE FROM PEKING: With Mireille Darc

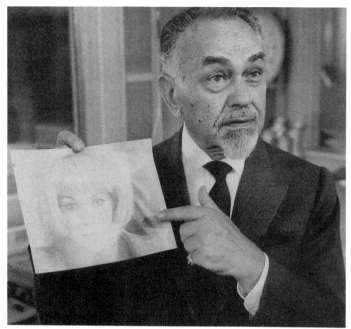

THE BLONDE FROM PEKING

CRITICAL VIEWS

"Spy shenanigans concern Chinese, Russian and Yank spies seeking errant Red Chinese missile data plus a priceless jewel. But all this does not quite have the verve, ironic comic twists or sheer suspense and action flair to bring it all off. It emerges possibly . . . on the color, scope and lure of the Edward G. Robinson name albeit he has a small role in the affair [as] the shrewd CIA chief."—*Variety*

AD OGNI COSTO
(In the U.S., GRAND SLAM)

1967   Paramount Pictures

A Co-production of Jolly Film (Rome)/Coral Producciones (Madrid)/ Constantin Films (Munich); Producers, Harry Colombo and George Papi; Director, Giuliano Montaldo; Screenplay, Mino Roli, Augusto Caminito, Marcello Fondato, Antonio De La Loma and Marcello Coscia; Photography, Antonio Macasoli; Art directors, Alberto Boccianti and Juan Alberto Soler; Music, Ennio Morricone; Sound, Umberto Picistrelli; Editor, Nino Baragli. Techniscope and Technicolor. 121 minutes

Prof. James Anders (*Edward G. Robinson*), Mary Ann (*Janet Leigh*), Mark Milford (*Adolfo Celi*), Erich Weiss (*Klaus Kinski*), Gregg (*Georges Rigaud*), Jean-Paul Audry (*Robert Hoffmann*), Agostino Rossi (*Riccardo Cucciolla*), Setuaka (*Jussara*), Manager (*Miguel del Castillo*)

As teacher-turned-criminal mastermind, Edward G. Robinson was given "special guest star" billing in this multi-national co-production. He is cast as Professor James Anders, retiring to New York from the convent school in Rio de Janeiro where he taught with such devotion over thirty years. In New York, he goes to see an old friend, Mark Milford, now a prominent racketeer, and lays out a plan he has concocted for a big heist—the bi-annual delivery of jewels to a Brazilian diamond company which he has watched from his classroom over the years. He needs backing, however, and four good men to do the job which he hopes to pull during Carnival. From Milford's extensive files come the names of Erich Weiss, who will be the team leader; Gregg, a safecracker; Agostino Rossi, an electronics expert; and Jean-Paul Audry, a playboy whose job it will be to seduce Mary Ann, the American secretary to the diamond company's manager. Mary Ann, it seems, holds a special magnetic key to the strongroom. The day before Carnival, the jewel delivery is made, but the gang discovers that a new security system, Grand Slam 70, has been installed in the strongroom, and they must formulate a new master plan. Anders goes back to the drawing board.

With a new plan in place, the gang executes the robbery. However, Mary Ann discovers that something is wrong and alerts the police. Before long, internecine rivalry engulfs the gang, and for all his efforts, Milford recovers only an empty jewel case. Back in Rome, Mary Ann meets Anders and is about to turn over to him the real jewel case, all according to his plan, when a purse-snatcher zooms by on a motorcycle and grabs it from her, leaving the two aghast and emptyhanded.

Shown in Europe in late 1967, screenplay-by-committee *Grand Slam* did not make it to the United States until after Robinson's next movie, *The Biggest Bundle of Them All*, was released.

CRITICAL VIEWS

"Edward G. Robinson, as a retired teacher who engineers the caper, smoothly ambles in early and returns for the fade-out."—Howard Thompson, *The New York Times*

"Edward G. Robinson, who just finished engineering a major heist in *The Biggest Bundle of Them All*, returns as the real mastermind in *Grand Slam*, portraying a mild school teacher [who] retires . . . and plots to rob a dia-

GRAND SLAM:
With Janet Leigh

GRAND SLAM: With Adolfo Celi

mond company across the way from his former class-room."—Ann Guarino, New York *Daily News*

"The opening sequence . . . is very strikingly done, with its exhilaratingly mysterious pursuit of Edward G. Robinson, from farewell chanted by nuns and school-

GRAND SLAM: With Riccardo Cucciolla

THE BIGGEST BUNDLE OF THEM ALL: With Vittorio DeSica and Raquel Welch

214

children at Rio airport to arrival on the New York sky-line (some brilliant helicopter footage) and prowl through city streets, ending up in a nightclub where the stripteaser performs to a decorous string quartet."— *Monthly Film Bulletin*

THE BIGGEST BUNDLE OF THEM ALL

1968   Metro-Goldwyn-Mayer

A Shaftel-Stewart Production; Producer, Josef Shaftel; Associate producer, Sy Stewart; Director, Ken Annakin; Screenplay, Josef Shaftel, Sy Salkowitz and Riccardo Aragno; Based on a story by Josef Shaftel; Photography, Piero Portalupi; Art director, Arrigo Equini; Music, Riz Ortolani; Sound, Kurt Doubravsky; Editor, Ralph Sheldon. Panavision and Metrocolor. 106 minutes

Harry Price (*Robert Wagner*), Juliana (*Raquel Welch*), Benjamin Brownstead (*Godfrey Cambridge*), Cesare Celli (*Vittorio De Sica*), Professor Samuels (*Edward G. Robinson*), Davy Collins (*Davy Kaye*), Antonio Tozzi (*Francesco Mule*), Captain Giglio (*Victor Spinetti*), Teresa (*Yvonne Sanson*), Joe Ware (*Mickey Knox*), Uncle Carlo's Bride (*Femi Benussi*), Signora Rosa (*Paola Borboni*), Carabiniere (*Andrea Aureli*), Capitano del Signore (*Aldo Bufi Landi*), Franco (*Carlo Croccolo*), Uncle Carlo (*Roberto De Simone*), Captain Capuano (*Piero Gerlini*), Lt. Naldi (*Giulio Marchetti*), Emma (*Ermelinda De Felice*), Signora Clara (*Gianna Dauro*), Maitre D'Hotel (*Carlo Rizzo*), Chef (*Nino Musco*), Inspector Bordoni (*Calisto Calisti*)

Edward G. Robinson, receiving special billing as Professor Samuels, is the mastermind behind a platinum heist on the Riviera in this comic caper movie which was mainly a vehicle for showing off the admirable figure of Raquel Welch. The Professor is brought into the proceedings to blueprint a heist after small-time con artist Harry Price and his inept crew of amateur criminals kidnap retired gangster Cesare Celli, living in Naples, in order to collect a ransom. But none of his cronies is willing to bail him out. Celli, in turn, has conceived the idea of a $5-million platinum robbery, both as a way to repay Price and his gang for their kidnapping efforts and to retaliate against a world that has passed him by. After taking command of the operation and putting the novice criminals through rigorous physical training, Celli brings aboard The Professor, an old friend and master crook.

THE BIGGEST BUNDLE OF THEM ALL: With Vittorio DeSica,
Robert Wagner and Raquel Welch

THE BIGGEST BUNDLE OF THEM ALL: With Raquel Welch

The Professor already has a plan for The Biggest Bundle Of Them All, but Celli decides the gang must pull off a number of small robberies first to know that they're prepared—and each one is bungled. The Professor's scheme, however, is put into effect: it involves intercepting the train carrying the platinum ingots by blocking the tracks with a tank and loading the loot onto a hijacked B-25 for transport to a fence in Morocco. Despite consistent bumbling and threats by Price and his bikini-clad girlfriend to double-cross Celli and abscond with the swag, the heist is successful and the plane makes its getaway. But the gang's efforts are for naught when the plane's bomb doors are accidentally opened and the ingots descend into the waiting arms of the police. After their initial disappointment, however,

215

MAD CHECKMATE: With Maria Grazia Buccella

MAD CHECKMATE: With Jorge Rigaud

Advertisement for MAD CHECKMATE under its TV title

the robbers are happy to learn that The Professor is working on a new plan for even a bigger heist.

CRITICAL VIEWS

"[It] begins like one of those really bad movies that are unintentionally funny. Then it becomes clear that it intends to be funny and isn't . . . By the time Edward G. Robinson appears, his wrinkled countenance, flat eyes and generally turtlish appearance make it seem everyone might be on location for *The Wind in the Willows*."—Renata Adler, *The New York Times*

"Godfrey Cambridge and Edward G. Robinson go through their criminal paces without the distinction that marks their work in other times."—Archer Winsten, *New York Post*

"Edward G. Robinson contributes one of his usual smooth performances as a professor in crime called in to blueprint the robbery."—*Variety*

"After an opening strikingly reminiscent of *The Happening*, this comedy thriller soon develops along the familiar lines of a robbery planned and executed as a high-spirited caper . . . Edward G. Robinson is in fine form as a smooth-talking, impeccably dressed master crook, and the minor characters are entertaining."—*Monthly Film Bulletin*

UNO SCACCO TUTTO MATTO

(In the U.S., MAD CHECKMATE*)*

1968   American-International Pictures

A Co-production of Kinesis Films (Rome)/Tacisa (Madrid Miniter); Producer, Franco Porro; Director, Robert Fiz;

216

Screenplay, Massimilliano Capriccoli, Ennio De Concini, Jose G. Maesso, Leonardo Martin, Juan Cesarabea and Robert Fiz; Photography, Antonio Macasoli; Art director, Rafael Ferri; Music, Manuel Asins Arbo; Editor, Mario Mora. Eastmancolor. 89 minutes

Sir George MacDowell (*Edward G. Robinson*), Pelocce (*Adolfo Celi*), Monique (*Maria Grazia Buccella*), Jerome (*Jorge Rigaud*), D'Origone (*Terry-Thomas*) and: (*Manuel Zarzo, Jose Bodalo, Loris Bazzocchi, Rossella Como*)

Yet another caper movie made in Europe (his last one) finds Edward G. Robinson again masterminding a grand plan. Playing a retired Englishman named Mac-Dowell, living in Majorca, he begins hatching a scheme to knock over his bank after being introduced, one day, to his butler's niece Monique and noticing her remarkable resemblance to the bank director's secretary. Six months later, three men arrive at MacDowell's villa from abroad, each resembling an employee of the bank. Through various subterfuges, MacDowell has each of the three and Monique swap places with their lookalikes, and a fairly complex heist is seemingly completed, but attempting to make their getaways they run into a series of unforeseen situations, and the briefcase stuffed with the stolen money changes hands innumerable times.

A short while later, MacDowell receives a visit from the police who have come on a tip that in his cellar three men and a girl are being held prisoners. The "prisoners" were secretly returned to the bank before the arrival of the police. The next day, the police have to pacify the four who claimed to have been kidnapped although the bank director swears that they were at their respective jobs as usual at the time of the robbery. MacDowell is present at the questioning, standing by impassively, until the safe is opened. Everything seems to be in order. Apparently there had been no robbery. The money is there. Then a noise is heard and a door opens. Out troop four men in white overalls, each quite dirty. They complain that they have been locked inside while repairing the bank's central heating unit. A surprised MacDowell receives profuse apologies from the bank officials and the police, and he is driven home to get over his puzzlement—and begin another grand scheme.

Mad Checkmate received virtually no theatrical release in the United States and was sold into television syndication under the title *It's Your Move*.

OPERATION ST. PETER'S: With Marie-Christine Barclay and Ugo Fancareggi

OPERAZIONE SAN PIETRO
(*In the U.S.*, OPERATION ST. PETER'S)

1968   Paramount Pictures

A Co-production of Ultra Film (Rome)/Marianne Productions (Paris)/Roxy Film (Munich); Producer, Turi Vasile; Director, Lucio Fulci; Screenplay, Ennio De Concini, Adriano Baracco, Roberto Gianviti, Paul Hengge and Lucio Fulci; Photography, Alfio Contini and Erico Menczer; Art director, Giorgio Giovannini; Music, Armando Trovaioli and Ward Swingle. Eastmancolor. 96 minutes

Napoleon (*Lando Buzzanca*), Joe (*Edward G. Robinson*), Cardinal Braun (*Heinz Ruhmann*), Cajella (*Jean-Claude Brialy*), The Baron (*Pinuccio Ardia*), The Captain (*Dante Maggio*), Agonia (*Ugo Fancareggi*), Marisa (*Marie-Christine Barclay*), Samantha (*Uta Levka*), Cesira (*Antonella Delle Porte*)

OPERATION ST. PETER'S:
With Dante Maggio, Pinuc-
cio Ardia, Heinz Ruhmann,
Lando Buzzanca and Ugo
Fancareggi

OPERATION ST. PETER'S

In still another European-made comedy caper movie, Edward G. Robinson plays Joe Ventura, an American gangster who has come to Italy with his henchmen and playmate, Samantha, on "business." Coming in contact with four small-time thieves who unaccountably have managed to pull off a big heist in Rome and have made off with Michelangelo's Pieta, worth $30-billion, and have found rather tough to fence, Joe offers to take it off their hands for forty bucks and spaghetti dinner. The Vatican of course doesn't want word to leak out that the statue had been stolen, so they send out their own priest to track it down. The investigation leads to Joe Ventura, who has taken the Pieta to a coastal town and then aboard a ship outside territorial waters, to later sell it back to the Vatican.

The Vatican calls upon all priests of the area to converge on the town—in a slapstick chase that becomes a series of crashes and automobile acrobatics. Even the gang that sold Joe the Pieta is enlisted by the Church for the statue hunt. At dockside, as the boat carrying the statue is pulling away, Cardinal Braun, who in his youth won the Indianapolis 500 (!), accelerates his car which lunges across the water onto the ship's deck. Meanwhile, the bands of priests, friars, nuns, Jesuits, Salesians and hoods approach the boat on anything that floats and in a free-for-all, retrieve the Pieta from Joe Ventura and his mob.

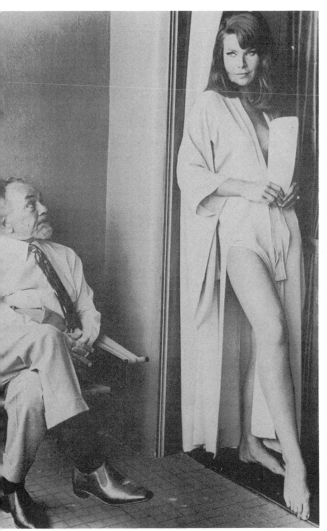

OPERATION ST. PETER'S: With Marie-Christine Barclay

CRITICAL VIEWS

"A very weak comedy . . . Robinson made several films in Europe during the mid-1960s, none of them particularly memorable, but this was surely one of the worst."—*Motion Picture Guide*

NEVER A DULL MOMENT

1968   Buena Vista

Producer, Ron Miller; Director, Jerry Paris; Screenplay, A. J. Carothers; Based on the novel *A Thrill a Minute with Jack Albany* by John Godey; Photography, William Snyder; Art

directors, Carroll Clark and John B. Mansbridge; Set decorators, Emile Kuri and Frank R. McKelvy; Music, Robert F. Brunner; Special effects, Eustace Lycett and Robert A. Mattey; Editor, Marsh Hendry. Technicolor. 100 minutes

Jack Albany (*Dick Van Dyke*), Leo Joseph Smooth (*Edward G. Robinson*), Sally Inwood (*Dorothy Provine*), Frank Boley (*Henry Silva*), Melanie Smooth (*Joanna Moore*), Florian (*Tony Bill*), Cowboy Schaeffer (*Slim Pickens*), Ace Williams (*Jack Elam*), Rinzy Tobreski (*Ned Glass*), Bobby Macoon (*Richard Bakalyan*), Francis (*Mickey Shaughnessy*), Fingers Felton (*Philip Coolidge*), Museum Director (*James Millhollin*), Prop Man (*Johnny Silver*), Tony Preston (*Anthony Caruso*), Lenny (*Paul Condylis*), 2nd T.V. Actor (Police Capt.

NEVER A DULL MOMENT: With Dick Van Dyke

Jacoby) (*Bob Homel*), 1st T.V. Actor (*Dick Winslow*), Sexy Girl (*Jackie Russell*), Sam (*Rex Dominick*), Police Lieutenant (*Ken Lynch*), Matron (*Eleanor Audley*), 1st Museum Guard (*John Cliff*), Police Chief Grayson (*Tyler McVey*), Police Photographer (*Jerry Paris*), 2nd Museum Guard (*John Dennis*)

Robinson's only picture for the Disney people (it was the first production after Walt's death) found him to be a wealthy comic gangster named Leo Joseph Smooth who has assembled a gang of bumblers to steal a priceless painting from the New York Museum. He only wants to keep it until his death, after which it will be returned, provided the trustees agree to rename the museum after him—his claim, he figures, to immortality. Into Smooth's gang comes a struggling actor, Jack Albany, mistaken by one of Smooth's hoods, Florian, for Ace Williams, the hired killer he was supposed to pick for smooth. Fearing for his life if his real identity is discovered, Albany goes along quietly to Smooth's mansion, and there he meets Sally Inwood, Smooth's pretty art instructor who has been "invited" to spend the night of the heist at the mansion because the boss

suspects she knows too much to be running loose. When Albany manages to get her alone, he tries in vain to tell her he is not a professional hood, just an out-of-work actor.

When the real Ace Williams turns up, smooth Leo Smooth suggests a bare hand contest in the library to determine who the real killer is. Albany emerges victorious, with the help of Sally, and they trap Ace in the cellar. The next day, Smooth puts his plan into action, the robbery is thwarted by Albany and Sally. The gang is picked up in mid-heist and Smooth soon is rounded up himself, accepting defeat graciously.

CRITICAL VIEWS

"Apparently determined to live up to the title, the Disney organization has settled for volume and slapstick in *Never a Dull Moment*, a brash and extremely broad romp [about] the robbery of an art museum. The idea of the theft itself has possibilities, with the gang masterminded by an old hand, Edward G. Robinson, as an art authority . . . [He] plays it cool and casual, wisely, and his hoodlums rough it up with Keystone Kops sub-

NEVER A DULL MOMENT: With Philip Coolidge, Henry Silva, Tony Bill, Ned Glass and Slim Pickens

220

NEVER A DULL MOMENT

NEVER A DULL MOMENT: With Dorothy Provine

tlety."—Howard Thompson, *The New York Times*

"Edward G. Robinson once again gives an effortless interpretation of a top criminal . . . [with] lines like 'Keep your hands to yourself or I'll take them away from you!'"—Ann Guarino, *New York Daily News*

"With no pretentions to being anything but a rollicking farce, this slight but intermittently amusing comedy largely succeeds on its own modest level . . . Edward G. Robinson, nostalgically cast as an art-loving racketeer, plays the part as straight as a die, and happily avoids the temptations offered by a zany action painting sequence."—*Monthly Film Bulletin*

MACKENNA'S GOLD

1969 Columbia Pictures

A Highroad Production; Producers, Carl Foreman and Dimitri Tiomkin; Director, J. Lee Thompson; Screenplay, Carl Foreman; Based on the novel by Will Henry; Photography, Joseph MacDonald; Art directors, Geoffrey Drake and

222

MACKENNA'S GOLD: With John Garfield, Jr.

MACKENNA'S GOLD

MACKENNA'S GOLD: With Burgess Meredith, John Garfield, Jr. and Raymond Massey on the set

Cary Odell; Set decorator, Alfred E. Spencer; Costumes, Norma Koch; Music, Quincy Jones; Special effects, Geoffrey Drake, John Mackey, Bob Cuff, Willis Cook and Larry Butler; Sound, Derek Frye and William Randall, Jr.,; Editor, Bill Lenny. Super Panavision and Technicolor. 128 minutes

Mackenna (*Gregory Peck*), Colorado (*Omar Sharif*), Sergeant Tibbs (*Telly Savalas*), Inga (*Camilla Sparv*), Sanchez (*Keenan Wynn*), Hesh-Ke (*Julie Newmar*), Hachita (*Ted Cassidy*), The Editor (*Lee J. Cobb*), The Preacher (*Raymond Massey*), The Storekeeper (*Burgess Meredith*), Older Englishman (*Anthony Quayle*), Old Adams (*Edward G. Robinson*), Ben Baker (*Eli Wallach*), Prairie Dog (*Eduardo Ciannelli*), Avila (*Dick Peabody*), Besh (*Rudy Diaz*), Monkey (*Robert Phillips*), Pima Squaw (*Shelley Morrison*), Young Englishman (*J. Robert Porter*), Adams's Boy (*John Garfield, Jr.*), Laguna (*Pepe Calla-*

han), Old Apache Woman (*Madeleine Taylor Holmes*), Lieutenant (*Duke Hobbie*), Old Man (*Trevor Bardette*), Narrator (*Victor Jory*)

In this bloated all-star Western about total greed, with assorted bands of gold-lusters in search of a fabulous treasure that may or may not exist in the desert, Edward G. Robinson is one of the "guest stars," a blind old prospector whose eyes were taken out by Apache warriors after, he claims, he actually saw the gold. Among the participants in the stellar search are Mackenna, the Sheriff of Hadleyburg (Gregory Peck), who has acquired a map from a dying Indian that shows the way to the legendary Valley of Gold; Colorado (Omar

Adams' son), the son of the onetime Warners tough guy during Robinson's heyday at the studio and with whom Robinson costarred in *The Sea Wolf* nearly three decades earlier.

CRITICAL VIEWS

"A Western of truly stunning absurdity, [it] is the work of J. Lee Thompson, a thriving example of that old Hollywood maxim about how to succeed by failing big . . . Although it is set in the Old West, it actually has the shape of French farce: various groups of characters pursuing each other in and out of ambushes in the kind of circular action so dear to Feydeau . . . [including] such people as Lee J. Cobb, Eduardo Ciannelli, Raymond Massey, Burgess Meredith, Anthony Quayle, Edward G. Robinson and Eli Wallach, each of whom does a sort of stagger-on and then dies."—Vincent Canby, *The New York Times*

"As it is, *Mackenna's Gold* is a standard Western. The plot is good, the acting adequate. It's the scenery—the vastness of the West—it's the use of cameras, of horses, it's the special effects which keep the viewer involved and entertained . . . and the scenery is breathtaking . . . There's enough action, suspense and grandeur to insure the film's success."—*Variety*

"Preposterous hotch-potch of every cliche known to the gold-lust book, with a broken-backed script which drags in a royal flush of guest stars but gets rid of them before they have time to earn their keep . . . It is almost—but not quite—bad enough to be enjoyable."—*Monthly Film Bulletin*

Sharif), a ruthless bandit who is so eager to get his hands on the treasure that he not only makes a hostage of the daughter of the town judge but also kidnaps the sheriff himself, dragging both of them across the desert; the Gentlemen of Hadleyburg, including the local newspaper editor (Lee J. Cobb), the town preacher (Raymond Massey), a storekeeper (Burgess Meredith), a couple of Englishmen (Anthony Quayle and J. Robert Porter), and the blind prospector, Old Adams (Robinson); plus the pursuing cavalry and a band of hostile Apaches.

Virtually everyone in the cast is killed (only five survive) in this beautifully photographed outdoor epic that also featured the intriguing bit of casting by having Robinson's "eyes" being John Garfield, Jr. (as Old

SONG OF NORWAY

1970   ABC Pictures/Cinerama Releasing Corp.

An Andrew and Virginia Stone Production; Producers, Andrew L. Stone and Virginia Stone; Writer-Director, Andrew L. Stone; Adapted from the stage musical by Milton Lazarus (book) and Robert Wright and George Forrest (music and lyrics), based on a play by Homer Curran; Photography, Davis Boulton; Art director, William Albert Havemeyer; Costumes, David Walker and Fiorella Mariani; Music based on the works of Edvard Grieg, performed by the London Symphony Orchestra; Music supervisor, Roland Shaw; Piano works played by John Ogden; Animation director, Jack Kinney; Choreography, Lee Theodore. Second-unit director, Yakima Canutt; Editor, Virginia Stone. Super Panavision and DeLuxe Color. 142 minutes

SONG OF NORWAY

226

SONG OF NORWAY: With Christina Schollin, Elizabeth Larner, Harry Secombe, Toralv Maurstad and Florence Henderson

Edvard Grieg (*Toralv Maurstad*), Nina Grieg (*Florence Henderson*), Therese Berg (*Christina Schollin*), Rikard Nordraak (*Frank Porretta*), Björnsterne Björnson (*Harry Secombe*), Berg (*Robert Morley*), Krogstad (*Edward G. Robinson*), Mrs. Björnson (*Elizabeth Larner*), Engstrand (*Oscar Homolka*), Henrik Ibsen (*Frederick Jaeger*), Franz Liszt (*Henry Gilbert*), Hans Christian Andersen (*Richard Wordsworth*), George Nordraak (*Bernard Archard*), Aunt Aline (*Susan Richards Chitty*), Hagerup (*John Barrie*), Mrs. Hagerup (*Wenke Foss*), Gade (*Ronald Adam*), Captain Hansen (*Carl Rigg*), Mrs. Thoresen (*Aline Towne*), Irate Woman (*Nan Munto*), Berg's Butler (*James Hayter*), Helsted (*Erik Chitty*), Violinist (*Manoug Parikian*), Councilman 1 (*Richard Vernon*), Councilman 2 (*Ernest Clark*), Björnson's Secretary (*Eli Lindtner*)

This rather misguided, big budget, Cinerama-style musical, closing out for good a memorable Hollywood era, was based on the 1944 Broadway fantasy that floated on the airs of Edvard Grieg. The Stones, Andrew and Virginia, chose apparently to forego the fantasy on the screen and aim for "true biography" and therein was their downfall. As one critic observed,

"This turns out to be the same old cliche-ridden life story that Liszt, Chopin and Schubert have already been given by Hollywood." Edward G. Robinson's contribution to the life of Edvard Grieg (portrayed by an unknown, Toralv Maurstad) was to play the kindly old piano dealer in the would-be composer's hometown, with a Norwegian accent that wasn't quite as good as the one he used back in the 1940s in *Our Vines Have Tender Grapes*. Later the same kindly old piano dealer, in the company of Franz Liszt, comes upon Grieg while on business in Rome and takes on the role of one of the now-recognized composer's patrons.

CRITICAL VIEWS

"*Song of Norway* is no ordinary movie kitsch, but a display to turn Guy Lombardo livid with envy . . . The cast includes Toralv Maurstad, Frank Porretta and Florence Henderson. Robert Morley, Edward G. Robinson and Oscar Homolka appear in non-singing roles. That they all appear to be a little more foolish than they need be is not only because of the scenario,

227

SONG OF NORWAY: With Florence Henderson

but also because of [Andrew] Stone's pursuit of realism, in this case, of scenery, which is so overwhelming that the people are reduced to being scenic obstructions."—Vincent Canby, *The New York Times*

". . . a magnificent motion picture. Unfortunately, [Andrew] Stone's screenplay imparts a frequently banal, two-dimensional note . . . Edward G. Robinson is kindly and concerned as the kindly, concerned old piano dealer."—*Variety*

". . . what we have is a Cinerama travelogue of old towns, snow-covered mountains, fjords, waterfalls and abundant wild flowers. Every prospect pleases, and only the script is vile . . . Grieg's music is vulgarised by the team responsible for *Kismet* to provide jolly songs and dance numbers . . . [but] the music is at its worst when it comes closest to Grieg . . . A good many of the

SONG OF NORWAY: With Florence Henderson

228

details in the film are perfectly authentic, but they're strung on such a ludicrous thread that even they come to sound false."—*Monthly Film Bulletin*

NEITHER BY DAY NOR BY NIGHT

1972   Motion Pictures International

An MPI/Mordechai Slonim Films Production; Producer, Mordechai Slonim; Associate producer, Mischa Asherov; Director, Steven Hilliard Stern; Screenplay, Steven Hilliard Stern and Gisa W. Slonim; Based on the play by Avraham Raz; Photography, Ammon Salomon; Set decorator, Gidi Levi; Music, Vladimir Cosma; Songs "Time" and "Innocent Friends" by Vladimir Cosma and Steven Hilliard Stern; Sound, Derrick Leather; Editor, Alain Jakubowicz. Eastmancolor. 95 minutes.

Adam (*Zalman King*), Hannah Sokolova (*Miriam Bernstein-Cohen*), Yael (*Dalia Friedland*), Adam's Father (*Edward G. Robinson*), Doctor (*Mischa Asheroff*), Akira (*Chaim Anitar*), and (*Eli Cohen, Jetta Luka, Zicha Gold, David Smadar*)

Edward G. Robinson, in this American/Israeli co-production, is an American furrier who flies to Tel Aviv to visit his son, an expatriate injured in a bomb attack while picking oranges on a kibbutz and who is soon to go blind. Their meeting in the hospital is short and strained. The father learns that there are only two other people there with whom his son has any real contact. One is an attractive nurse whose parents died in Auschwitz, and whom he grows to love; the other, an elderly woman who suffers from cataracts and mistakes the disillusioned American for an Israeli soldier she once loved, and whom he enjoys as a companion, encouraging her fantasies.

This obscure, downbeat film, based on an Israeli play, was shown first at the 1972 Berlin Film Festival and got spotty theatrical distribution in the United States after Robinson's death the next year and after the release of his valedictory film, *Soylent Green.*

CRITICAL VIEWS

"*Neither by Day Nor by Night* is a mawkish melodrama at its most unpalatable; maybe a degree of humor in the script and performances would have made it easier to swallow, but the Jewish ability to find laughter in adversity seems to have deserted everybody both before and behind the cameras . . . Edward G. Robinson's neatly etched cameo provides a morsel of pleasure."—*Monthly Film Bulletin*

"A conventional tale of a young battle-wounded American trying to adjust to impending blindness in an Israeli hospital . . . It's actually the superlative performance of Miriam Bernstein-Cohen which gives pic its extra dimension, raising an otherwise over-sudsy tale by several notches . . . Edward G. Robinson makes the most of a cameo scene as [Zalman King's] estranged father."—*Variety*

NEITHER BY DAY NOR BY NIGHT

SOYLENT GREEN

1973   Metro-Goldwyn-Mayer

Producers, Walter Seltzer and Russell Thacher; Director, Richard Fleischer; Screenplay, Stanley R. Greenberg; Based on the novel *Make Room! Make Room!* by Harry Harrison;

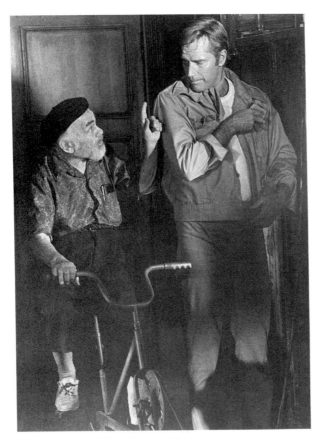

SOYLENT GREEN: With Charlton Heston

SOYLENT GREEN: With Charlton Heston

Photography, Richard H. Kline; Art director, Edward C. Carfagno; Set decorator, Robert Benton; Costumes, Pat Barto; Music, Fred Myrow; Symphonic music director, Gerald Fried; Action scenes coordinator, Joe Canutt; Special photographic effects, Robert R. Hoag and Matthew Yuricich; Sound, Charles M. Wilborn and Harry W. Tetrick; Editor, Samuel E. Beetley. Panavision and Metrocolor. 97 minutes

Detective Thorn (*Charlton Heston*), Shirl (*Leigh Taylor-Young*), Sol Roth (*Edward G. Robinson*), Tab Fielding (*Chuck Connors*), William Simonson (*Joseph Cotten*), Hatcher (*Brock Peters*), Martha (*Paula Kelly*), Gilbert (*Stephen Young*), Kulozik (*Mike Henry*), Priest (*Lincoln Kilpatrick*), Donovan (*Roy Jenson*), Charles (*Leonard Stone*), Governor Santini (*Whit Bissell*), Exchange Leader (*Celia Lovsky*), First Usher (*Dick Van Patten*), First Book (*Morgan Farley*), Second Book (*John Barclay*), Third Book (*Belle Mitchell*), Fourth Book (*Cyril Delevanti*), Attendants (*Forrest Wood, Faith Quabius*), Mrs. Santini (*Jane Dulo*), Brady (*Tim Herbert*), Wagner (*John Dennis*), Bandana Woman (*Jan Bradley*), New Tenant (*Carlos Romero*), Fat Guard (*Pat Houtchens*), Furniture Girls (*Joyce Williams, Erica Hagen, Beverly Gill, Suesie Eejima, Cheri Howell, Kathy Silva, Jennifer King, Marion Charles*)

His final role was in the futuristic *Soylent Green*, adapted from sci-fi writer Harry Harrison's terrific novel *Make Room! Make Room!*, which is set in the year 2022. New York City has a population of forty million and has been turned into a police state. Edward G. Robinson is Sol Roth, harried space age detective Thorn's ancient, scholarly research assistant (a veritable walking encyclopedia) who remembers what things were like way-back when. Thorn is investigating the death of wealthy William Simonson, and learns through Sol that the victim had been director of the giant Soylent company, a manufacturer of synthetic foods. Becoming involved with Simonson's mistress, Shirl, part of the "furniture" in the industrialist's super-luxurious apartment, Thorn runs afoul of his superior, Hatcher, who has been pressured to drop the Simonson case.

Thumbing through his books, Sol uncovers the secret that drove Simonson to despair and made him a threat to his own company, which had him killed by his own bodyguard, Fielding. Leaving a message for Thorn, Sol has himself admitted to a clinic where death is administered in blissful surroundings. Arriving at the clinic in time to be told the secret by Sol, Thorn follows a truck-load of corpses to a Soylent plant where he discovers that they are processed into the latest product called Soylent Green. Fielding's thugs catch up with and severely wound him, but he survives to pass on the secret to the world.

Robinson's on-screen death speech, before passing into a pleasant demise amid beautiful scenes of the nature that used to be back in the 20th century and music of one's choice being piped into the chamber of dreams, remains one of the most poignant final monologues in movies. He died in real life several months before the release of *Soylent Green*.

CRITICAL VIEWS

"New Yorkers certainly have problems these days . . . but nothing like the horrors due in 2022 as depicted in *Soylent Green* . . . Unfortunately the script, direction and the principals involved in this struggle for survival often are as synthetic as *Soylent Green* [which] projects essentially simple, muscular melodrama a good deal more effectively than it does the potential of man's seemingly witless destruction of the earth's resources . . . Mr. Robinson is pitiably natural as the realistic, sensitive oldster facing the futility of living in dying surroundings."—A. H. Weiler, *The New York Times*

"To the late Edward G. Robinson went the best part, to which he gave a fine display of his talents in what turned out to be a valedictory performance."—*Variety*

". . . for a film so devoid of any thematic strategy or even plain story-telling flair, *Soylent Green* does turn up the occasional delight . . . [One is] a scene where the grim warning note for the rest of the film is given an edge of delirious fantasy as Sol, a crumpled survivor from another world gruffly personified by Edward G. Robinson in his last appearance, gives himself up to death in a strongly affecting moment of romantic kitsch . . ."—*Monthly Film Bulletin*

SOYLENT GREEN

With David Ben-Gurion during the filming of ISRAEL (1959)

SHORT FILMS

THE STOLEN JOOLS aka
THE SLIPPERY PEARLS (1931)

A Paramount 2-reeler

Produced by Chesterfield Cigarettes

Written and directed by E.K. Nadel and William McGann. Wallace Beery, Buster Keaton, Edward G. Robinson, George E. Stone, Eddie Kane, Laurel and Hardy, Polly Moran, Norma Shearer, Hedda Hopper, Joan Crawford, Robert Ames, Irene Dunne, Bebe Daniels, Ben Lyon, Loretta Young, Douglas Fairbanks Jr., Maurice Chevalier, Frank Fay, Barbara Stanwyck, Fifi D'Orsay, Warner Baxter, Winnie Lightner, Wynne Gibson, Claudia Dell, Edmund Lowe, Victor McLaglen, El Brendel, Wheeler and Woolsey, Gary Cooper, Charles "Buddy" Rogers, Eugene Pallette, William Haines, Richard Dix, Richard Barthelmess, Charles Butterworth, Louise Fazenda, Lowell Sherman, Fay Wray, Jack Oakie, Joe E. Brown, George "Gabby" Hayes, Mitzi Green, and Members of the Keystone Kops and Members of Our Gang

VERDENSBEROMTHEDER I KOBENHAVEN (1939)

Produced by Dansk Films in Denmark

with Robert Taylor, Myrna Loy, Edward G. Robinson, Charles Lindbergh, Duke Ellington, Alice Babs Nilsson, Edvard Persson

SCREEN SNAPSHOTS (1942) (Series 22, No. 4)

Produced by Columbia Pictures

Ten minute performance of Russian music with Edward G. Robinson providing humorous introductions.

MOSCOW STRIKES BACK (1942)

Feature-length documentary of the Russian winter counter-offensive of 1941. Narrated by Edward G. Robinson, with English commentary by Albert Maltz and music by Dimitri Tiomkin. Produced by Central Studios, Moscow. Edited by Slavko Vorkapich. Released by Artkino.

THE RED CROSS AT WAR (1943)

Narration spoken by Edward G. Robinson

PROJECTION OF AMERICA (1943)

For the overseas division of the Office of War Information, Edward G. Robinson talked about this country, about cowboys, about Chicago, etc.

SCREEN SNAPSHOTS (1944) (Series 23, No. 9)

Produced by Columbia Pictures

A one-reel record of cinema history, celebrating the Golden Jubilee of the film industry. Edward G. Robinson appeared along with Fred Astaire, John Barrymore, Carole Lombard, Irene Dunne, Rosalind Russell, Cary Grant, Mary Pickford, Rita Hayworth, Lillian Gish, Lionel Barrymore, Hedy Lamarr, Wallace Beery, Humphrey Bogart, others.

SCREEN SNAPSHOTS (1948) (Series 27, No. 8)

Produced by Columbia Pictures

"Hollywood Honors Hersholt" (aka "Jean Hersholt Party")

SCREEN SNAPSHOTS (1948) (Series 27, No. 10)

Produced by Columbia Pictures

"Hollywood Friars Honor George Jessel"

WHERE DO YOU GET OFF (1948)

One-reel short for United Jewish Appeal with Edward G. Robinson narrating.

SCREEN SNAPSHOTS (1950)

Produced by Columbia Pictures

Advertisement for ISRAEL

Edward G. Robinson, Dan Duryea, Dana Andrews and Wanda Hendrix, among others, appear in "Ice Capades Premiere."

SCREEN SNAPSHOTS (1951)

Produced by Columbia Pictures

Robinson narrated "Hollywood Memories"

THE HEART OF SHOW BUSINESS (1957)

Produced by Columbia Pictures

40-minute documentary on the history of Variety Clubs International. Edward G. Robinson was one of the narrators, along with Bing Crosby, Bob Hope, James Stewart, Burt Lancaster and Cecil B. DeMille. Stars who also participated included Harry Belafonte, Victor Borge, Maurice Chevalier, Lena Horne, Art Linkletter, Sophie Tucker, Jimmy Durante, and Edgar Bergen and Charlie McCarthy.

ISRAEL (1959)

Produced and written for Warner Bros. by Leon Uris and directed by Sam Zebba

Edward G. Robinson narrated 29-minute pictorial tour of Israel, combining picturesque sites of Biblical times and the scope of the country's dramatic modern day achievements. Score arranged and conducted by Elmer Bernstein. Filmed in WarnerScope and Technicolor.

OTHER FILMS USING CLIPS OF PREVIOUS EDWARD G. ROBINSON PERFORMANCES

OKAY FOR SOUND (1946)

Twenty minute Vitaphone short produced by Gordon Hollingshead to commemorate the anniversary of the pioneer Warner talking motion pictures.
Among clips from past films produced by the company were one from *Little Caesar* and one from *Dr. Ehrlich's Magic Bullet*.

WHEN THE TALKIES WERE YOUNG (1956)

Seventeen minute Vitaphone short produced by Robert Youngson.
A clip from *Five Star Final* was incorporated into it.

MYRA BRECKENRIDGE (1970)

Feature-length 20th Century-Fox film produced by Robert Fryer.
Scenes from earlier 20th Century-Fox pictures were utilized, among them, a portion of the Edward G. Robinson episode in *Tales of Manhattan*.

CARTOONS UTILIZING THE ANIMATED CHARACTER LIKENESS OF EDWARD G. ROBINSON

THE COO-COONUT GROVE (1936)

Merrie Melodies cartoon directed by I. Freleng

THUGS WITH DIRTY MUGS (1939)

Merrie Melodies cartoon supervised by Fred Allen (Edward G. Rob'em some as The Killer)

WHAT'S COOKIN' DOC? (1944)

Merrie Melodies cartoon supervised by Robert Clampett (Bugs Bunny imitates Robinson)

HUSH MY MOUSE (1946)

Looney Tunes cartoon directed by Charles M. (Chuck) Jones

HOLLYWOOD CANINE CANTEEN (1946)

Merrie Melodies cartoon directed by Robert McKimson

RACKETEER RABBIT (1946)

Looney Tunes cartoon directed by I. Freleng

In THE FIREBRAND (1924)

236

STAGE APPEARANCES

PAID IN FULL (as Sato)

Binghamton, NY
April 1913

THE GAMBLER
(as Thomas, the Butler,
and Hicks, the Plain-
clothesman)

Binghamton, NY
April 1913

Stock in Cincinnati
(22 weeks)
Shows included ALIAS
JIMMY VALENTINE
(as Dick the Rat)

Season 1913-14

Stock Tour of Canada

UNDER FIRE
(as Andre Lemaire)

1914

Hudson Theatre, NYC
August 12, 1915

UNDER SENTENCE
(as Fagan)

Harris Theatre, NYC
October 3, 1916

THE PAWN (as Hushmaru)

Fulton Theatre, NYC
September 8, 1917

DRAFTED (as Lieutenant
Haenkel)

(on tour)   October 1917

THE LITTLE TEACHER
(as Batiste)

Playhouse Theatre, NYC
February 4, 1918

FIRST IS LAST (as Steve)

Maxine Elliott Th., NYC
September 17, 1919

NIGHT LODGING
(as Satin)

Plymouth Theatre, NYC
December 22, 1919

POLDEKIN (as Pinsky)

Park Theatre, NYC
September 9, 1920

SAMSON AND DELILAH
(as The Director)

Greenwich Village
Theatre, NYC
November 17, 1920

THE IDLE INN
(as Mendel)

Plymouth Theatre, NYC
December 20, 1921

THE DELUGE
(as Nordling)

Plymouth Theatre, NYC
January 27, 1922

BANCO (as Louis)

Ritz Theatre, NYC
September 20, 1922

PEER GYNT (as The
Button Moulder and
Von Eberkopf)

Garrick Theatre, NYC
February 5, 1923

THE ADDING
MACHINE (as Shrdlu)

Garrick Theatre, NYC
March 19, 1923

Stock in Chicago
LAUNZI (as Louis)

Summer 1923
Plymouth Theatre, NYC
October 10, 1923

A ROYAL FANDANGO
(as Pascual)

Plymouth Theatre, NYC
November 12, 1923

STELLA DALLAS
(as Ed Munn)

(in Baltimore, MD)
January 20, 1924

THE FIREBRAND
(as Octaviano)

Morosco Theatre, NYC
October 15, 1924

ANDROCLES AND THE
LION (as Caesar)

Klaw Theatre, NYC
November 23, 1925

THE MAN OF DESTINY
(as Giuseppe) (in repertory)

THE GOAT SONG
(as Reb Feiwell)

Guild Theatre, NYC
January 25, 1926

THE CHIEF THING
(as Stage Director)

Guild Theatre, NYC
March 22, 1926

WE AMERICANS
(as Morris Levine)
(Because of his commit-
ment to the Theatre
Guild, Robinson did
not play the role on
Broadway; it went to
Muni Weisenfreund aka
Paul Muni)

(in Atlantic City)
April 1926

THE STOLEN LADY
(as Col. Virgilio
Hermanos Barroso)

(in Atlantic City)
July 1926

HENRY BEHAVE
(as Wescott P. Bennett)

Nora Bayes Th., NYC
August 23, 1926

JUAREZ AND
MAXIMILIAN
(as Porfirio Diaz)

Guild Theatre, NYC
October 11, 1926

NED McCOBB'S
DAUGHTER
(as Lawyer Grover)

John Golden Th., NYC
November 29, 1926

THE BROTHERS
KARAMAZOV
(as Smerdiakov)

Guild Theatre, NYC
January 3, 1927

RIGHT YOU ARE IF

Guild Theatre, NYC

YOU THINK YOU ARE (as Ponza)	March 2, 1927
KIBITZER (as Lazarus)	(in Atlantic City) Summer 1927
THE RACKET (as Nick Scarsi)	Ambassador Th., NYC November 22, 1927 West Coast, Spring 1928
A MAN WITH RED HAIR (as Mr. Crispin)	Ambassador Th., NYC November 8, 1928
KIBITZER (as Lazarus)	Royale Theatre, NYC February 18, 1929
MR. SAMUEL (*Le Marchand de Paris*) (as Samuel Brisach)	Little Theatre, NYC November 10, 1930
DARKNESS AT NOON (as Rubashov)	opened McCarter Theatre, Princeton, NJ September 28, 1951; closed Cox Theatre, Cincinnati April 26, 1952
MIDDLE OF THE NIGHT (as The Manufacturer)	ANTA Theatre, NYC February 8, 1956; (tour) opened Shubert Theatre, New Haven October 9, 1957; closed Curran Theatre, San Francisco March 29, 1958

In PEER GYNT (1923)

In THE GOAT SONG (1926)

With George Gaul, Alfred Lunt and Morris Carnovsky in THE BROTHERS KARAMAZOV (1927)

With Nancy R. Pollack and Betty Walker in MIDDLE OF THE NIGHT (1957)

In THE KIBITZER (1929)

In MIDDLE OF THE NIGHT

With Ona Munson and ZaSu Pitts on *Big Town*

DRAMATIC RADIO WORK

November 7, 1933—*California Melodies* (CBS)

February 1, 1935—*Hollywood Hotel* (CBS):
"The Whole Town's Talking" with Jean Arthur

January 13, 1936—*Lux Radio Theater* (CBS):
"The Boss"

January 30, 1936—*The Standard Brands Hour* (NBC):
"The Inner Voice" with Ruth Easton and Len Hollister

May 8, 1936—*Hollywood Hotel* (CBS): "Bullets or
Ballots" with Joan Blondell, Kay Kenney (songbird of
Hawaii) and James Melton

January 18, 1937—*Lux Radio Theater* (CBS):
"Criminal Code" with Beverly Roberts

April 29, 1937—*Kate Smith A&P Bandwagon* (CBS):
"Thunder in the City"

June 4, 1937—*Hollywood Hotel* (CBS):
"Kid Galahad" with Joan Blondell

August 2, 1937—*CBS Shakespeare Theater* (CBS):
"Taming of the Shrew" with Frieda Inescourt

October 19, 1937 to July 2, 1942—Starred as Steve
Wilson on "Big Town" (CBS)

March 10, 1938—*Hollywood Showcase* (CBS):
Anniversary for Jean Hersholt

December 19, 1938—*Lux Radio Theater* (CBS):
"Kid Galahad" with Wayne Morris, Andrea Leeds, Joan
Bennett

April 17, 1939—*Lux Radio Theater* (CBS):
"Bullets or Ballots" with Mary Astor, Humphrey Bogart,
Otto Kruger

February 25, 1940—*Gulf Screen Guild Theater* (CBS):
"Blind Alley" with Joseph Calleia, Isabel Jewell, Leatrice
Joy

November 2, 1941—*Gulf Screen Guild Theater* (CBS):
"The Amazing Dr. Clitterhouse" with Humphrey Bogart,
Marsha Hunt

March 16, 1942—*Lux Radio Theater* (CBS):
"Manpower" with Marlene Dietrich and George Raft

January 4, 1943—*Lockheed's Ceiling Unlimited* (CBS):
(substitute narrator for host Orson Welles)

February 8, 1943—*Lux Radio Theater* (CBS):
"The Maltese Falcon" with Laird Cregar and Gail Patrick

March 15, 1943—*DuPont Cavalcade of America* (NBC):
"A Case for the FBI"

April 18, 1943—*Radio Reader's Digest* (ABC)

April 26, 1943—*Lockheed's Ceiling Unlimited* (CBS):
As Steve Wilson in "World of Tomorrow"

June 30, 1943—As narrator and master of ceremonies
on program of Motion Picture Committee for Hollywood
War Savings Staff (NBC)

July 4, 1943—*U.S. Rubber Hour* (CBS): "Our
American Scriptures" (doing readings from the Constitu-
tion and from Jefferson's letters)

April 3, 1944—*Lux Radio Theater* (CBS): "Destroyer"
with Marguerite Chapman, Dennis O'Keefe

June 5, 1944—*Lady Esther's Screen Guild Theater* (NBC):
"The Amazing Dr. Clitterhouse" with Claire Trevor, Lloyd
Nolan

October 2, 1944—*DuPont Cavalcade of America* (NBC):
"Voice On the Stairs" narrated by Walter Huston

March 1, 1945—*Suspense* (CBS): "My Wife
Geraldine"

April 8, 1945—*P. Lorillard Comedy Theater* (NBC):
"A Slight Case of Murder"

April 16, 1945—*Lux Radio Theater* (CBS):
(guest producer)

April 30, 1945—*DuPont Cavalcade of America* (NBC):
"The Philippines Never Surrender"

June 25, 1945—*Lux Radio Theater* (CBS): "The
Woman in the Window" with Joan Bennett, Dan Duryea

October 13, 1945—*Lady Estlier Screen Guild Players* (CBS):
"Flesh and Fantasy" with Dame May Whitty, Vincent
Price

March 11, 1946—*DuPont Cavalcade of America* (NBC):
"The Man With Hope in His Hands"

March 26, 1946—*Colgate Theater of Romance* (CBS):
"The Woman in the Window"

October 17, 1946—*Suspense* (CBS): "The Man

With Claire Trevor in "The Million Dollar Dog Stealing Racket" episode of *Big Town*

Who Thought He Was Edward G. Robinson"

November 18, 1946—*Lady Esther Screen Guild Players* (CBS): "Blind Alley" with Broderick Crawford, Isabel Jewell, Frank Albertson

December 7, 1946—*Proctor and Gamble's This Is Hollywood* (CBS): "The Stranger" with Ruth Hussey

November 25, 1947—*Gulf's We the People* (CBS)

March 14, 1948—*The Eternal Light* (NBC): "The Island in the Wilderness" (narrator)

April 12, 1948—*Camel's Screen Guild Players* (CBS): "The Great Man Votes" with Edmund Gwenn, Frank McHugh

November 11, 1948—*Camel's Screen Guild Players* (NBC): "All My Sons" with Burt Lancaster

January 28, 1949—*Ford Theater* (CBS): "The Woman in the Window" with Linda Darnell, Stephen McNally

February 27, 1949—*NBC Theater* (NBC): "Night Has a Thousand Eyes" with William Demarest

November 28, 1949—*Lux Radio Theater (CBS):*

"Key Largo" with Claire Trevor, Edmond O'Brien

December 2, 1949—*Screen Director's Playhouse* (NBC): "All My Sons" with Jeff Chandler

February 3, 1950—*Screen Director's Playhouse* (NBC): "The Sea Wolf" with Paul Frees and Lurene Tuttle

January 25, 1951—*Screen Director's Playhouse* (ABC): "House of Strangers" with Victor Mature, June Havoc

December 7, 1952—*Eternal Light* (NBC): As Chaim Weizmann in "Trial and Error"

October 21, 1953—State of Israel Bond Program (NBC): "Jerusalem Is Her Name" with Paul Muni (taped broadcast of special Madison Square Garden Show)

December 7, 1953—*Lux Radio Theater* (CBS): "Man on a Tightrope" with Terry Moore

December 20, 1953—*The Eternal Light* (NBC): "Face to Face with Gabriel"

January 24, 1954—*NBC Star Playhouse* (NBC): "A Slight Case of Murder" with Elspeth Eric, Pat Hosley, William Redfield, Wendell Holmes, Larry Haines

With Ona Munson (the second Loreli Kilbourne) on *Big Town*

As Steve Wilson on CBS Radio's *Big Town* series

With son Manny and "Big Town" co-star Claire Trevor at KNX studios in Hollywood in 1939

With Claire Trevor and Gale Gordon on *Big Town*

With wife Gladys Robinson and producer William Spier during a 1940s rehearsal for radio's *Suspense*

With Ida Lupino and Robert Young in ONLY YESTERDAY on *Lux Radio Theater*

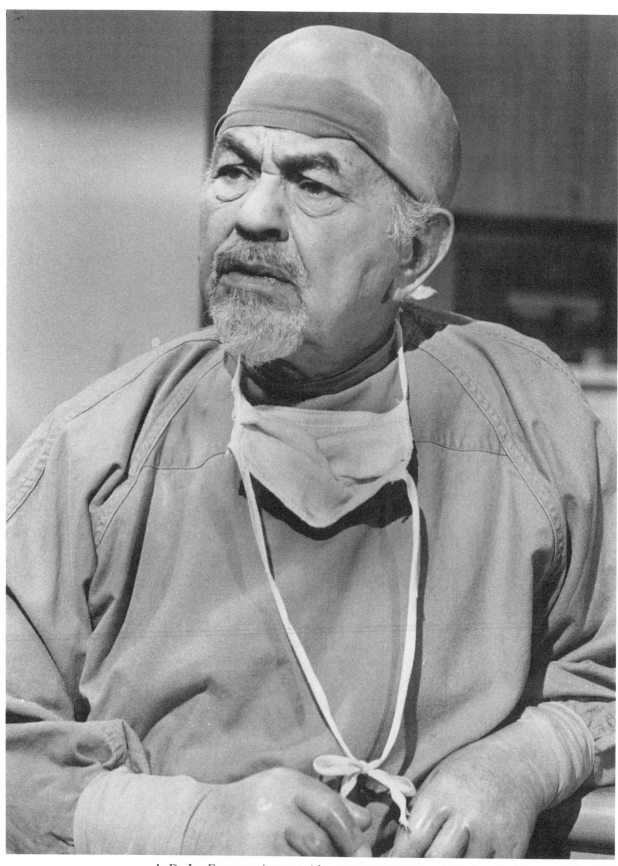

As Dr. Lee Forestman in U.M.C. (aka OPERATION HEARTBEAT), his first television movie (in 1969) and the pilot to the hit series, *Medical Center*

DRAMATIC TELEVISION APPEARANCES

9/17/53 LUX VIDEO THEATER (CBS):
"Witness for the Prosecution" (60 M.)

1954 FOR THE DEFENSE: "The Case of Kenny Jason"
(pilot for proposed weekly series) 30 M.
Director: James Neilson
Producer: Samuel Bischoff
Teleplay: Donn Mullally

Cast:

EDWARD G. ROBINSON (Matthew Considine), GLENN
VERNON (Kenny Jason), ANN DORAN (Mrs. Jason), JOHN
HOYT (Captain Thomas Hardy), ROBERT OSTERLOH
(Duke), VIC PERRIN (Barney), HERBERT HEYES (Judge),
MORRIS ANKRUM (District Attorney), TOM DUGAN (Desk
Sergeant)

12/9/54 CLIMAX! (CBS): "Epitaph for a Spy" 60 M.
Director: Allen Reisner
Producer: Bretaigne Windust
Teleplay: Donald S. Sanford
Novel: Eric Ambler

Cast:

EDWARD G. ROBINSON (Josef Vadassy), MELVILLE
COOPER, ROBERT F. SIMON, IVAN TRIESAULT, NICHOLAS
JOY, NORMA VARDEN, DAVID O'BRIEN, MARJORIE LORD,
MAURICE MARSAC

1/13/55 FORD THEATER (NBC): ". . . And Son" 30 M.
Story: I.A.R. Wylie
Adapted for television by Peter Packer and Robert Bassing

Cast:

EDWARD G. ROBINSON (John Derwent), JOHN BAER (Larry
Derwent), ERIN O'BRIEN-MOORE (Elsa Derwent), WILLIS
BOUCHEY (Charlie Crichton), J.P. O'DONNELL (Recep-
tionist)

12/29/55 FORD THEATER (NBC): "A Set of Values"
30 M.

Cast:

EDWARD G. ROBINSON (Baron Carter), ANN DORAN (Sue
Carter), TOMMY COOK (Jerry Carter), PAUL FIX (Franklin), JOSEPH DOWNING (Arnie)

9/30/56-10/28/56 THE $64,000 CHALLENGE (CBS)
30 M.
EDWARD G. ROBINSON and VINCENT PRICE vie in the category of art. (Price had previously triumphed over famed
jockey Billy Pearson in the same category.)

10/23/58 PLAYHOUSE 90 (CBS): "Shadows Tremble"
90 M.
Director: Herbert Hirshman
Producer: Herbert Brodkin
Teleplay: Ernest Kinoy

Cast::

EDWARD G. ROBINSON (Oscar Bromek), RAY WALSTON
(Lyle Patridge), BEATRICE STRAIGHT (Grace Tyburn),
FRANK CONROY (John Tyburn), PARKER FENNELLY
(George Putnam), ROBERT WEBBER (Malcolm Field)

3/2/59 GOODYEAR THEATER (NBC): "A Good Name"
30 M.
Director: Eliot Silverstein
Producer: Winston O'Keefe
Teleplay: Richard Alan Simmons

Cast:

EDWARD G. ROBINSON (Harry Harper), LEE PHILIPS (Vin-
cent Harper), PARLEY BAER (Walter Brodsky), JAC-
QUELINE SCOTT (Ann Harper), CARLETON G. YOUNG
(Gene Morley), GLENN TAYLOR (Mike Hudson), OLAN
SOULE (Thin Member)

4/2/59 ZANE GREY THEATER (CBS): "Loyalty" 30 M.

Cast:

EDWARD G. ROBINSON (Victor Bers), EDWARD G. ROBIN-

With Ann Doran and Glenn Vernon in his prospective/TV series pilot *For the Defense* in 1954

With emcee Ralph Storey and Vincent Price on *The $64,000 Challenge* in 1956

SON JR. (Hunt), JOHN HACKETT (Lieutenant), ROBERT BLAKE (Michael Bers), DAN BARTON, GEORGE WALLACE, LEW GALLO, QUENTIN SONDERGAARD

2/17/60 NBC-TV SPECIAL: "The Devil and Daniel Webster" 60 M. (repeated CBS-TV 4/30/62)

Director: Tom Donovan
Teleplay: Phil Reisman Jr.
Story: Stephen Vincent Benet

Cast:

EDWARD G. ROBINSON (Daniel Webster), DAVID WAYNE (Devil), TIM O'CONNOR (Jabez Stone), JOHN HOYT (Middle Selectman), LORI MARCH (Felicia Field), WALTER BALDWIN (Left Selectman), BYRON FOULGER (Frank Post), BETTY LOU HOLLAND (Dorcas Stone), ROYAL BEAL (Justice Hawthorn), STUART GERMAIN (Stevens), HOWARD FREEMAN (Pinkham), and EDGAR BERGEN, host

10/24/60 THE RIGHT MAN (CBS) 60 M. Historical revue of U.S. presidential campaigns

Director: Burt Shevelove
Producer: Fred Freed
Narrator: Garry Moore

EDWARD G. ROBINSON played Theodore Roosevelt

1/29/61 GENERAL ELECTRIC THEATER (CBS): "The Drop-Out" 30 M.

Director: Richard Irving
Producer: Stanley Rubin
Teleplay: Roger O. Hirson

Cast:

EDWARD G. ROBINSON (Bert Alquist), BILLY GRAY (Jerry Alquist), CARMEN MATTHEWS (Mrs. Alquist), RAY MONTGOMERY (Cooper)

10/6/61 THE DETECTIVES (NBC): "The Legend of Jim Riva" 60 M.

Director: Richard Carlson
Producer: Arthur Nadel
Teleplay: John K. Butler and Boyd Correll
Story: Arthur Browne Jr.

Cast:

EDWARD G. ROBINSON (Jim Riva), RUDY SOLARI (Nathan Riva), BUTCH PATRICK (Bobby), ROBERT TAYLOR (Captain Matt Holbrook), TIGE ANDREWS (Lt. Johnny Russo), MARK GODDARD (Sgt. Chris Ballard), ADAM WEST (Nelson)

3/18/62 PROJECT TWENTY (NBC): "Cops and Robbers" 60 M.

Director: Don Hyatt
Producer: Don Hyatt
Written by Phil Reisman Jr.
EDWARD G. ROBINSON as the narrator

12/1/63 THE WORLD'S GREATEST SHOWMAN (NBC) 90 M.

Tribute to Cecil B. DeMille. Hosted by EDWARD G. ROBINSON, BETTY HUTTON, CORNEL WILDE and BARBARA STANWYCK

1/9/65 HOLLYWOOD PALACE (ABC) 90 M.

Dramatic reading of patriotic essay, "This Is It"

2/19/65 XEROX SPECIAL (ABC): "Who Has Seen the Wind" 90 M.

Director: George Sidney
Producer: George Sidney
Teleplay: Don Mankiewicz
Story: Tad Mosel

Cast:

EDWARD G. ROBINSON (Captain), STANLEY BAKER (Janos), MARIA SCHELL (Maria Radek), THEODORE BIKEL (Josef Radek), VERONICA CARTWRIGHT (Kiri), GYPSY ROSE LEE (Proprietress), LILIA SKALA (Nun), SIMON OAKLAND (Inspector), PAUL RICHARDS (Father Ashton), VICTOR JORY (Peralton)

6/17/67-6/24/67 EYE ON ART (CBS) 30 M.

EDWARD G. ROBINSON as narrator of two of six parts of this series, and tour guide of galleries, museums and art studios in Chicago on first show and Los Angeles on second.

4/17/69 CBS MOVIE WORLD PREMIERE: "U.M.C." 120 M.

Director: Boris Sagal
Producer: A.C. Ward
Teleplay: A.C. Ward

Cast:

RICHARD BRADFORD (Dr. Joseph M. Gannon), EDWARD G. ROBINSON (Dr. Lee Forestman), JAMES DALEY (Dr. Paul Lochner), KIM STANLEY (Joanna Hanson), MAURICE EVANS (Dr. George Barger), KEVIN MCCARTHY (Coswell), J.D. CANNON (Jarris), WILLIAM WINDOM (Hanson), DON QUINE (Martin), SHELLEY FABARES (Mike), JAMES SHIGETA (Chief Resident), WILLIAM MARSHALL (Dr. Tawn), ALFRED RYDER (Dr. Corlane), ROBERT EMHARDT (Judge)

10/13/70 ABC MOVIE OF THE WEEK: "The Old Man Who Cried Wolf" 90 M.

Director: Walter Grauman
Producer: Walter Grauman
Teleplay: Luther Davis
Story: Arnold Horwitt
Executive Producer: Aaron Spelling
Assistant to the Executive Producer: Edward G. Robinson Jr.

Cast:

EDWARD G. ROBINSON (Emile Pulska), MARTIN BALSAM (Stanley Pulska), DIANE BAKER (Peggy Pulska), PERCY RODRIGUES (Frank Jones), RUTH ROMAN (Lois), EDWARD ASNER (Dr. Morheim), MARTIN E. BROOKS (Hudson Ewing), PAUL PICERNI (Detective Green), SAM JAFFE (Abe Stillman), ROBERT YURO (Detective Seroly), BILL ELLIOTT (Carl), JAMES A. WATSON (Leon), NAOMI STEVENS (Mrs. Raspili), VIRGINIA CHRISTINE (Miss Cummings), JAY C. FLIPPEN (Pawnbroker), JASON WINGREEN (Arthur)

10/23/70 BRACKEN'S WORLD (NBC): "The Mary Tree" 60 M.

With Ray Walston in "Shadows Tremble" on *Playhouse 90* in 1958 . . .

Director: Paul Henreid
Producer: Stanley Rubin
Teleplay: Jerry Ziegman

Cast:

EDWARD G. ROBINSON (Elstyn Draper), DIANA HYLAND (Mary Draper), LESLIE NIELSEN (John Bracken), PETER HASKELL (Kevin Grant), ELIZABETH ALLEN (Laura Dean), EDWARD G. ROBINSON JR. (Bill Lawrence), CLAUDIA BRYAR (Housekeeper), TIM HERBERT (Connie Rose), JEFF DONNELL (Joan Elliot)

10/23/70 THIS IS TOM JONES (ABC) 60 M.

Dramatic reading of "I Will Not Go Back" and Kipling's poem "The Betrothed"

5/4/71 HOLLYWOOD TELEVISION THEATRE (PBS) 150 M.

John Dos Passos's "U.S.A."
Director: George Schaefer
EDWARD G. ROBINSON delivered the prologue and epilogue.

. . . and with Beatrice Straight

12/15/71 ROD SERLING'S NIGHT GALLERY (NBC):
"The Messiah on Mott Street" (One segment of multipart weekly series)

Director: Don Taylor
Producer: Jack Laird
Teleplay: Rod Serling
EDWARD G. ROBINSON was Abraham Goldman, an impoverished old man who refused to die until the coming of the Messiah.

Cast:

YAPHET KOTTO (Buckner), RICKY POWELL (Mikey), TONY ROBERTS (Dr. Levine), ANNE TAYLOR (Miss Moretti)

3/18/73 AMERICA'S ROMANCE WITH THE LAND (ABC)

EDWARD G. ROBINSON narrated this special that was telecast posthumously.

Robinson also made cameo appearances as himself on "The Lucy Show" (2/7/66), "Batman" (3/2/67) and "Bracken's World" (9/26/69)

On the set of "Loyalty," an episode of *Zane Grey Theater* (1959)

With Billy Gray in the *General Electric Theater* episode, "The Drop-Out" (1961)

With Ruth Roman in the TV movie THE OLD MAN WHO CRIED WOLF (1970)

As Abraham Goldman in "The Messiah on Mott Street" (1971), an episode of Rod Serling's *Night Gallery*, and Robinson's final television appearance